Unto the Thousandth Generation

American University Studies

Series X
Political Science

Vol. 43

PETER LANG
New York • Washington, D.C./Baltimore • San Francisco
Bern • Frankfurt am Main • Berlin • Vienna • Paris

Bruce Edward Auerbach

Unto the Thousandth Generation

Conceptualizing Intergenerational Justice

PETER LANG
New York • Washington, D.C./Baltimore • San Francisco
Bern • Frankfurt am Main • Berlin • Vienna • Paris

Library of Congress Cataloging-in-Publication Data

Auerbach, Bruce Edward.
Unto the thousandth generation : conceptualizing intergenerational justice / Bruce Edward Auerbach.
p. cm. — (American university studies. Series X, Political science ; vol. 43)
Includes bibliographical references.
1. Justice. 2. Intergenerational relations. I. Title. II. Series: American university studies. Series X, Political science; v. 43.
JC578.A94 320'.01'1—dc20 93-2300
ISBN 0-8204-2228-2
ISSN 0740-0470

Die Deutsche Bibliothek-CIP-Einheitsaufnahme

Auerbach, Bruce Edward:
Unto the thousandth generation : Conceptualizing intergenerational justice / Bruce Edward Auerbach. - New York; San Francisco; Bern; Baltimore; Frankfurt am Main; Berlin; Wien; Paris: Lang.
(American university studies : Ser. 10, Political science ; Vol. 43)
ISBN 0-8204-2228-2
NE: American university studies / 10

Cover design by Scott Conner.

The paper in this book meets the guidelines for permanence and durability of the Committee on Production Guidelines for Book Longevity of the Council of Library Resources.

Printed in the United States of America.

To my father and the memory of my late mother,
who taught me the meaning of justice
and
to my nieces and nephews,
Julie, Jeff, Debbie, and Dan,
in the hope they may help make this world more just

ACKNOWLEDGMENTS

On the road to completing this book I benefited from the generosity and assistance of many people. I owe special thanks to Dr. Heidi Burns, acquisitions editor at Peter Lang, first for encouraging me to publish this work, and second for her helpful comments on drafts of each of the chapters.

I received encouragement from many other people, as well, including Professor Neal Riemer, who chaired a panel at the annual meeting of the American Political Science Association at which I presented a paper on Derek Parfit's non-identity problem. The arguments presented in that paper form the foundation for Chapter VI.

Professor Terence Ball was most generous in reading and commenting extensively on an early draft of this book. This work has benefited greatly from his criticism as well as his encouragement.

I am fortunate to have the support of two special friends, Professors Carol Creedon of Reed College and Max Mehlman of Case Western Reserve University Law School. To Carol Creedon, I am indebted for her sage advice and warm encouragement during the good times and the bad. To Max Mehlman, I am indebted for his steadfast friendship and his comments and suggestions on various chapters of this book.

In completing this work, I was assisted by two former students. Shawn Zanicky displayed courage and humor in drawing attention to both obvious and subtle deficiencies of early drafts. Becky Steinberger helped proofread the final draft of this book.

These acknowledgments would be incomplete without recognizing the debt I owe to my former teacher and mentor, the later Professor Mulford Q. Sibley, who encouraged me to ask important and difficult questions, and to value my own answers to these questions.

Finally, I would like to express my gratitude to my wife, Theresa, for her encouragement, assistance, and suggestions, all of which helped make this a better book than it otherwise would have been.

CONTENTS

Preface

Few moral concepts are as fascinating or as elusive as intergenerational justice. The concept is fascinating, in part, because it defies single-discipline answers. Although one can examine questions of intergenerational justice from the perspective of a single discipline, such as political theory or philosophy, the search for fuller answers inevitably leads one to ask questions traditionally the province of the natural sciences (such as limits on the capacity of this planet to support the human population) or theology (such as the value of the existence of posterity or the sources of meaning in life). Because the question "What do we owe to remote generations?" cannot be answered fully without addressing philosophical, scientific, and theological questions simultaneously, answers are often elusive.

Answers to questions of intergenerational justice are elusive for other reasons, as well. Many of the conceptual difficulties associated with intergenerational justice are the result of attempting to address intergenerational questions with moral theories which were developed in an era largely unconcerned with that issue. As several thinkers including Ernest Partridge, Peter Laslett and James Fishkin have noted, the question of intergenerational justice was nearly absent from the philosophical literature and popular discourse until the 1960s. It was then that the combination of the threat of nuclear annihilation and a loss of faith in the inevitability of progress brought the question of intergenerational justice to the fore in the West. Indeed, this combination of circumstances made it almost inevitable that intergenerational justice would become an important concern among philosophers and forward-looking political scientists.

Although some thinkers have argued that the problem of intergenerational justice is new to our era, my own view is somewhat different; we have not invented or discovered the problem of intergenerational justice, as much as we have rediscovered it. A concern with achieving justice in an intergenerational community has informed the writings of political philosophers since the Biblical era. A remarkable faith in progress, engendered by the industrial revolution, obscured the problem of intergenerational justice throughout much of the nineteenth and early twentieth centuries. As this faith faded, the question of intergenerational justice reemerged and now demands our attention.

What is unique to our age, then, is not the concern with intergenerational justice, but the way we understand intergenerational justice. In contrast to the traditional concern with acting justly in an intergenerational community, the contemporary understanding defines intergenerational justice as meeting our obligations to those who will live in the future. This understanding of intergenerational justice treats obligations to future generations as not fundamentally different from our obligations to contemporaries. Many of the difficulties and paradoxes associated with intergenerational justice stem from this change in the way intergenerational justice is understood. My analysis suggests that the principal problem with this understanding is not so much its lack of coherence, as its narrowness of focus. In other words, the problem is not that we are wrong to be concerned with meeting our obligations to those who will inherit the Earth from us, but that we are wrong to focus on this question to the exclusion of other, broader questions.

This book sets forth the case for a broader understanding of intergenerational justice, which recognizes the moral significance of our ability to determine the size and the identity of future generations, as well as our capacity to affect the conditions under which future persons will live. Our capacity to shape the future makes intergenerational action sufficiently different from intragenerational action that a new approach to intergenerational justice is called for, which treats future generations not as strangers, but as members of our community. In Chapters Eight and Nine, I suggest that a Kantian understanding of intergenerational relations may help move us in the right direction. Specifically, I argue that the we ought to act towards posterity in such a way that future generations are most likely to choose voluntarily to honor the commitments and build upon the moral traditions of their ancestors.

I

INTRODUCTION

IN THE LAST TWENTY YEARS the problem of intergenerational justice has re-emerged from a period of intellectual neglect. This re-emergence resulted largely from the realization that the welfare and even the existence of future generations are threatened by the public policies of the United States and other industrialized nations. The proliferation of nuclear weapons, the pollution of the natural environment, and the growth of our national debt hold out the very real prospect that if future generations exist at all, their lives will be significantly poorer than those of the present generation of Americans.

The renewal of concern with intergenerational justice represents a comparatively recent change in the thinking of Western nations, in general, and of the United States, in particular. As recently as the 1960s there was little discussion of intergenerational justice in the scholarly or the popular literature.[1] While the recent lack of interest in the problem of intergenerational justice may seem shocking from the vantage point of the 1990s, it is not difficult to explain. Until the 1970s, Americans generally assumed that the next generation would have a better, more prosperous life than the present generation and that this situation would continue for the foreseeable future. This faith in "progress" was largely unchallenged during the later half of the nineteenth century and the first two-thirds of the twentieth century.

An important consequence of our faith in progress was the willingness to entrust our future to the hands of science, technology, and private industry. Despite the exploitation of workers and the pollution of the natural environment throughout this period, our faith in technology was rewarded with an astounding increase in the standard of

---

[1]Ernest Partridge remarks on this fact in the Introduction to his *Responsibilities to Future Generations*. Ernest Partridge, ed., *Responsibilities to Future Generations: Environmental Ethics*, (Buffalo, NY: Prometheus Books, 1980), 10.

living of most Americans. Just as material prosperity and social mobility undermined revolutionary movements in the United States, so our faith that the next generation would be better off than the present generation undermined concern with intergenerational justice. Given the assumption of inevitable economic and even "moral" progress, there appeared to be little reason to be concerned about justice to future generations. Indeed, if anything seemed "unjust," it was that future generations would inherit a world improved by the labor of their ancestors.

The events of recent decades have shaken our faith in the inevitability of progress. Despite recent efforts at arms reduction and the collapse of the Soviet Union, the proliferation of nuclear weapons and the existence of large nuclear arsenals continue to threaten the survival of our own and other species. Nor are nuclear weapons the only threat to our survival. In recent decades we have discovered that many of the chemicals, so important in creating and maintaining our high standard of living, threaten the ozone layer protecting this planet, cause cancer and birth defects, or are otherwise toxic to human beings, animals and vegetation. We have also become aware that the agricultural practices which made the United States the "breadbasket of the world," threaten the survival of our lakes and rivers and permit top-soil erosion at a rate which imperils the long-term productivity of our agricultural land. The net result of these discoveries is that it no longer seems inevitable or even probable that future generations will enjoy greater material prosperity and a generally better quality of life than the present generation of Americans.

Once we accept that our legacy to posterity may be a world considerably less fit for human habitation than the world we enjoy, it ceases to be morally acceptable to allow the future to care for itself. Instead, it becomes essential to raise, once again, the question of intergenerational justice.

DEFINING THE TOPIC

As a working definition, we may say that intergenerational justice is what we owe to remote past and future generations as a matter of justice. By remote generations, I mean generations who are not alive at the same time, or in the words of Martin Golding, generations that do not share a "common life."[2] Intergenerational justice thus consists of our obligations to our great-grandchildren and their descendants rather than to our children or our grandchildren.

The reason for focusing on remote generations is two-fold. First, this focus emphasizes problems that are too easily neglected by our political system, such as long-term environmental concerns and the shifting of the costs of our prosperity onto future generations. Because the policies and actions of the present generation will affect the lives of future persons for hundreds and even thousands of years,[3] it is essential that we ask what obligations we have to those distant future persons who will be affected by our actions and our policies.

The second reason for the long-term focus is that this focus generally precludes relying on reciprocal exchanges among generations as a solution to questions of intergenerational justice. An example of reciprocal exchange among generations is the obligation of a child to care for her parents when they are no longer able to care for themselves. The care a child owes her parents is a form of repayment for the care she received from them when she was a child. While reciprocal exchange is often a desirable approach to resolving allocation problems among contiguous generations, it is generally unavailable to remote or noncontiguous generations. By focusing on justice to remote generations, we can ensure that any principles and policy recommendations will be applicable to both proximate and remote generations and not limited to contiguous generations.

---

[2]Martin P. Golding, "Obligations to Future Generations," *Responsibilities to Future Generations*, ed. Ernest Partridge, (Buffalo, NY: Prometheus Books, 1980), 61–62.

[3]Some nuclear waste, for example, will remain hazardous for hundreds of thousands of years.

The question of intergenerational justice has been discussed under a variety of different titles in the last two decades. In addition to "intergenerational justice," the more popular titles include "obligations to future generations," and "duties to posterity." To some extent the different titles represent merely the stylistic preferences of different authors. Contemporary approaches to the study of intergenerational ethics share much in common. Virtually all contemporary studies of intergenerational ethics are concerned with how the actions of the present generation will affect those persons who will live in the future. Similarly, almost all contemporary studies of intergenerational ethics are concerned with what the present generation owes to future generations. These two questions (how our actions affect remote generations and what we owe to remote generations) represent the "core" issues for most contemporary thinkers concerned with intergenerational justice.

Contemporary approaches to intergenerational justice differ principally in what problems are addressed beyond the core questions. Many thinkers limit their concern to these core questions.[4] Others adopt a broader understanding of the problem of intergenerational ethics, including not only obligations to future generations, but also obligations to past generations, and even the obligation to procreate.

In part, these different approaches are reflected in the ways different authors define their topic. Thinkers who are concerned only with how our actions will affect future persons and the nature of our obligations to future persons are likely to define their topic as "obligations to future generations" or "obligations to posterity." On the other hand, those who are concerned about obligations to past generations, or who are critical of the limitations inherent in focusing on future persons are more likely to define their topic as "intergenerational justice" or

---

[4]Some thinkers go so far as to argue that we have no (or almost no) obligations to distant future generations. Two thinkers who make such arguments are Martin P. Golding, "Obligations to Future Generations," *Responsibilities to Future Generations*, ed. Ernest Partridge, (Buffalo, NY: Prometheus Books, 1980), 61–72; and John Passmore, *Man's Responsibility for Nature*, (New York: Charles Scribner's Sons, 1974).

"intergenerational ethics." Given the variety of different ways that the question of intergenerational ethics can be approached, it is important to spell out my understanding of the scope of the problem and my reasons for defining my topic as intergenerational justice in preference to other possible definitions.

The explanation comes in two parts. The first part concerns the use of the term "*intergenerational*" justice as opposed to justice to "*posterity*" or justice to "*future generations.*" The second part concerns why I have chosen to focus on the question of "*justice*" and not on "*obligations*" to future generations or more generically on intergenerational "*ethics.*"

By defining my topic as *intergenerational* justice, I seek to avoid foreclosing consideration of the question of what the present generation owes to past generations. While the idea that we might have obligations to past generations strikes many contemporary thinkers as nonsensical, this idea is actually rooted deeply in Western thought. Even if we conclude that we have only the most limited obligations to past generations, respect for our intellectual traditions makes it appropriate for us to give serious consideration to the question of what we owe to past generations.

Another reason for defining the topic as *intergenerational* justice rather than justice to *future generations* or justice to *posterity* is that it encourages us to inquire broadly into our capacity to shape the future and not to limit our focus to how our actions will affect those individuals who actually will exist in the future. Some of the most difficult and important questions of intergenerational ethics arise from the power of the present generation to determine the size of the future population and the identity of those individuals who will exist in the future. If we limit the scope of our inquiry to the effects of our actions on those persons who actually will exist in the future, as do many contemporary thinkers, we make it more difficult to come to terms with the ethical issues associated with policies and actions such as nuclear war, genocide, population control, and genetic engineering. Because the capacity of the present generation to determine the size and the identity of future generations constitutes an essential aspect of the relationship among generations, it is important to define the scope of our inquiry in a manner that facilitates discussion of these questions.

The second part of my explanation concerns why I have chosen to focus on the question of *justice* and not on *obligations* to future generations or more generically on intergenerational *ethics*. There are several reasons why it is desirable to focus on the concept of justice. The first is the historic importance of the concept of justice and of the application of that concept to intergenerational questions. Perhaps no concept has been more thoroughly examined and debated in the Western literature than the concept of justice. When we apply the concept of justice to intergenerational actions we build on a tradition dating back to the Biblical Prophets and the Greek philosophers.

The concept of justice is not of historic importance only. Justice continues to be seen as the most important virtue of social arrangements.[5] The importance of the concept of justice for intergenerational action was explained well by Brian Barry who points out that

> claims based on justice are commonly regarded as having a higher priority than claims based on considerations of humanity.... If future generations were held to be ... 'outside the scope of the theory of justice' their claims would be reduced to the same residual status as the claims of animals....[6]

Even if we conclude that the concept of justice is not an appropriate standard by which to judge intergenerational actions in all situations, it is important to understand under what circumstances it is appropriate to speak of intergenerational justice and under what circumstances other concepts should be employed.

---

[5]John Rawls states that "justice is the first virtue of social institutions, as truth is of systems of thought." John Rawls, *A Theory of Justice*, (Cambridge, MA: Harvard University Press, 1971), 3.

[6]Brian Barry, "Circumstances of Justice and Future Generations," *Obligations to Future Generations*, ed. R. I. Sikora and Brian Barry, (Philadelphia: Temple University Press, 1978), 205.

THE MEANING OF "JUSTICE"

The word justice is one member of a family of words which have their root in the Latin *ius (jus)*, *iustitia (justitia)* and *iustus (justus)*. The root word *ius* in Latin means right, law, or justice. The term *iustitia* means justice or righteousness; and the term *iustus* means just.

In addition to the word *ius*, the Romans also used the word *lex* to refer to laws. *Ius* and *lex* referred to two different kinds of laws. *Lex* referred to civil law or ordinances. These were laws which existed to regulate the affairs of the state. *Ius* referred to both civil and natural law. The distinction between *lex* and *ius* corresponds roughly to the distinction which is made in modern law between acts which are *malum prohibita* (wrong because prohibited) and acts which are *malum in se* (wrong in themselves).

The English family of words which are derived from the Latin *ius* (via the French) includes just, unjust, justly, justness, justice, and injustice. The extended family includes terms such as juridical, jurisdiction, jurisprudence, jurist and jury, justiciable, as well as words such as justify, justification, and justificatory. Among the different meanings of the adjective *just* listed in the *Oxford English Dictionary* are: morally right or righteous; that which is equitable; what conforms to the standard of right, proper or correct; in accordance with reason, truth or fact; appropriate or suitable; exact; equal, even or level; complete in amount or character, full, proper or regular.

In the Roman natural law, the various meanings of the word *ius* were closely connected. For the Romans to say that an act was right or just (*ius*) implied that it was legal. By contrast, in contemporary usage we make a sharper distinction between the concepts of justice and right, on the one hand, and legality, on the other. In contemporary usage, to say that an action is just or right does not imply that the action is legal and vice versa. Thus it is perfectly coherent to say that it is just or right to assist an aged and infirm parent to end her or his own life, but that doing so would be illegal.

In other respects, there continues to be a strong connection between justice and law, as there was for the Romans. We consider justice to be the highest virtue of the law. Therefore, the most serious criticism that can be made of a law is that it is unjust. This connection between justice and the law is symbolized by the fact that we call judges on our highest courts "justices."

A noteworthy feature of our usage of the words *just* and *unjust* is that there is an asymmetry between the praise we bestow upon an action when we describe it as just, and the condemnation we heap on an action when we describe it as unjust. When we say that an action is unjust we necessarily condemn that action. Thus, we would not say that the punishment a convict received was unjust unless we thought that the judge ought to have given a different sentence. On the other hand, we might say that an action was just without indicating that the action was mandatory. For example, the parents of a man sentenced to twenty years in jail might concede that the twenty-year sentence given to their son was just (in light of the crimes he had committed), without giving up their belief that it would have been preferable for the judge to have given a lighter sentence.[7]

We may contrast the imbalance between the concepts just and unjust with the much closer balance between the terms good and bad. The praise we bestow on an action when we say that the action is good is equal to and opposite of the criticism we make of an action when we describe it as bad. This can be seen best by looking at the negations. When we say that an action is not good, we are criticizing that action, though less strongly than if we had said that the action was bad. When we say that an action is not bad, we are praising but less strongly than if we said that the action was good.

---

[7]One way of expressing this is to say that there are circumstances which may justify departing from what justice requires (as by tempering justice with mercy). On the other hand, there are few circumstances short of dire necessity which would *justify* acting unjustly towards another person.

There is something of a paradox in this statement since the words justify and just are closely related and of common origin. In this context, to *justify* an action means *to show that there are adequate grounds for* taking an action.

The asymmetry in our usages of the words just and unjust can also be seen from the fact that while it is never acceptable to act unjustly, it is not always appropriate to act "justly." A man who is said to treat his family unjustly is a person one would not want for a friend. On the other hand, a man who is described as treating his family justly, might well be suspected of being somewhat cold and stodgy.

The reason for this suspicion is that we associate acting justly with a commitment to reason and to principle. In our culture members of a family are supposed to share an emotional bond based on an unlimited commitment to their mutual welfare. Members of a family are supposed to see their individual good as inextricably interwoven with the good of other members of the family. We expect a person to treat family members with kindness and love rather than with justice. By contrast, questions of justice generally arise in the context of relations among individuals more distant from each other than members of a family. More specifically, questions of justice generally arise among individuals to whom impersonal rules apply. To apply impersonal rules to members of one's family is to act in a manner that we consider inappropriate.

What, then, do we mean when we speak of an act being just or unjust? When we say that an action is just we are indicating approval for that action. Conversely, when we say that an action is unjust we are condemning that action. However, when we say that an action is just or unjust we are doing more than simply signaling our approval or condemnation of the action; we are also indicating that we have reasons for approving or condemning the action. As Hanna Pitkin points out, concepts like justice imply standards of judgment. "Where someone considers a situation unjust, we expect him to be able to tell us how it is unjust, what is unjust about it."[8]

The standards of judgment implicit in the concept of justice are not merely personal but interpersonal. Actions are not just "to me" in the same way that a wine may taste bitter "to me." We accept that persons

---

[8]Hanna Fenichel Pitkin, *Wittgenstein and Justice*, (Berkeley: University of California Press, 1972), 185.

differ in their likes and dislikes for food. Thus, the fact that I find a food delicious, does not imply that you are wrong if you find the same food unpalatable. By contrast, even though people disagree about questions of justice, we are not prepared to accept such disagreement without further examination. We expect people to be able to give reasons for holding an action to be just or unjust, but not for saying that a food is either delicious or unpalatable.

When we say that an action is just or unjust we are not expressing merely our personal preference, we are also making a claim that we expect to bind the judgments and actions of others. When we say that an action is unjust we are indicating that persons of good conscience ought to condemn the action because it fails to meet culturally defined minimum ethical standards. Thus, to say that an action is unjust is to make a very powerful statement against *anyone* taking that action. Conversely, to say that an action is just is to provide a powerful defense of that action.

Another characteristic of the concept of justice is the type of situation in which it is appropriate to speak about justice. We do not speak of actions being just or unjust in all situations. Rather, we speak of justice when an action affects other human beings or when an action affects sentient creatures.[9] We sometimes use the word justice to characterize actions which do not directly affect human beings, as when we speak of "doing justice to a meal." But even in this "poetic" usage of the word justice, a relationship to another human being (the preparer of the meal) looms in the background.

When we speak about justice, one of our central concerns is how our actions affect other human beings and our obligations to other

---

[9]Some thinkers argue that it is also appropriate to raise questions of justice concerning our treatment of animals. Among the thinkers who take this position are Tom Regan in his "Introduction," Tom Regan, ed., *Earthbound: New Introductory Essays in Environmental Ethics*, (New York: Random House, 1984); Peter Singer in "Utilitarianism and Vegetarianism," *Philosophy and Public Affairs* 9 (1979–1980), 325–337; and Joel Feinberg, "The Rights of Animals and Unborn Generations," *Responsibilities to Future Generations*, ed. Ernest Partridge, (Buffalo, NY: Prometheus Press, 1980), 139–150.

human beings. In this context, when we say that an action is just we are indicating that the action meets culturally sanctioned standards for treating other human beings or that the action fulfills culturally defined obligations to other human beings.

We defend our judgment in these situations by advancing those criteria which would lead others to the same judgment. Thus, we might defend our judgment that a punishment was just by explaining how the punishment fit the crime, or how the punishment would lead to the rehabilitation of the criminal, or how the punishment would deter the criminal or others from committing similar crimes. When we present arguments which explain why an action was just we are said to "justify" the action.

It is apparent from these examples that there is often a lack of agreement about the criteria we ought to apply to determine whether actions are just. To the extent that people disagree about the criteria we ought to apply in determining whether actions are just, people will inevitably disagree about the justice of those actions. More importantly, to the extent that we do not agree on the criteria by which we ought to judge actions, we also do not agree about the meaning of the concept of justice.

The fact that there is disagreement about the meaning of the concept of justice is not cause for alarm. As W. B. Gallie has argued, the meanings of many moral concepts are inherently matters of dispute.[10] We cannot avoid contestable concepts without abandoning moral discourse altogether. What we can do is to recognize that moral concepts have areas of contest and attempt to understand how these areas of contest reflect different understandings of our moral concept.

A very important feature of justice is that it is not only a duty or obligation owed to our fellow human beings, it is also a right which can be demanded and obtained even from those unwilling to act justly. In

---

[10]See W. B. Gallie, "Essentially Contested Concepts," *Proceedings of the Aristotelian Society* 56 (1955–6), 167–98, for a discussion of the essential contestability of moral concepts.

this sense justice is different from other moral concepts such as love, respect, and charity. People have obligations to honor their parents, respect their elders, and give charity to the needy. It is also possible for those to whom those obligations are due to demand love, honor, respect, and charity. But neither love, nor honor, nor respect, nor charity can be obtained from an individual against her will. A person may be obligated to treat others with respect, and she may even be punished for being disrespectful, but respect can only come from the will of the individual. The same is true of love, honor, and charity.[11] Justice is unique, in that justice can be obtained from a person even when that individual remains unwilling to grant justice voluntarily.[12] Thus it is possible to have courts of justice, but not courts of love, honor, respect, or charity.[13]

On the other hand, while there are courts of justice in every nation, no nation has a court of intergenerational justice. There are no courts of intergenerational justice for very different reasons than there are no courts of love, honor, respect, or charity. While it is possible theoretically to require persons to act in an intergenerationally just manner against their will, by the time future generations suffer harm at the hands of their ancestors, those ancestors will be beyond the reach of any court. The problem, in other words, is the practical one of mootness.[14] There is no inherent reason why contemporary judges could not hear claims raised *in the name of future generations* before those

[11]The obligation to love cannot be enforced. Honor and respect can be given grudgingly, but they cannot be extracted against a person's will. One can force a person to give money to another. But forced charity is a contradiction in terms.

[12]This is not to say that justice can always be enforced successfully. No enforcement mechanism is ever perfect, and enforced justice is almost always less complete than justice voluntarily given.

[13]This is not to say that we do not sometimes try to enforce obligations to love, honor, and respect in court. But such efforts are notoriously unsuccessful.

[14]Martin Golding makes this point somewhat differently. He argues that there is a fundamental difference between having a claim and making a claim. Future generations can have a claim against us, but they are incapable of making that claim now or in the future. By contrast, at least some contemporaries, who do not have a claim on our resources, nonetheless make claims on us. Martin P. Golding, "Obligations to Future Generations," 64.

future generations come into existence. Indeed, as I argue elsewhere,[15] there may well be good and sufficient reasons why we ought to permit suits to be brought on behalf of future generations before those generations come into existence.

Nonetheless, one might be led to ask whether the lack of an institutional mechanism for enforcing judgments against prior generations diminishes our obligation to act justly towards other generations? I would suggest that it does not. The argument that the obligation to act justly towards others is dependent on the existence of an institutional mechanism for enforcing judgments rests on a Hobbesian understanding of the nature of justice. It runs roughly as follows: If there were no mechanisms for enforcing justice, or if the institutional mechanisms which dispense justice were incompetent, those individuals who act "justly" would be at the mercy of those who are unconcerned about justice. In such a situation, there can be no imperative to act justly. Instead the only imperative is to preserve oneself.[16]

What makes this Hobbesian argument inappropriate in the case of intergenerational action is the fact that the present generation cannot be threatened by the lack of an institutional mechanism for enforcing justice to future generations. To the extent that future generations cannot harm the present generation, the present generation cannot use the lack of a "common judge" as an excuse for failing to act justly towards future generations.[17]

---

[15]Bruce E. Auerbach, "Standing for Future Generations." *Pennsylvania Political Science Association Annual Meeting.* (Harrisburg, PA: 1992).

[16]See Thomas Hobbes, *Leviathan*, ed. Michael Oakeshott (New York: Collier Books, 1962), 103–124.

[17]A more complex problem is posed by the lack of a common standard of justice among remote generations. This problem is explored more thoroughly in Chapter III. At this point, it is sufficient to note that for Hobbes (as for Locke) the lack of agreement on the meaning of justice was a problem principally because it rendered persons insecure and made enforcement of law difficult, if not impossible. Lack of agreement on the meaning of justice is a less severe problem with respect to intergenerational justice insofar as disagreement over the meaning of justice may render the efforts of the present generation to act justly towards its

Even if we believed that the obligation to act justly originally grew out of the conditions of equality and mutual terror that characterize the Hobbesian understanding of the state of nature, the scope of the civilized obligation to act justly transcends this original condition.[18] Indeed, questions of justice are most appropriately raised not when natural equality ensures a fair competition, but in those situations in which natural conditions render competition unfair. Thus the obligation to act justly is most important in our dealings with those who are unable to defend themselves. We may admire the person who could "con" a Donald Trump, but we consider a person who "cons" elderly persons out of their savings or orphans out of their inheritance to be a scoundrel and a thief.

Future generations stand in a comparable position to orphans. Remote future generations are dependent on us and can do us no harm. Indeed, at present they do not even have the protection of courts of justice which might enforce our obligations against our will. But these are not reasons for absolving the present generation of the obligation to act justly towards (past or) future generations. On the contrary, they are reasons for us to be even more scrupulous in fulfilling our obligation to act justly towards other generations.

THE PROBLEM OF APPLYING THE CONCEPT OF JUSTICE TO INTERGENERATIONAL ACTION

The study of intergenerational justice is both rewarding and frustrating. It is rewarding because questions of intergenerational justice are among the most important and interesting philosophical questions of our era. It is frustrating because many of the questions which one expects to be simple often turn out to be surprisingly complex. At the

---

distant descendants futile, but such disagreement cannot pose a threat to the security of the present generation.

[18]See Brian Barry, "Circumstances of Justice and Future Generations," *Obligations to Future Generations*, ed. R. I. Sikora and Brian Barry, (Philadelphia: Temple Univ. Press, 1978), 204–248.

root of the difficulty lies the problem of understanding intergenerational action.

When we think about intergenerational justice we begin with our familiar understandings of justice among contemporaries. When we ask questions about justice we are concerned with how our actions will affect other persons and with the nature of our obligations to those persons. Generally, we consider actions to be just to the extent that the effects of our actions on others are benign and to the extent that those actions meet our obligations to other persons.

It is important to distinguish between saying that the effects of an action are benign and saying that the action meets our obligations to other generations. We generally would describe the effects of actions as benign if, at a minimum, the actions do not harm other persons. But in some circumstances we may have an affirmative obligation to provide specific benefits to other persons. In these circumstances, merely causing no harm may not be sufficient for an action to be considered just.

Most approaches to intergenerational justice seek to apply these same criteria to intergenerational actions. Thus, when we think about intergenerational justice we think about the effects of our actions on other generations and about the nature of our obligations to other generations. Generally, we hold that our actions are just to the extent that the effects of those actions on other generations are benign and to the extent that our actions meet our obligations to other generations.

The problem with this approach to intergenerational justice is that the circumstances of *inter*generational action are different from the circumstances of *intra*generational action. Our actions can shape the distant future in more and different ways than our actions can shape the near future. For example, our actions can determine the size and the identity of the distant future generations, as well as the conditions in which future generations will live. By contrast, we confront a more limited range of policy choices with respect to contemporaries. We cannot cause a decrease in the size of the present population without violating the most fundamental ethical prohibition against murder. Nor can we alter the identity of the present population without violating similarly fundamental prohibitions. As a result, the primary focus of intragenerational policies is on altering the conditions in which contemporaries live.

To the extent that we approach questions of intergenerational justice as if they were questions of intragenerational justice, there is "imperfect fit" between the assumptions which underlie our theories and the circumstances of intergenerational action. This imperfect fit has two consequences. The first is that it causes us either to recognize more limited obligations to remote generations than to contemporaries or to place a lower priority on acting justly towards remote generations than on acting justly towards contemporaries. The second is that it makes it difficult to address important intergenerational issues as questions of justice.

Perhaps the most obvious consequence of our understanding of intergenerational justice is that it makes it difficult for us to take seriously the question of obligations to past generations. In contrast to Edmund Burke and to most of the classical thinkers, many contemporary thinkers are concerned primarily with obligations to contemporaries and secondarily with obligations to future generations. Only a handful of contemporary thinkers have addressed the question of obligations to past generations.[19] Our lack of concern with the question of justice to past generations is largely a result of adhering to person-affecting principles[20]

---

[19]Among the authors who have raised the question of obligations to past generations are Joel Feinberg, "The Rights of Animals and Unborn Generations," *Responsibilities to Future Generations*, ed. Ernest Partridge., (Buffalo, NY: Prometheus Press, 1980), 139–150; and *Harm to Others, The Moral Limits of the Criminal Law*, Vol. 1, (New York: Oxford University Press, 1984); Barbara Baum Levenbook, "Harming Someone after His Death," *Ethics* 94 (1984), 407–419; and "Harming the Dead, Once Again," *Ethics* 96 October (1985), 162–164; Don Marquis, "Harming the Dead," *Ethics* 96 October (1985), 159–161; Ernest Partridge, "Posthumous Interest and Posthumous Respect," *Ethics* 91 (1981), 243–264; George Pitcher, "The Misfortunes of the Dead," *American Philosophical Quarterly* 21 (1984), 183–188; and John O'Neill, "Future Generations: Present Harms," *Philosophy* 68 January (1993), 35–51.

[20]A moral principle is a "person-affecting principle" if it considers to be morally relevant only the effects of actions on persons. Thus an act would be considered

and of our secular belief that the present generation can neither benefit nor harm persons once they are dead.[21] Even though the present generation may have obligations to past generations, we believe that it is not possible for the present generation to either benefit or harm past generations. As a result, most contemporary thinkers either ignore the question of justice to past generations or see it as a *non sequitur*.

The fact that "person-affecting principles" form the basis of most contemporary understandings of justice also tends to limit the scope of our concern with intergenerational justice in more subtle ways. To the extent that a person-regarding morality requires that we be concerned with how our actions will affect future persons, a precondition for acting justly is the ability to foresee the likely consequences of our actions for future persons. If we are unable to foresee whether a course of action is likely to be beneficial or harmful to future generations, we have no basis for holding that the action is either just or unjust to posterity.

In many cases it may be more difficult to foresee the long term effects of our actions than the short term effects. When we make policies that will affect distant future generations, we are acting towards generations who may have different cultural values than we do, and who may be affected by our actions in ways that we cannot foresee. In addition, the material world of future generations may be different from

---

wrong if and only if it harmed some person. Conversely an act would be considered good if and only if it made some person better off. Actions which neither benefit nor harm persons, or actions which do not affect persons, are considered to be morally neutral. Derek Parfit, *Reasons and Persons*, (Oxford: Clarendon Press, 1984), 393–5.

[21] This is a matter of secular faith. Not every society has held this belief. Traditional Confucian beliefs held that the worship of one's ancestor could ensure the immortality of those ancestors. The Ancient Egyptians evidently believed that the manner in which a person was buried could affect the quality of that person's afterlife. Closer to home, the Catholic religion holds that the prayers of the living may shorten the time a deceased loved one spends in purgatory. Among the contemporary thinkers who argue that the actions of the present generation can harm the dead are Barbara Baum Levenbook, "Harming Someone after His Death," 407–419, Joel Feinberg, *Harm to Others*, and "The Rights of Animals and Unborn Generations," 139–150, George Pitcher, "The Misfortunes of the Dead," 183–188; and John O'Neill, "Future Generations: Present Harms," *Philosophy* 68 January (1993), 35–51.

ours in unanticipatable ways. Just as our ancestors could not foresee the invention of the electric light bulb, so we cannot foresee future inventions that may transform the world of our descendants. The greater the uncertainty we have about the effects of our actions on remote generations, the more likely it is that we will choose to discount the value of policies that will affect remote generations.

Another problem is presented by how we define our obligations to future generations. We recognize at least four sources of obligation to other persons. The first is promises or contracts. We have obligations to other persons if we have made a promise to them, or a contract with them. A second important source of obligations is gratitude for the benefits others have bestowed upon us. A third source of obligations is a relationship of mutual trust and dependence to other persons; a fourth, universal duties owed to all human beings.

The first two sources of obligations are not normally relevant for our obligations to future generations. We cannot have promissory or contractual obligations to remote future generations, since future generations cannot sign contracts or alter their expectations based on our promises.[22] While gratitude may be a source of obligations to our ancestors, it cannot be a source of obligations to future generations. As a result, most contemporary thinkers rest their case for obligations to future generations either on our relationship with posterity or on universal duties owed to all persons.

One problem with basing obligations to future persons on our relationship with posterity is that it is not clear how we should define that relationship. Are our remote descendants members of our community with the same rights as we, entitled to consideration as the equals of present members of our community; or are remote generations strangers to us, entitled only to the minimal consideration we give to strangers?

---

[22]We can, however, make promises to our immediate ancestors to care for posterity. The validity of such promissory obligations depends on the validity of obligations to past generations.

Several arguments support the view that remote generations stand as strangers to us. The first is the fact that our distant descendants are unknown to us. Indeed, this is a matter of definition since remote generations are typically defined as those generations with whom we do not share a common life.[23] Second, remote generations may be culturally different from us. Remote generations may have different understandings of the good life[24] and of justice.[25] Remote generations may even see us as part of their barbarian past. Finally, reciprocity between remote generations is impossible. We can affect remote future generations, but remote future generations cannot affect us.

Whether we see remote generations as members of our community or as strangers is a critical issue. Our obligations to members of our family and to our community are both more extensive and generally of higher priority than our obligations to strangers. While defining future generations as strangers would not eliminate all obligations to them, it would place severe limitations on those obligations. Undoubtedly, we would recognize a general obligation to avoid causing harm to future generations just as we recognize a general obligation to avoid harming strangers. But if we considered future generations to be strangers, we would recognize no particular obligation to promote their good, just as we recognize no particular obligation to promote the good of contemporary strangers.

Contemporary thinkers are divided over the question of whether future generations should be considered to be strangers or members of our community. Many hold that future generations stand as strangers to us. Others argue that we ought to treat those who will exist in the future as members of our extended community.[26] But even those who adopt

---

[23]See for example, Martin Golding, "Obligations to Future Generations," 61–62.

[24]Ibid., 70.

[25]Terence Ball, *Transforming Political Discourse*, (New York: Basil Blackwell, 1988), 142–160.

[26]Among those who adopt such a position are Daniel Callahan and Richard Routley and Val Routley. Daniel Callahan, "What Obligations Do We Have to Future Generations?," *Responsibilities to Future Generations*, ed. Ernest Partridge, (Buffalo,

the later position have some difficulty coming to grips with the special circumstances which make it difficult to treat future generations as full members of our community. Because the circumstances of *inter*generational action are different from those of *intra*generational action, when we apply the paradigm of justice to contemporaries to intragenerational actions, the fit is less than perfect. The effect of approaching intergenerational justice in the same way we approach justice to contemporaries is to make our obligations to remote generations seem more limited than our obligations to our contemporaries.

An even more severe problem with contemporary approaches to intergenerational justice is that they fail to address important dimensions of intergenerational action which have no analogies in intragenerational action. For example, a concern with the effects of actions on other persons assumes the existence of a stable reference population against which to measure the consequences of actions. But future generations are not a stable reference population. Our actions affect not only the conditions in which future generations will live, but also the size and the identity of that population. Indeed, it is our act of procreation which brings future generations into existence in the first place. If, instead of procreating, we act to prevent the existence of future persons, a strict application of person-affecting principles would make it impossible to measure the morality of our actions.

Similar problems exist with respect to our power to affect the identity of future persons. Policies such as genocide and genetic engineering represent attempts to alter the identity of the future population. To the extent that our approach to intergenerational ethics and justice is tied to measuring the effects of our actions on actual (but future) persons, we may have difficulty addressing coherently the ethical implications of actions which prevent the existence of segments of the

---

NY: Prometheus Books, 1980), 73–85. Richard Routley and Val Routley, "Nuclear Energy and Obligations to the Future," *Responsibilities to Future Generations*, ed. Ernest Partridge, (Buffalo, NY: Prometheus Books, 1980), 277–301.

human population or which bring one set of individuals into existence in preference to another.

While some thinkers have struggled to extend our theories of justice in an effort to address questions such as the obligation to procreate, a commitment to person-regarding principles has led other thinkers to argue that actions which prevent the existence of future persons raise no questions of intergenerational justice.[27] Thinkers such as Mary Warren argue that we ought to confine our discussion of intergenerational ethics to the effects of our actions on those persons who will actually exist in the future, and not be concerned with the intergenerational ethics of preventing the existence of merely "potential" persons.[28] An even more common response is simply to ignore the issues raised by our capacity to determine the size and identity of the future population, by focusing on those questions which our theories of justice allow us to address more easily. As I argue in the second half of this book, such a response is unacceptable. In an era in which the human and other species face the threat of possible extinction from nuclear weapons and environmental pollution, the survival of the human species is an essential question of intergenerational justice.

The emerging science of genetic engineering also makes it imperative that we develop ethical standards to cover actions which seek to alter the identity of the future population. At a minimum, a theory of intergenerational justice must enable us to distinguish between attempts to eliminate genetic diseases and policies which seek to eliminate racial, ethnic or "genetic" minorities. While the power to determine the size and the identity of the human population can be discussed from the point of view of justice to contemporaries, any attempt to deal with these questions solely from the perspective of the current generation is inherently inadequate. We must extend our understanding of

---

[27] Actions which prevent persons from procreating may, of course, raise questions of justice to contemporaries.

[28] Mary Warren, "Do Potential People Have Moral Rights?," *Obligations to Future Generations*, ed. R. I. Sikora and Brian Barry, (Philadelphia: Temple Univ. Press, 1978), 24–28.

intergenerational justice to include a concern with the ethical dimensions of our capacity to affect the size and identity of the future population. We must also begin the task of developing ethical standards for actions that affect the size and identity of the future population.

II

The Historical Roots of Intergenerational Justice

"Know therefore that the Lord your God is God, the faithful God who keeps covenant and steadfast love with those who love him and keep his commandments, to a thousand generations...." Deuteronomy 7:9

OUR MODERN UNDERSTANDING of intergenerational justice has its roots in Biblical writings and, to a lesser extent, in the writings of Ancient Greece. We can trace the antecedents of our contemporary concern with the environment to Biblical prohibitions against deforestation as a tactic of war[1], and to the injunctions to allow the land to lie fallow every seven years.[2] Contemporary concerns with the effects of pollution on future generations have striking parallels to the concerns of the Biblical prophet Jeremiah, who wrote that "the fathers have eaten sour grapes, and the children's teeth shall be set on edge."[3] More generally, we have inherited from the Hebraic and the Greek traditions an outlook towards nature and towards our fellow human beings which continues to influence our thinking on intergenerational justice.[4]

Although there are a great many differences between the Hellenic and the Hebraic traditions, they also have several characteristics in common. The first is their concern with community. Both the Hebrews and the Greeks saw membership in a community as the most important feature of their social world. The community was seen as the conveyer

[1] *Deuteronomy* 20, 19.

[2] *Exodus* 23, 10–11.

[3] *Jeremiah* 27, 29.

[4] Among the more important perspectives we have inherited from the Hebraic traditions is the notion that human beings have dominion over nature. This concept is explored later in this chapter.

of those values which made life worth living. Communities could be based on membership in a tribe, on citizenship in a polis, on a shared history or Covenant, or a combination of these and other characteristics. Members of a community shared bonds which united them and which differentiated them from members of other communities. Communities had histories. Members of a community shared habits and attitudes which developed when people were raised under similar conditions or shared common experiences.[5] Thus the Hebrew people wandered forty years in the desert before they could enter the promised land. The experience of the exodus and the deprivation of the desert forged the bonds necessary to establish a community out of former slaves and the children of former slaves.

The Hellenic and Hebraic traditions also shared an understanding that communities had an existence and a reality which extended beyond that of individual members of the community at any given moment. This was so in two senses. First, the Classical thinkers recognized that communities could perish even if the individuals who made up the community at any given time survived. Thus, if a city was conquered and its citizens dispersed and sold into slavery, the community, which was the city, would perish just as surely as if the city had been sacked and all the citizens killed. For the Ancient world, the death of a community in the first manner was no less real than its death in the second.

The other sense in which classical thinkers recognized communities as having a reality beyond that of the individual, is that they understood communities to be inherently intergenerational. Communities were made up not only of those alive at any given time, but also of those who had lived in the past, and those who would live in the future.

The intergenerational nature of community was not a mere abstraction; it was an essential part of what was meant by a community. Thus, the Covenant which God made with Abraham extended not only to Abraham, but also to Abraham's descendants. Similarly, the polis is

---

[5]See for example, Plato's discussion of new colonists in *The Laws*, (Book IV, 708), 163.

described by Plato as being made up of clans composed of the present generation, its ancestors, and its descendants.[6]

A third characteristic which Hellenic and Biblical writers share is that they were concerned not only with the physical survival of the community, but also with the health and justice of the community. Of all the Hellenic writers, this is most true of Plato. In *The Laws*, the Athenian states that "we do not hold the common view that a man's highest good is to survive and simply continue to exist. His highest good is to become as virtuous as possible and to continue to exist in that state as long as life lasts."[7] While a few isolated individuals, such as a Socrates, might become just despite living in an unjust polis, the more general situation is that persons can only become as virtuous as possible when they live in a just polis.[8] A central task of both *The Republic* and *The Laws* is to inquire into the types of institutions and legislation required for citizens to become "as virtuous as possible and to continue to exist in that state as long as life lasts."[9]

Perhaps the most important characteristic which Plato and the Biblical authors share is the understanding that justice is necessary for the long term health and survival of the community. In *The Republic*, Plato argues that the polis decays in proportion to its departure from justice, though it is equally accurate to say that the departure from justice is both the cause and the symptom of decay in the polis.[10] The Hebrew Prophets, too, never ceased warning of the intergenerational consequences to the community of injustice, and of the benefits to the community of acting justly. For example, the prophet Jeremiah states

> ... if you truly amend your ways and your doings, if you truly execute justice with one another, if you do not oppress the alien, the fatherless or the widow, or shed innocent blood in this place, and if you do not go after

---

[6]Plato, *The Laws*, (Book XI, 923), 464.

[7]Plato, *The Laws*, (Book IV, 707), 168.

[8]Plato, *The Republic*, (Book VI, 487–496), 194–204.

[9]Plato, *The Laws*, (Book IV, 707), 168.

[10]Plato, *The Republic*, (Book VIII, 546), 269.

> other gods to your own hurt, then I will let you dwell in this place, in the land that I gave of old to your fathers for ever.[11]

From the modern perspective what is striking about the Ancient understanding of intergenerational justice is that neither the Prophets nor Plato described the problem of intergenerational justice principally in terms of acting justly towards future persons. Certainly this is not due to the failure of the Ancient thinkers to be aware that the actions of one generation affect future generations. On the contrary, it is quite clear from the writings of Plato and the Prophets that they understood well that the actions of the present generation affect the welfare of posterity.[12] Nor were Plato and the Prophets unconcerned with the welfare of future generations. If anything, they were more concerned with the welfare of their descendants than we are with the welfare of ours.

The Biblical Prophets and Plato did not conceive of the problem of intergenerational justice in terms of acting justly towards future persons because they had a different understanding of the role of justice in the community. Their understanding linked the perpetuation of the community to the achievement of justice. For both the Prophets and Plato, intergenerational justice consisted primarily of achieving justice in an intergenerational community. In this sense, we might say that the Ancients had *an intergenerational conception of justice* rather than *a concept of intergenerational justice*.

The Prophets and Plato believed that if the survival and prosperity of the community were to be assured, the community must adhere strictly to the standards of justice. Communities which departed from the standards of justice, inevitably would suffer the consequences of their

---

[11] *Jeremiah* 7, 5–7.

[12] For example, the compilers of the Bible recognized that human beings are capable of making significant and destructive changes in the ecology of the planet which would affect future generations. Thus the Bible prohibits the destruction of food bearing trees even when besieging a city asking "Are the trees in the field men that they should be besieged by you?" *Deuteronomy* 20, 20. More generally, both the Platonic and the Biblical writings saw acts of injustice as having negative consequences for future members of their respective communities.

unjust actions. Those consequences might be felt by the present generation or by future generations. In either case, it was the community which would reap the consequences of its injustice.

THE BIBLICAL UNDERSTANDING OF INTERGENERATIONAL JUSTICE

The Hebrew understanding of intergenerational justice has at least three essential components. The first is the Covenant. The Covenant is a compact between God and Abraham which binds not only Abraham but also the descendants of Abraham.[13] The Covenant establishes the Hebrew Community as an intergenerational community.

The second component is the laws of the Hebrew people. The Torah includes laws which either prohibit or require certain actions in order to establish justice in the community. Many of these laws regulate actions which are intergenerational in nature.

The final component is the prophetic tradition. The principal concern of the writings of the Hebrew prophets is justice in the community. More specifically the Prophets are concerned with warning the Hebrew people that their departures from righteousness would bring destruction on themselves and their descendants.

The Covenant between God and Abraham is the foundation of the Hebrew community. The Covenant is a compact not only between God and Abraham, but between God and Abraham and the descendants of Abraham, through his son, Isaac. In the Covenant, God promises to protect Abraham and his descendants and Abraham promises that he and his male descendants will be circumcised as a sign of the Covenant with God.

God said to Abraham,

> 'As for you, you shall keep my Covenant, you and your descendants after you throughout their generations. This is my Covenant which you shall keep, between you and your descendants after you: Every male among you shall be circumcised. You shall be circumcised in the flesh of your

[13]Later Covenants were made between God and Isaac and God and Moses.

> foreskins, and it shall be of the Covenant between me and you. He that is eight years old shall be circumcised; every male throughout your generations, whether born in your house or bought with your money from any foreigner who is not of your offspring, both he that is born in your house and he that is bought with your money shall be circumcised. So my Covenant shall be in your flesh an everlasting Covenant. Any uncircumcised male who is not circumcised in the flesh of his foreskin shall be cut off from his people, he has broken my Covenant.'[14]

From the perspective of intergenerational justice, the Covenant presents a major theoretical problem. This is the idea that the promise of one individual can bind the actions of the descendants of that individual. Our normal assumption is that a person cannot make promises for another and that an individual can only be bound by his or her own promises. The Covenant which God makes with Abraham departs from this model in that Abraham promises not only that he will keep the Covenant, but that his descendants will do so, as well.

The questions we must ask of the Covenant of God with Abraham are the same questions we should ask of commitments the present generation makes for future generations. "What is the basis for the authority to make a Covenant binding on future generations?" and "What makes this Covenant an exercise of legitimate authority?"[15]

One possible justification for the authority of Abraham to make the Covenant with God is that as the patriarch of the family, Abraham has the authority to speak for his descendants. His word is binding on future generations because future generations will owe their existence to his actions.

This answer would likely have not satisfied the Ancient Hebrews any more than it would satisfy contemporary thinkers. The role of the tribal head of Ancient Israel was to provide moral leadership to the

---

[14]*Genesis* 17, 9–14.

[15]It could be argued that Abraham did not have any say in the terms of the Covenant, that Abraham had no choice but to accept the covenant as a commandment of God. But this interpretation would distort beyond all recognition the concept of a covenant. Abraham must have accepted the Covenant with God voluntarily, in order for the concept of a covenant to be meaningful.

community. Only in time of war did the tribal chief have the authority to command. "In time of peace, the tribal chief could not impose his decisions."[16]

For most modern thinkers, the notion of patriarchal authority is unacceptable. We see appeals to patriarchal authority as illegitimately equating intergenerational justice with the will of the older generation, much as Thrasymachus equates justice as the will of the stronger in Plato's *Republic*. Defining justice as the will of the older generation says nothing about how that older generation ought to act towards posterity.[17] Unless we have a reason to hold that Abraham acted justly towards posterity when he agreed to the Covenant with God, we cannot conclude that future generations have a duty to fulfill the terms of that Covenant.

A second answer we might give is that Abraham had the authority to make a Covenant for future generations because Abraham was presented with the choice of either agreeing to or rejecting the Covenant. It was God who chose the terms of the Covenant. If Abraham agreed to the Covenant his agreement would bind the choices of future generations. But if Abraham did not agree, his choice would deprive his descendants of the benefits of the Covenant. Whatever Abraham's "existential" choice, his descendants would live with its consequences.

This understanding of Abraham's choice is strikingly similar to some of the dilemmas we face today. Our technology has developed to the point that many of our public policy choices will have a significant impact on remote generations. The choice of leaving the world as we found it, and thus not affecting remote generations, is no longer available to us. In this situation, intergenerational justice requires us to give due consideration to the interests of future generations when choosing among the options available to us.

---

[16] George Horowitz, *The Spirit of Jewish Law*, (New York: Central Book Co., 1973), 68–69.

[17] See Pitkin, 169–192.

We can justify Abraham's decision to bind his descendant in similar terms. Given the choices which Abraham faced, Abraham's substantive responsibility to posterity was to give due consideration to the interests of his descendants. Even though the Covenant binds his descendants, Abraham acted justly in agreeing to the Covenant because he made the choice he felt would be in the best interests of his descendants. Indeed, Abraham is revered by both Jews and Arabs as the great Patriarch of their peoples.

But even this answer does not dispose of our concerns, entirely. For it is not clear that it would be just for Abraham to agree to a Covenant which deprived future generations of the liberty to choose whether to be bound by the Covenant, even if Abraham felt that this might be in the best interests of his descendants. Considerations of procedural justice may well have prohibited Abraham from making certain kinds of promises for posterity. For Abraham to bind himself to God is an act of autonomy. For Abraham to bind his descendants may be an act of tyranny by past generations over future generations.

Once again there are striking analogies between the choices facing Abraham and those we face today. For example, most contemporary American conservatives oppose spending on social welfare programs. Many of these same conservatives supported the tax cuts and defense spending increases of the Reagan years. These conservatives were willing to tolerate annual federal deficits of several hundred billions of dollars. Indeed, some so-called conservatives went further and argued that one of the fringe benefits of the record deficits of the Reagan era was that the burden of financing the national debt would deprive future generations of the ability to expend resources on new social welfare programs, thus making permanent the "conservative" policies of the Reagan administration.

Commitments made by one generation, which bind future generations, raise a number of issues which are as important today as they were three thousand years ago. One issue is whether we have an obligation to attempt to act in a manner which will benefit future generations, and, if so, how we can know whether future generations will actually find our actions beneficial.

Many of the policies of the present generation bind and restrict the choices of future generations. At the same time, the actions of one generation can open up new options for posterity and leave to future generations the possibility of altering the course of history in ways that reflect their wisdom and their judgment. Intergenerational justice requires the present generation to make those choices which reflect its best judgment of what is desirable for the future, without unduly restricting the capacity of future generations to make their own policy choices.

Fundamental questions of intergenerational procedural justice arise when the actions of the present generation restrict the options available to future generations. Such actions must be justified more carefully than other substantive choices. The more one generation deprives future generations of the ability to chart their own course, the greater the burden of justification that generation must meet. Because the capacity to exercise autonomous judgment is a fundamental right valued by human beings, there is some point beyond which it may become impossible to justify binding the choices of future generations regardless of how great the supposed benefits to posterity.

The Covenant does not exceed this limit primarily because the obligations of the Covenant must be assumed voluntarily by successive generations.[18] Later generations retain the capacity to abandon the Covenant by abandoning its obligations, including the circumcision of male children. On the other hand the fact that successive generations must choose to renew the Covenant does not mean that the Covenant is not binding on the Hebrew community, and on those who would remain within the community. To be a member of the Hebrew community meant to accept the responsibilities of the Covenant. Individual members of the community could be required to live by the law of the

[18]In fact the Covenant is not simply renewed but enhanced with the giving and acceptance of the Law at Mount Sinai.

Covenant, just as individuals in other communities are required to live by the laws of those communities. If the people as a whole break the Covenant by abandoning the laws and practices made obligatory by the Covenant, they would be cut off from past generations who had observed the Covenant and from future generations of the Hebrew community, who would not exist.

The second element of the Hebraic understanding of intergenerational justice is to be found in the Torah, the law of the Hebrew people. Many of the injunctions of the Torah are concerned with regulating conduct that has an impact on future generations. The Torah includes a prohibition against the cutting down of trees as a tactic of war, and a specific prohibition against the cutting of food trees for building siegeworks.[19] The Hebrew people are also prohibited from taking a bird and its chicks from a nest on the same day.[20] These prohibitions are complemented by affirmative obligations such as the requirement that the land be allowed to lie fallow every seven years.[21] Together these prohibitions and injunctions indicate a concern with the impact of human actions on the natural environment, which is comparable in many ways to contemporary concern over the use of defoliants in war and with the impact of modern farming techniques on soil erosion. The Biblical writers quite clearly were concerned with ensuring practices which were compatible with the long-term prosperity of their community.

The Torah also includes prohibitions and injunctions aimed at regulating policies which directly affected other human beings and other

---

[19]"When you besiege a city for a long time, making war against it in order to take it, you shall not destroy its trees by wielding an axe against them; for you may eat of them, but you shall not cut them down. Are the trees in the field men that they should be besieged by you? Only the trees which you know are not trees for food you may destroy and cut down that you may build siegeworks against the city that makes war with you, until it falls." *Deuteronomy* 20, 19–20.

[20]*Deuteronomy* 22, 6–7.

[21]The principal stated purpose of the injunction to allow the land to lie fallow every seventh year is to feed the poor. The secondary stated purpose is to allow wild beasts to eat. *Exodus* 23, 10–11.

generations. For example, the Rabbis interpreted the Biblical commandments regarding the conduct of war as prohibiting cutting off all paths of retreat when besieging a city.[22] War was not to be waged against future generations.[23] The Bible also enjoins fathers to teach their children to love and fear God.[24] These elements of the Hebrew Law are designed to ensure the perpetuation and survival of the intergenerational community which the Covenant established.

The third component of the Hebrew understanding of intergenerational justice is the Prophetic tradition. The most important function of the Hebrew Prophets was to admonish the Hebrew people to keep the Covenant with God and to act justly. Their message was that if the Hebrew people did not mend their ways, they or their offspring would be punished by God. On the other hand, if the people did mend their ways, God would bless them and their descendants and restore them to prosperity.

An important characteristic of the Hebrew understanding is that reward and punishment were most often foreseen as befalling not only the present generation, but future generations as well. Thus in Exodus, God is quoted as commanding the following to Moses:

> 'I am the LORD your God, who brought you out of the land of Egypt, out of the house of bondage.
> You shall have no other gods before me.
> You shall not make for yourself a graven image, or any likeness of anything that is in heaven above, or that is in the earth beneath, or that is in the water under the earth; you shall not bow down to them or serve them; for I the Lord your God am a jealous God, visiting the iniquity of the fathers upon the children to the third and the fourth generation of

---

[22]Horowitz, 150–1.

[23]The exception to this rule is that the Hebrew people were commanded to exterminate the seven original tribes of Canaan so "that they may not teach you to do according to all their abominable practices which they have done in the service of their gods and so to sin against the Lord your God." Deuteronomy 20, 18. As Horowitz points out this was never carried out. Horowitz, 147.

[24]*Deuteronomy* 6, 1–9.

> those who hate me, but showing steadfast love to thousands of those who love me and keep my commandments.'[25]

On the other hand, in the Prophetic writings we also see unhappiness with the idea that a person should be punished for the sins of the father. For example in Ezekiel we read the following words:

> Yet you say, 'Why should not the son suffer for the iniquity of the father?' When the son has done what is lawful and right, and has been careful to observe all my statutes, he shall surely live. The soul that sins shall die. The son shall not suffer for the iniquity of the father, nor the father suffer for the iniquity of the son; the righteousness of the righteous shall be upon himself, and the wickedness of the wicked shall be upon himself.[26]

We see similar concerns expressed in the Book of Jeremiah in the form of a prophesy of a new covenant:

> In those days they shall no longer say: 'The fathers have eaten sour grapes, and the children's teeth are set on edge.'
> But every one shall die for his own sin; each man who eats sour grapes, his teeth shall be set on edge.[27]

Despite the unhappiness of some of the prophetic writers with the idea that the children should be punished for the iniquities of their parents, there is a recognition that the welfare of future generations, in fact, is tied to the actions of the present generation. In this regard, the prophetic vision has striking parallels to present-day concerns that future generations will inherit an environment rendered toxic by our pollution.

An important difference between the Prophetic understanding of intergenerational justice and the contemporary understanding is that, for us, what makes a policy such as the depletion of the ozone layer unjust, is that future persons will be harmed by these actions. By contrast, for the Prophets such a policy would be unjust because it violated the Covenant with God and departed from the ways of righteousness. For us, the suffering of future generations *is* the evil, whereas for the Prophets the

---

25 *Exodus* 20, 2–6.

26 *Ezekiel* 18, 19–20.

27 *Jeremiah* 31, 29–30.

failure to keep the Covenant was the evil, and the suffering of future generations, God's punishment for the inequities of prior generations.

The Prophetic and contemporary approaches to intergenerational justice also rest on different understandings of our relationship to posterity. The Prophetic model assumes that the people care intensely about what happens to their community and their descendants. Indeed, the Prophetic model assumes that people care at least as intensely about the fate of their community and their descendants as they do about their own fate. If people did not care intensely about the fate of their descendants, then the threat of God's punishment falling on their descendants would not be an effective spur to action. For the Ancient Hebrews a prophesy that future generations would become like strangers to them would have been a powerful condemnation of their actions.

By contrast, our modern understanding of intergenerational justice does not assume that we care as much about posterity as we do about ourselves. On the contrary, most contemporary understandings of intergenerational justice start with the premise that future generations *are* like strangers to us. According to most contemporary understandings, our principal obligation is to avoid acting in ways that cause harm to future generations. For us, the problem of intergenerational justice arises only when we become aware our actions may result in injury to those persons who will exist in the future.

PLATO'S CONCEPTION OF INTERGENERATIONAL JUSTICE

Compared to the profoundly historical world view of the Prophets, the Platonic understanding of intergenerational justice seems static and ahistorical. For Plato, the overriding problem was to establish justice in the polis. Once justice was established, intergenerational justice consisted primarily of not changing the existing institutions or deviating from existing practices.

To avoid the dangers of innovation, Plato would have the guardians of the laws censor or discourage almost every activity which could lead people to depart from the existing practices of the just polis. Thus, Plato favors censorship of poetry, story telling, and music.[28] Plato would also have the guardians of the laws regulate the games children play to guard against the introduction of innovations.[29] Clearly, this is a conservative position.

It is important to recognize that Plato's conservatism is based on the assumption that the polis is already just. Plato is concerned with eliminating innovation which may lead to an unthinking departure from justice. Plato does not propose stifling innovation which would improve the polis. If the existing order is unjust, Plato is not hesitant about prescribing the most radical changes in those institutions and practices. This is clearest in *The Republic*, where Plato proposes the most profound changes to the existing social and political order of the polis. But it is also true where the existing order more closely approximates justice. For example, in *The Laws*, Plato allows for changes in the laws of Magnesia to remedy the inevitable deficiencies in the work of the legislator.[30]

For Plato, a polis, by its very nature, is an intergenerational community; and a just polis is an intergenerationally just community. An essential part of Plato's examination of justice in *The Republic* and *The Laws* concerns the relationship among the generations. Thus, Plato dwells at length on questions such as the best way to educate children in music, athletics and the art of war. Plato's concern with education arises from the belief that an essential function of a community is to educate

---

[28]Plato, *The Laws*, (Book VII, 800–802), 287.

[29]Ibid., 284.

[30]Ibid., 247. Plato sees more room for innovation in the early years of Magnesia than in its later years. The Athenian proposes that the process of remedying deficiencies "should continue until every detail is thought to have received its final polish. After that, they must assume that the rules are immutable, and observe them along with the rest of the code which the legislator laid down and imposed on them originally. Not a single detail should be altered, if they can help it; but if they ever believe that the force of circumstances has become irresistible, they must consult all the officials, the entire citizen body and all the oracles of the gods. If the verdict is unanimously in favor, they may amend, but never in any other condition whatever; the law will be that the opposition must always win the day." *The Laws*, (Book VI, 772), 251. As might be expected Plato is considerably less hostile to innovation in *The Republic* where he makes the assumption that the rulers are philosophers who understand the Forms.

the next generation to be good citizens. To do this, the next generation needs to acquire not only the skills required of citizens, but also the attitudes and habits which make a person a good citizen. A polis which fails to educate the youth properly inevitably will change. For Plato, if the laws of the polis are just, change necessarily entails a falling away from justice.

A just community is also concerned about the proper relations between adults and children.[31] Thus, Plato devotes considerable attention to the problem of selecting the next generation of guardians, in *The Republic*, and new members of the nocturnal council, in *The Laws*.

An important objective of these sections is to set forth those conditions which permit the just polis to perpetuate itself. But it is a mistake to interpret these sections of Plato's work as dealing only with the perpetuation of the polis, as if the question of the perpetuation of the polis were separate and distinct from the question of justice in the polis. For Plato, a polis which fails to transmit its laws and its institutions to the next generation, without those laws and institutions undergoing fundamental change, is an unjust polis. This is true both for the ideal world of *The Republic*, and for the practical world of *The Laws*. Thus, an important test of the justice of the laws is whether future generations consider the laws worth preserving and perpetuating.[32]

The notion that justice concerns only how actions affect our contemporaries is as alien and as antagonistic to the thought of Plato as to the thought of the Hebrew Prophets. For Plato, to be unconcerned with the perpetuation of the laws and institutions of the polis was to be unconcerned not only with intergenerational justice, but with justice itself. The polis was an intergenerational community, and a concern with the proper relations among generations is an integral part of what it meant to be concerned with justice in a community. If we want to understand Plato's views on intergenerational justice we need to look not

---

[31]See for example Plato, *The Laws*, (Book IV, 716–718), 174–176.

[32]See Plato, *The Laws*, (Book IV, 707–708), 163–164.

only to his discussion of the dangers of intergenerational change, but also to his understanding of the polis as an intergenerational community.

Nowhere is the intergenerational nature of the polis more apparent than in a passage from *The Laws* in which the Athenian addresses the question of how questions of inheritance should be regulated. The Athenian, who speaks for Plato in this dialogue, suggests that people be told the following when they come to death's door and wish to dispose of their property:

> 'Friends, you "creatures of a day" in more senses than one, it is difficult for you in your present circumstances to know the truth about your own property and also "know yourselves," as the Delphic inscription puts it. Therefore, I, as legislator, rule that neither you nor this property of yours belongs to yourselves, but to your whole clan, ancestors and descendants alike; and your clan and its property in turn belong, even more absolutely, to the state. That being so, I should be reluctant to tolerate someone worming himself into your good graces when you are smitten with illness or old age, and wheedling you into making a will that is not for the best. I shall legislate with a view to nothing except the interest of your clan and the entire state, relegating (as is only right) that of the individual to second place. So as you go on your journey, which is the way of all flesh, show restraint and goodwill towards us: we will look after your affairs for the future and guard your interests with the utmost care, down to the smallest detail.'[33]

What is clear from both *The Republic* and *The Laws* is that the survival of the polis and the justice of the polis are inextricably linked. A just polis will endure far longer than an unjust one.[34] In an unjust polis, the laws exist to serve the interests of the stronger and not the interests

---

[33]Ibid., 464–465.

[34]Even a just polis will inevitably decay. To explain this decay in *The Republic*, Plato introduces an imperfection (in the form of a failure of the guardians to understand the mysteries of the proper timing of conception) in order to explain how it is that the Republic could fall from its condition of virtue. The consequence of this imperfection is the birth of less worthy children, who are incapable of understanding fully the forms. As a result of having less worthy guardians, the polis begins to fall away from justice in accelerating stages through the various degenerate forms of government. *The Republic*, (Book VIII, 546), 269.

of the whole state.[35] When this is the case, there is constant strife, the polis is weak, and its collapse not far off. On the other hand, "if law is the master of the government and the government is its slave, then the situation is full of promise and men enjoy all the blessings that the gods shower on a state."[36]

Just laws, like the just polis, endure longer than unjust laws. The endurance of the laws in turn brings about greater respect for the law.

> When the laws under which a people are brought up have by some heaven-sent good fortune remained unchanged over a very long period, so that no one remembers or has heard of things being any different, the soul is filled with such respect for tradition that it shrinks from meddling with it in any way. Somehow or other the legislator must find a method of bringing about this situation in the state.[37]

EDMUND BURKE

Perhaps no thinker is more closely associated with the concept of intergenerational justice than Edmund Burke. The concept of intergenerational justice is the cornerstone of Burke's political theory and of his critique of the French Revolution. This, alone, would make Burke's writings worth examining in a study of intergenerational justice. What makes Burke's writings especially important is the fact that they also serve as a transition between the classical concern with justice in an intergenerational community, and the modern concern with obligations to future persons.

Burke's understanding of intergenerational justice echoes many of the themes we saw in the writings of Plato and in the Bible. Like Plato and the Biblical writers, Burke understands society (and the state) to be inherently an intergenerational community. Thus, Burke argues that the state

---

[35]Plato, *The Laws*, (Book IV, 715), 173.
[36]Ibid., 174.
[37]Ibid., 284.

> ... is to be looked upon with reverence, because it is not a partnership in things subservient only to the gross animal existence of a temporary and perishable nature. It is a partnership in all science; a partnership in all art; a partnership in every virtue and in all perfection. As the ends of such a partnership cannot be obtained in many generations, it becomes a partnership not only between those who are living, but between those who are living, those who are dead, and those who are to be born. Each contract of each particular state is but a clause in the great primeval contract of eternal society, linking the lower with the higher natures connecting the visible and invisible world, according to a fixed compact sanctioned by the inviolable oath which holds all moral natures, each in their appointed place.[38]

Because society is intergenerational, justice also must be intergenerational. If people act as if the Earth were the sole possession of the present generation, if they fail to respect the value of what they have inherited from the past and ignore the needs and interests of future generations, they act unjustly.

> ... [O]ne of the first and most leading principles on which the commonwealth and the laws are consecrated is, lest the temporary possessors and life-renters in it, unmindful of what they have received from their ancestors or of what is due to their posterity, should act as if they were the entire masters, that they should not think it among their rights to cut off the entail or commit waste on the inheritance by destroying at their pleasure the whole original fabric of society, hazarding to leave to those who come after them a ruin instead of a habitation—and teaching these successors as little to respect their contrivances as they had themselves respected the institutions of their forefathers. By this unprincipled facility of changing the state as often, and as much, and in as many ways as there are floating fancies or fashions, the whole chain and continuity of the commonwealth would be broken. No one generation could link with the other. Men would become little better than the flies of summer.[39]

38Edmund Burke, *Reflections on the Revolution in France*, (New York: Bobbs-Merrill, 1955), 110.

39Burke, 108.

These passages from Burke are strikingly similar to the "creatures of a day" speech in Plato's *Laws* [40] and to other passages in *The Laws* which are critical of unthinking innovation.[41]

But if Burke shares the classical view that society is intergenerational in nature, Burke also adds something to the classical understanding. What Burke adds is the recognition that future generations have rights and that we have obligations to future members of our community. Speaking of Dr. Price and other advocates of "the rights of man," Burke states that

> [i]n denying their false claims of right, I do not mean to injure those which are real, and are such as their pretended rights would totally destroy. If civil society be made for the advantage of man, all the advantages for which it is made become his right. It is an institution of beneficence; and law itself is only beneficence acting by a rule. Men have a right to live by that rule; they have a right to do justice, as between their fellows, whether their fellows are in public function or in ordinary occupation. They have a right to the fruits of their industry and to the means of making their industry fruitful. The have a right to the acquisitions of their parents, to the nourishment and improvement of their offspring, to instruction in life and to consolation in death.[42]

Burke's innovation is to argue that the present generation is morally responsible for the consequences to future generations of the present generation's unjust assault on the political community. In Burke's hands an act of injustice, such as the revolutionary overthrow of the political order, which causes the decline of civilization, becomes a double injustice. First, it is an act of injustice to overthrow the existing political order because the existing order is based on a partnership or contract among the generations. Because the contract is a sacred one, beyond the

---

[40]Plato, *The Laws,* (Book XI, 923), 464–465.

[41]See for example *The Laws,* (Book IV, 708) 163, in which Plato argues that a colony populated by settlers from different cities "haven't the unity of a swarm of bees," and (Book VII, 797–8) 283–4, in which Plato argues that constant change is equally unhealthy for the body and the polis.

[42]Burke, 67.

reach of any individual or even any generation, to abrogate this contract is a grave injustice.

Second, it is an act of injustice to overthrow the existing order because to do so would cause injury to future generations. When the existing political order is overthrown, forces and passions are unleashed which threaten to destroy the collective inheritance which is a civilization. Those who undertake to make a revolution are responsible for depriving future generations of the benefits of civilization to which they are entitled.

Burke's first argument evokes the classical understanding that the present generation is bound by the terms of an intergenerational compact, just as the Hebrews were bound by the Covenant. To break such a contract is sinful and unjust. If the present generation abrogates the intergenerational contract, the community inevitably will decline.

Burke's second argument goes beyond the first in making explicit that the harm which will befall future generations is the moral responsibility of those who abrogate the intergenerational contract. The second argument states that it is wrong to break the intergenerational contract *because* future generations have a right to inherit the benefits of a civilization which is not the creation of any one generation, but the product of a partnership of many generations. Once we recognize that future generations have a right to the benefits of that intergenerational partnership, we cannot deny that the suffering of future generations, caused by the breaking of the intergenerational contract, constitutes an injustice.

THE TRANSITION TO THE MODERN APPROACH

An important characteristic of the traditional approaches to intergenerational justice is that one's obligations to past and future generations were based on membership in a community. For the Biblical writers and for Plato, intergenerational justice consisted of acting justly in an intergenerational community. If the community were just, then it would perpetuate itself and its traditions across the generations. If the community were unjust, if the children were not taught the ways of justice, the community would depart from the path of righteousness, and hard times would befall it.

Burke shared the traditional view that intergenerational justice consisted of acting justly in an intergenerational community. But with Burke there is a subtle shift in the way intergenerational justice is understood. Even though Plato and the Biblical writers cared intensely about how their actions would affect their descendants, they did not hold that to permit their respective communities to decline was to perpetrate an act of injustice *upon their descendants.* Instead, the classical thinkers saw the suffering of future generations either as the natural and tragic consequence of the injustices of their ancestors or as a punishment God meted out to the community for the iniquities of their ancestors.

Burke represents a pivotal figure in the transition from the traditional to the contemporary understanding of justice. Burke based his theory of intergenerational justice on the traditional view that the community is inherently an intergenerational enterprise. Burke added to the traditional understanding the insight that if the present generation takes actions which imperil civilization, they also act unjustly *towards* those who will live in the future by depriving those persons of benefits to which they are entitled.

For Burke the decline of the community is not only a consequence of the injustice of the community, it is also an injustice *to* future generations. Because future generations have a right to the benefits of civilization, the actions of revolutionaries who seek to break with the past are unjust to those who will live in the future. The fact that civilization is an inherently intergenerational enterprise means that the present generation has an obligation *to* future persons to preserve civilization and not to squander the accumulated wisdom of centuries of cultural evolution.

It is clear that Burke's position represents an extension of the classical understanding of intergenerational justice, rather than a radical departure from that understanding. On the other hand, by extending the classical understanding, Burke also introduces a tension into (or recognizes a tension in) the concept of intergenerational justice that did not previously exist (or was not previously recognized). At the heart of the classical understanding of intergenerational justice was the belief that just as each generation was indissolubly bound to its ancestors and its descendants, so justice among contemporaries was inseparable from justice among the generations. In the writings of Burke we see, for the first time, the possibility of an opposition between a concern with justice to contemporaries and a concern with intergenerational justice. For Burke, this tension is properly resolved by subordinating the demands of the present generation to the longer range goal of achieving intergenerational justice. Thus, Burke opposes revolutionary demands for distributional justice among contemporaries by arguing that to accede to these demands would be to act in an *intergenerationally* unjust manner. Nonetheless, after Burke, it is possible to speak of intergenerational justice as a problem distinct from the problem of justice.

Two critical elements of the contemporary understanding of intergenerational justice, thus, are already present in the writings of Edmund Burke. The first is the idea that different generations may have different interests, and that what may be advantageous to the present generation may not be just to future generations. The second is the understanding that we have obligations *to* those persons who will live in the future. The concept of *obligations to future persons* is at the core of most contemporary understandings of intergenerational justice.

The last elements which make up the contemporary understanding of intergenerational justice are not present in Burke. These are the decline of the pillars of traditional morality: religion-based ethics, community and authority, and their replacement by anthropocentric ethics and individualism.

We no longer understand ethics in terms of the fulfillment to religious duties. We also no longer see ourselves as existing in coherent intergenerational communities. Reciprocal obligations to other human beings have replaced religious authority as the cornerstone of our ethics. This has had a dramatic impact on how we understand intergenerational justice.

The decline of authority also played a pivotal role in undermining Burke's notion of an intergenerational contract. We no longer accept the legitimacy of an intergenerational contract because we do not accept that one generation has the authority to bind the actions of its descendants. In the absence of such authority, intergenerational contracts among remote generations become far more problematic.

In abandoning the concept of an intergenerational contract as the basis for civilization, we also undermine Burke's argument that future generations have a contractual right to the benefits of civilization. For Burke, the claims of future generations grew out of the recognition that civilization is an intergenerational enterprise. Because all generations were seen as having a claim to the benefits of civilization, no one generation had the right to abandon that enterprise. While many contemporary thinkers retain the idea that future generations have rights, most contemporary thinkers who speak of the "rights of future generations" seem to have in mind something closer to the understanding of rights embodied in the French Revolution's *Declaration of the Rights of Man and Citizen*, than to Burke's contractual rights of citizenship.

Where the present generation is understood to have duties to God or to past generations, we can speak of intergenerational justice, but not of obligations to future persons. By contrast, where the present generation is understood to have obligations to persons who will live in the future, or where those future generations are seen as having rights and the present generation as having corresponding duties, intergenerational justice tends to be equated with obligations to future persons.

Much of the current literature on intergenerational justice can be understood as an effort to work out the implications of having reconceptualized intergenerational justice as obligations to future persons. Much remains to be done to complete this process.

THE DEVELOPMENT OF MODERN UNDERSTANDINGS OF INTERGENERATIONAL JUSTICE

A concern with justice is characteristic of virtually every society and every epoch. The same may not be said of intergenerational justice. In some periods there is considerable interest in intergenerational justice; in others, little or none.

Nowhere is the episodic nature of the concern with intergenerational justice more apparent than in the last two centuries. Intergenerational justice lay at the heart of Edmund Burke's political philosophy, in general, and of his critique of the French Revolution, in particular. Today a concern with intergenerational justice once again is the focus of academic and political debate. Yet, in the period between Edmund Burke and the 1970s, remarkably little was written about intergenerational justice.[43]

It is not clear whether the absence of interest in intergenerational justice is a phenomenon peculiar to the period in question or part of a recurring cycle in human history. My research supports the conclusion that a concern with intergenerational justice is not a recent development, as some contemporary theorists have argued.[44] However, it is difficult to determine whether the lack of interest in intergenerational justice in the

[43]One piece which does address the question of intergenerational justice is Nicolai Hartmann, *Ethics*, (Atlantic Highlands, NJ: Humanities Press, 1932), Vol. 2.

As I indicated in the first chapter, it is possible to explain our immediate ancestors' lack of interest in the question of intergenerational justice in terms of the faith in progress which characterized the intellectual climate in Europe and especially in the United States during the nineteenth and the first half of the twentieth century. This faith in progress gave people confidence that each succeeding generation would have a better life than its ancestors. Under such conditions, questions of intergenerational justice were overwhelmed by the faith that future generations would have the means to solve those problems which they inherited from their ancestors.

[44]See for example the argument of Hans Jonas, "Technology and Responsibility: The Ethics of an Endangered Future," *Responsibilities to Future Generations*, ed. Ernest Partridge, (Buffalo, NY: Prometheus Books, 1980), 23–36. See also Peter Laslett, and James S. Fishkin, "Introduction: Processional Justice," *Justice between Age Groups and Generations.*, ed. Peter Laslett and James S. Fishkin. (New Haven: Yale University Press, 1992), 14–15.

past century and a half is a unique occurrence or part of a cyclical pattern. If the waxing and waning of interest in intergenerational justice is part of a cyclical pattern in history, one would expect to find that certain types of conditions are associated with rising interest in intergenerational justice and others with declining interest. It seems probable that rapid social change, which produces anxiety about the future, would be associated with rising interest in questions of intergenerational justice. Certainly the writings of Plato, the Prophets, and Edmund Burke date from such eras. One might also expect that eras of stability or eras in which there is great confidence in the future would be characterized by declining interest in intergenerational justice.

On the other hand, it may be the case that most eras have been characterized by a concern with the issue of intergenerational justice, and that the absence of interest in intergenerational justice in our recent past is anomalous. Without undertaking an extensive study of the history of the concept of intergenerational justice, it is not possible to resolve this question. We may leave its resolution safely to future research, since the inability to resolve this question does not stand in the way of addressing other, more pressing issues.

Perhaps the most important issue which needs to be addressed is the conceptual difficulties associated with contemporary understandings of intergenerational justice. Among the conceptual issues which have been raised are concerns about the coherence of the concept of intergenerational justice,[45] the paradox of the non-identity problem,[46]

---

[45] Terence Ball, *Transforming Political Discourse*, (New York: Basil Blackwell, 1988), 142–160.

[46] The "non-identity problem" is a paradox described by Derek Parfit. This paradox arises when we define our moral concerns as a concern with whether our actions harm or benefit future persons. Parfit argues that any policy which is sufficiently significant to harm or benefit remote future generations will simultaneously have the effect of altering the identity of those persons who will exist in the future. (If a policy produces "benefits" or "harms" to future persons that policy must inevitably alter the course of people's lives sufficiently to affect the timings of conceptions and therefore the identities of subsequent generations.) Consequently, we cannot say that remote future persons will be either better off

the problems associated with the concept of obligations to potential persons,[47] and the concern that by focusing almost exclusively on obligations to future persons, we fail to address essential ethical questions arising from our capacity to shape the future.

While no moral concept is entirely free of conceptual difficulties, intergenerational justice would seem to have more than its share. Much of the contemporary literature is devoted to exploring and attempting to resolve these and other conceptual problems.

One reason conceptual difficulties surround the concept of intergenerational justice is that our moral understandings (including our understanding of the concept of justice) changed profoundly in the period between the late eighteenth century and the middle of the twentieth century.[48] Significantly, this was also an era in which concern for intergenerational justice was largely absent, in large measure due to the faith in progress engendered by the industrial revolution. The fact that a conceptual revolution in our understanding of justice took place in an era which was largely unconcerned with intergenerational justice has important implications for the development of this concept.

The normal course of conceptual development subjects new moral theories and understandings to criticism based on the ability of those

---

or worse off than they would otherwise be as a result of our policies (since those individuals would not exist if our policies were significantly different).

Parfit goes on to argue that the fact of non-identity ought not make a moral difference. He argues, however, that this is a reason for abandoning person-affecting principles in favor of utilitarian ethics. Derek Parfit, *Reasons and Persons*, (Oxford: Clarendon Press, 1984), 351–379.

Elsewhere I have argued that the non-identity problem can be addressed without abandoning person-affecting principles. Bruce E. Auerbach, "Intergenerational Justice and the Prophetic Tradition," *Annual Meeting of the American Political Science Association*, (New Orleans, LA: 1985).

[47]See, for example, the debate over the preservation of mankind in R. I. Sikora and Brian Barry, eds., *Obligations to Future Generations*, (Philadelphia: Temple University Press, 1978).

[48]For example, utilitarianism dates from the early Nineteenth Century writings of Jeremy Bentham and James Mill. While theories of justice based on individual rights are somewhat older, their widespread acceptance is also a comparatively recent phenomenon.

theories and understandings to confirm our intuitive moral judgments.[49] In order for moral theories to gain wide acceptance they must conform to the intuitive judgments of large numbers of persons. New theories which depart from those judgments in significant ways tend to be rejected.

However, this confirmation process is only as good as the questions we ask of our ethical theories. An era which is unconcerned with intergenerational justice will not test new ethical theories rigorously for their ability to conform to intuitive judgments concerning justice to other generations. Because many of our contemporary ethical theories either were developed or were changed in the period between the late eighteenth century and the middle of the twentieth century, when concern with intergenerational justice was at its nadir, those ethical theories have not been tested and critiqued as thoroughly for their ability to guide *inter*generational actions as for their ability to guide *intra*generational actions.[50]

When the question of intergenerational justice is taken up, once again, in the later half of the twentieth century, we are not simply picking up where traditional thinkers left off. Instead, we are seeking to address the problem of justice to other generations with concepts which are different in significant ways from those which had served as the basis for traditional discussions.[51] We discover new issues and new problems

---

[49]John Rawls describes this process as reflective equilibrium. John Rawls, *A Theory of Justice*, 20–22, 48–51.

[50]For example, James S. Fishkin points out that "the liberty to procreate is problematical because our notions of individual human interests have not been refined to deal with problems involving future possible people. Our ordinary criteria either break down or yield bizarre results." James S. Fishkin, "The Limits of Intergenerational Justice," Justice between Age Groups and Generations, ed. Peter Laslett and James S. Fishkin. (New Haven: Yale University Press, 1992), 63.

[51]Laslett and Fiskin are thus quite correct in pointing out that *the particular definition of intergenerational justice they use* ["an obligation on all present persons to conduct themselves in recognition of the rights of all future persons, regardless of geographical and temporal position"] "did not exist as a subject of analysis discussion, or even as a concept before ... the 1960s at the earliest." Peter Laslett, and James S. Fishkin, "Introduction: Processional Justice," 14–15.

not only because our world has changed, but also because the moral perspectives from which we view the world are different, in fundamental ways, from those of our ancestors.

What makes the change in our conceptual framework particularly important for the study of intergenerational justice is the fact that the meaning of the concept of intergenerational justice is linked to and derived from the meaning of the concept of justice. As our understanding of justice changes, so does our understanding of intergenerational justice. But this is not the only way that the concept of intergenerational justice can change. Changes may also take place along a second plane, in the *way* the concept of intergenerational justice is derived from the concept of justice. We can see such a dual change in the concept of intergenerational justice by comparing the ways in which traditional and contemporary understandings of intergenerational justice are linked to and derived from their respective concepts of justice.

As we have seen, the classical thinkers generally did not have a separate concept of intergenerational justice. Rather, they understood intergenerational justice to consist of acting justly in an intergenerational community. This understanding reflected the classical idea that justice was the virtue that allowed the (intergenerational) community to function well.

The classical understanding of intergenerational justice also generally rested on a religious foundation and on the primacy of the community as an object of moral concern. For example, the Hebraic understanding of the obligation to act justly towards one's fellow human beings was rooted in divine commandment. Thus in Deuteronomy, the Hebrew people are commanded "[Y]ou shall not pervert justice; you shall not show partiality; and you shall not take a bribe, for a bribe blinds the eyes of the wise and subverts the cause of the righteous. Justice, and only justice, you shall follow, that you may live in the land which the Lord your God gives you."[52] To show partiality or to take a bribe was to

---

[52] *Deuteronomy* 16, 19–20.

violate one's duties to God, and thereby to subject oneself and one's community to God's punishment.[53]

Traditional thinkers also stressed the importance of membership in a community and the role of justice in ensuring the long term health and survival of the community. The decay of the community was seen as the most severe consequence of injustice.[54]

By contrast, contemporary thinkers generally understand intergenerational justice to consist of meeting one's obligations to future persons or respecting the rights of future persons. Unlike the classical understanding of intergenerational justice, we understand the concept of intergenerational justice to be separate from the concept of justice. This is to say that our understanding of intergenerational justice and justice allows for the possibility of conflict between the obligation to act justly towards contemporaries and the obligation to act justly towards remote generations. The traditional understanding of intergenerational justice did not permit such an opposition. Because traditional thinkers recognized that the community was intergenerational, they understood justice to require that one focus not on the welfare of contemporaries alone but on the intergenerational health of the community.

Contemporary theories of justice also no longer rest on the traditional pillars of religious duties and community ties. Instead, most contemporary understandings of intergenerational justice are rooted in secular values. More specifically, most contemporary understandings of intergenerational justice are based on person-affecting principles.

Our understanding of intergenerational justice is based on person-affecting principles insofar as actions are considered to be intergenerationally just if the effects of our actions meet our obligations to persons of remote generations, and intergenerationally unjust if the effects of those actions fail to meet our obligations to persons of remote generations. We do not raise questions of intergenerational justice

---

[53]The Platonic understanding of justice was not based on divine command. But it, too, was far removed from the contemporary understandings of justice.

[54]A substantially similar understanding of the relationship between justice and the health of the community is central to Plato's *Republic.*

about actions which do not affect other generations. We also do not raise questions of intergenerational justice if we considered ourselves to have no moral obligations to other generations.

The central issue in the contemporary debate over intergenerational justice is the nature of our obligations to future persons. Thinkers from different schools of thought have very dissimilar understandings of what we owe to future persons. Utilitarians argue that our obligations to future persons consist of acting in a manner which brings about the greatest amount of happiness (or good) for the greatest number of future persons. Thinkers in the individual rights tradition argue that our obligation is to respect the rights of future individuals. Still others adhere to the view that we have an obligation to treat future persons as equals.

The shift from a religious based concern with community to a secular concern with obligations to individuals has a number of important consequences. As we have seen, perhaps the most obvious consequence is that most contemporary thinkers are not concerned with the question of obligations to past generations. The principal reason for our lack of concern with obligations to past generations is that our secular assumptions about the nature of life lead us to conclude that the actions of the living cannot affect those who have died.[55] While there is some debate among contemporary thinkers over the question of whether we can harm the dead,[56] the dominant view is that we can neither affect nor harm the dead. Since person-affecting principles hold that actions which do not affect other persons are morally neutral, we are led to conclude that our actions can be neither just nor unjust to past generations.

---

[55] Some contemporary religions, most notably Catholicism, do hold that it is possible to intercede with God on behalf of the dead through prayer.

[56] Among the contemporary thinkers who argue that the actions of the present generation can harm the dead are Barbara Baum Levenbook, "Harming Someone after His Death," 407–419, Joel Feinberg, *Harm to Others*, and "The Rights of Animals and Unborn Generations," 139–150 and George Pitcher, "The Misfortunes of the Dead," 183–188; John O'Neill, "Future Generations: Present Harms," *Philosophy* 68(263) January (1993), 35–51.

Another important consequence of the shift from religious and community based understandings of intergenerational justice to a secular understanding is that by defining intergenerational justice as obligations to future persons, we enhance the probability of an opposition between the demands of justice and those of intergenerational justice. Future persons may have different interests than contemporaries. To give only one obvious illustration, it may be in the interest of the present generation to finance federal spending programs by long-term borrowing on the credit of the United States Government, but it is most definitely not in the interests of future generations to inherit this debt.

While the traditional understanding of justice in an intergenerational community did not eliminate conflicts among generations, the traditional understanding tended to deny the imprimatur of "justice" to benefits which accrued to the present generation at the expense of posterity.[57] By contrast, to the extent that contemporary understandings of intergenerational justice are concerned principally with the interests of future persons, one effect of separating the questions of justice and intergenerational justice is to diminish the salience of intergenerational justice.

A more subtle effect of the shift from the traditional to the contemporary understanding of intergenerational justice is to narrow what is meant by intergenerational justice. According to the contemporary view, in order to say that an action is intergenerationally unjust, we must be able to establish a link between that action and an undesirable consequence for some future person to whom we have an obligation. Unless we are concerned with how our actions will affect future persons or about whether our actions will meet our obligations to future persons, we do not raise questions of intergenerational justice. Thus, contemporary thinkers who are concerned about intergenerational justice focus typically on issues such as the effects of present energy

---

[57]See for example Plato's "creatures of a day" speech quoted earlier in this chapter. Plato, *The Laws*, (Book XI, 923), 464–465.

policies on future generations or the effects of environmental pollution on future generations.

However, not all actions which shape the future of the human community take the form of actions which affect "actual but future" persons. To take only the most glaring example, a nuclear holocaust which exterminates the human species would have the most profound effect on the future of the human community. Yet, because such a holocaust would prevent the existence of future generations, there would be no harm to any actual future person. Similar dilemmas appear when examining the implications of genocide and to a lesser extent population control.

Contemporary approach to intergenerational justice also make it more difficult to apply the concept of justice to policies and actions that shape the size and the identity of the future population. Ironically, this class includes many actions which traditionally had been understood to raise the most serious questions of intergenerational justice. Indeed, the traditional understanding of intergenerational justice was much broader and therefore better suited to dealing with such twentieth-century evils as nuclear war and genocide.[58] The traditional understanding of intergenerational justice included not only a concern with meeting one's obligations to past generations but also a concern with the survival and the development of the community in the future. Since the community was seen as transcending the lives of the individual members and as giving those lives meaning,[59] actions which harmed the community were considered to be unjust.

---

[58]Unlike nuclear war, genocide was not invented in the twentieth century. However, genocide does seem to have become an epidemic in the twentieth century.

[59]This is clearly the case for the Hebrew people who saw themselves as "the chosen people." This view is also present in the writings of Edmund Burke who states that "[e]ach contract of each particular state is but a clause in the great primeval contract of eternal society, linking the lower with the higher natures connecting the visible and invisible world, according to a fixed compact sanctioned by the inviolable oath which holds all moral natures, each in their appointed place." Burke, 110.

III

Contemporary Approaches to Intergenerational Justice

WITH THE RECENT REVIVAL OF INTEREST in the question of intergenerational justice has come a proliferation of articles advocating one or another philosophical approach to the question of intergenerational justice. Prominent in the literature are arguments advocating a contract model,[1] an individual rights approach,[2] and two variants of utilitarianism.[3] This chapter examines the debate over intergenerational justice in an effort to assess the adequacy and coherence of contemporary understandings of this concept.

A significant obstacle to assessing contemporary understandings of intergenerational justice is the fact that there is no single contemporary theory of intergenerational justice. It cannot even be said that there are competing contemporary theories of intergenerational justice. The situation is more muddled than that. What exists is a debate over intergenerational justice. This debate is characterized by agreement on a

---

[1]See John Rawls, *A Theory of Justice*, (Cambridge, MA: Harvard University Press, 1971), 284–293.

[2]Among those who adopt a rights-based approach are Joel Feinberg, "The Rights of Animals and Unborn Generations," *Responsibilities to Future Generations*, ed. Ernest Partridge, (Buffalo, NY: Prometheus Press, 1980), 139–150 and "Harm and Self-Interest," *Law, Morality and Society: Essays in Honour of H. L. A. Hart*, ed. P. M. S. Hacker and J. Raz. (Oxford: Clarendon Press, 1977), 284–308; Galen K. Pletcher, "The Rights of Future Generations," *Responsibilities to Future Generations*, ed. Ernest Partridge., (Buffalo, NY: Prometheus Books, 1980), 167–170; and Annette Baier, "The Rights of Past and Future Persons," *Responsibilities to Future Generations*, ed. Ernest Partridge. (Buffalo, NY: Prometheus Books, 1980), 171–183.

[3]Specifically, total and average utilitarianism. For a discussion of the differences between these two variants of utilitarianism, see Derek Parfit's *Reasons and Persons*, (Oxford: Clarendon Press, 1984), 391–417. See also L. W. Sumner, "Classical Utilitarianism and the Population Optimum," *Obligations to Future Generations*, ed. R. I. Sikora and Brian Barry, (Philadelphia: Temple University Press, 1978), 91–111, for an argument in defense of total utilitarianism.

number of important propositions and by disagreement on other equally important propositions. Many thinkers have contributed to this debate. But, as yet, no contemporary thinker has set forth a comprehensive theory of intergenerational justice along the lines of John Rawls's *Theory of Justice*.

Before we can assess contemporary understandings of intergenerational justice, it is necessary to discover the dominant patterns and common assumptions that characterize contemporary thinking on this question. At the outset I would remind the reader that my conclusions are based on my own interpretation of the literature. I make no claim that mine is the only valid interpretation, and I would be the first to recognize that some contemporary thinkers do not fit the pattern of this analysis. Nonetheless, it is worthwhile attempting to extrapolate the dominant understandings of intergenerational justice from the contemporary literature, if we hope to develop a more adequate understanding of this concept.

SHARED ASSUMPTIONS OF CONTEMPORARY THINKERS

Three assumptions (or preconditions) are common to most contemporary understandings of intergenerational justice. The first is that our actions will affect future persons. The second is that we have the capacity to choose among different courses of action based on their moral preferability. The third is that we have some affirmative obligations to future persons. Unless these three preconditions are met, contemporary thinkers generally do not raise questions of intergenerational justice.

The first precondition, that our actions will affect future persons, expresses an important feature of our contemporary moral outlook.[4] We regard as morally relevant only those actions that affect other persons. If we knew that no persons would exist in the distant future or that our actions could have no effect on future persons, we would assume that we

[4]See my discussion of person-affecting principles in Chapter II.

have no moral obligation to consider the long-term effects of our actions. Actions that affect oneself, but no other person, are termed self-regarding, and self-regarding actions are not generally considered to be proper objects of moral scrutiny.[5] Similarly, actions that affect the present generation, but not future generations, do not raise problems of intergenerational justice. Finally, to the extent that we cannot know whether persons will exist in the future, our moral obligations to posterity can be said to be contingent or conditioned on the existence of future generations.

On its surface, the assumption that our actions will affect persons in the future would seem to raise few difficulties.[6] Intuitively, it seems clear that our actions can either benefit or harm those who will live in the future.[7] If we pollute our waters, future generations will drink poisoned water. If we develop alternate energy sources, future persons may have a better quality of life than our own.[8]

---

[5]The classical statement on this question is, of course, John Stuart Mill's *On Liberty*. John Stuart Mill, "On Liberty," *Essential Works of John Stuart Mill*, ed. Max Lerner, (New York: Bantam Books, 1961) 249–360.

[6]On the other hand, in Chapter II we saw that our inability to "affect" those who have died leads many contemporary thinkers to dismiss the notion that we can have obligations to past generations.

[7]One way that our actions might have no effect on future persons is if no persons existed in the future. For example, if we were certain that the sun would explode within the next 50 years, we would consider ourselves to be under no obligation to conserve resources for remote future generations. Apparently a similar confidence in the coming of the Apocalypse undergirded James Watt's willingness to develop the wilderness. J. Adler, et al., "James Watt's Gold Rush," *Newsweek*, (June 29, 1981), 29.

[8]At least one philosopher has challenged the assumption that our actions can be said to either benefit or harm remote generations. In his book *Reasons and Persons*, as well as in various articles, Derek Parfit argues that there exists a "non-identity problem" which makes it impossible for us to say that our actions either benefit or harm remote persons. Parfit argues that any policy important enough to affect how remote future generations will live will also have the effect of altering the genetic identity of those individuals who will exist in the future (because such a policy would incidentally affect the timings of conceptions). To the extent that we are dealing with unique futures, populated by unique persons, we cannot really say that distant future persons will be either better off or worse off as a result of our policies. See Derek Parfit, *Reasons and Persons*, (Oxford: Clarendon Press, 1984).

But moral responsibility requires more than the fact that our actions affect other persons. It also requires that we be able to do something about *how* our actions affect others. Even if our actions cause harm to other persons, we would not consider ourselves to be morally responsible for that harm unless we could have pursued a different course of action and it was reasonable for us to have done so.

There are several reasons why we might lack the ability to pursue a different course of action. First, a particular course of action may be the only one open to us. Under such circumstances we would speak of acting out of necessity. Second, an alternate course of action may be available but we may be unaware of the existence of that alternative. We do not hold a person responsible for failing to choose a morally preferable course of action unless that person either was aware, or should have been aware, that another course of action was both possible and morally preferable.

In order to hold a person morally responsible for the effects of her actions, it must have been possible for her to have foreseen the likely effects of those actions[9] and to have acted differently from the way she did. The inability to foresee the possible effects of a course of action, to be aware of the risks inherent in a course of action, or to pursue a different course action excuses a person of moral responsibility for her or

---

Elsewhere, I have argued that while the non-identity problem does not represent a fundamental moral problem, Derek Parfit does point us in the direction of a different moral problem which is fundamental. This is the fact that we have the capacity to alter the identity of future persons as a matter of deliberate policy and not just as the random by-product of other policies. When people engage in policies such as eugenic breeding or genocide, or when they engage in broader social policies knowing that they will alter the reproductive patterns of discrete social groups, we cannot ignore the effects of such policies on the identity of future generations. Bruce E. Auerbach, "Intergenerational Justice and the Prophetic Tradition," *Annual Meeting of the American Political Science Association*, (New Orleans, LA: 1985). These questions are addressed at some length in Chapter VI.

[9]It is not necessary that we be able to foresee the possible effects of an action with great specificity. The ability to see that there are substantial and unjustifiable risks inherent in a course of action is generally sufficient for holding a person responsible for the consequences of her or his actions.

his actions. Finally, even if we are aware of the risks inherent in our actions, and even if we are aware of the existence of alternate courses of action, we would be free to chart our own course unless we had reason to believe that some courses of action were morally preferable to others.

Most contemporary thinkers hold that these conditions of moral responsibility are met with respect to distant future generations. This is to say, we have the capacity to choose among different courses of action based on their moral preferability. Even though we can neither foresee the future in detail, nor even be certain how future generations will react to the world they inherit, we are not ignorant of the fact that some policies involve a greater risk of harm to future generations than others. Science and common sense tell us that the continued pollution of this planet will have undesirable consequences for future generations. Even though it is conceivable that remote future generations may turn our garbage dumps into a valuable resource, it is irresponsible and unethical for us to count on such good fortune and creative adaptation by future generations when weighing the morality of our public policies.

The fact that our actions will affect future persons and that we have the capacity to choose among different courses of action means that most of the preconditions for moral responsibility to future generations are met. However, meeting these preconditions does not establish that we have an obligation to consider the interests of future generations when framing our public policies. Nor does it determine the extent and nature of our obligations to future generations. Before we can conclude that we have obligations to future generations, we must still accept that future persons are the types of beings to whom we can have obligations. It is this premise which is the subject of the greatest amount of debate among contemporary thinkers. For many thinkers, the existence of obligations to future persons follows directly from the recognition of the common humanity of all generations. For other thinkers, the existence of obligations to future generations is less obvious.

THE ANALYTICAL FRAMEWORK

Perhaps the most important division in the contemporary literature on intergenerational justice is between those who understand our obligations to posterity to be a function of our relationship to future persons and those who understand those obligations to be based on universal principles which govern our conduct towards all persons. I use the term *relational model* (or *approach*) to describe the first understanding and the term *universalistic model* (or *approach*) to describe the second.

The relational model of intergenerational justice is based on the proposition that our obligations to other persons are a function of our relationship to those persons. Just as we can have more or less extensive obligations to our contemporaries, so we can have more or less extensive obligations to members of future generations, depending on our relationship to them. In general, we have more extensive obligations to those persons with whom we share bonds of mutual trust and affection than to those with whom we share no such bonds. For example, we recognize the obligation to provide for the education of our children and to help pay for the education of the children of other members of our community. A community may even employ criminal sanctions against parents who fail to provide for the education of their children or who refuse to help pay for the education of the children of others. By contrast, we recognize more limited obligations to strangers. Although we accept that there is some obligation to help strangers in distress (when this can be done at minimal cost to ourselves), we generally do not understand this obligation to extend to providing for the education of their children, nor to providing for their general welfare. In a similar vein, we see ourselves as being obligated to tend the graves of our parents and of other deceased members of our community, but not to tend the graves of strangers. For thinkers who adopt a relational approach to intergenerational justice, a critical issue is how we define our relationship to posterity because how we define this relationship determines the extent of our obligations to future generations.

The universalistic approach to intergenerational justice holds that our obligations to other (future) generations are based on universal principles which govern our conduct towards other persons. Thinkers who adopt a universalistic approach tend to emphasize the moral equality of all persons regardless of the place or time of their birth. They argue that it is just as wrong to cause harm to remote future persons as it is to cause comparable harm to contemporaries.[10]

Two critical issues for thinkers who adopt a universalistic approach are how we define those universal principles which govern human interactions and how we apply those principles to actions which affect future persons. There is little agreement among proponents of the universalistic approach about which principles we ought to adopt nor about how those principles ought to be applied to the special circumstances of intergenerational action.

It is important to recognize that the relational and universalistic approaches to intergenerational justice are polar positions and not mutually exclusive categories. Even those who adopt a strongly relational approach may recognize that we have some obligations to strangers (and hence to remote generations) based on universal principles.[11] Similarly, those who base their theories of intergenerational justice on universalistic principles may accept that we can have special obligations to persons who are close to us, in addition to the universal obligations owed to all human beings.

Much of the difference between these approaches lies in the emphasis placed on one basis for obligation or the other. Those who base their ethical theories on relational models tend to minimize the

---

[10]See for example the argument of Richard Routley and Val Routley, "Nuclear Energy and Obligations to the Future," *Responsibilities to Future Generations*, ed. Ernest Partridge, (Buffalo, NY: Prometheus Books, 1980), 277–301.

[11]For example, Martin Golding recognizes that our actions may be bound by general duties to perform actions that are intrinsically right, but he distinguishes these general duties from the obligation to promote the good of future generations, which can only arise from our relationship to future generations. Martin P. Golding, "Obligations to Future Generations," *Responsibilities to Future Generations*, ed. Ernest Partridge, (Buffalo, NY: Prometheus Books, 1980), 62–63.

importance of universal ethical principles as a source of obligations to posterity. By contrast, those who base their theories on universalistic principles tend to minimize the importance that special relationships play in ethical decision making. One way that universalistic thinkers do this is by defining their universal principles more elaborately, so that these principles incorporate the flexibility to allow one to treat different persons differently.[12]

It is also worth noting that there are important similarities between contemporary relational approaches to intergenerational justice and the traditional understandings which we examined in the last chapter. An important assumption of both the traditional and the contemporary relational approaches is that obligations to other persons arise from membership in a community and that such obligations as we do have to other generations arise from membership in an intergenerational community. To the extent that this is the case, a critical question becomes who is a member of our intergenerational community. To recognize all or some of our descendants as members of our community is to recognize the existence of special obligations to those generations. By contrast, to hold that remote future generations are not members of our community is to accord remote future generations no more than the minimal consideration one would accord strangers.

In view of the similarities between traditional and contemporary relational approaches to intergenerational justice, it is striking that many contemporary relational thinkers agree that remote future generations (as contrasted with our immediate descendants) are more like strangers than members of our community. For example, Martin Golding states that it is "highly doubtful" that remote future persons will be members

---

[12]An excellent example of this approach is found in Ronald Dworkin's *Taking Rights Seriously*. Dworkin argues that there is a constitutionally based obligation to treat others as equals. However, the obligation to treat other persons as equals does not mean that all persons must receive the same treatment regardless of their circumstances. On the contrary, to treat others as equals may require that persons be treated differently in different circumstances. Ronald Dworkin, *Taking Rights Seriously*, (Cambridge, MA: Harvard University Press, 1977), 223–239.

of our moral community, "for we probably do not know what to desire for them."[13] Although Terence Ball comes to a different conclusion than Golding, Ball makes a similar point when he states that he suspects that "[w]e can know very little about remote future generations, save that they will probably be composed of beings quite unlike ourselves and with a different mix of claims and dissimilar conceptions of the human good."[14]

The exclusion of remote future generations from membership in our community leads those who are committed to a relational approach to de-emphasize our obligations to remote generations. Because bonds of mutual dependence, expectations and trust weaken with the time separating generations, relational thinkers hold that we have greater obligations to proximate generations than to remote generations. What follows is that we should place greater emphasis on acting justly towards our contemporaries and our immediate descendants than on acting justly towards remote generations. Another way of expressing this same idea is to say that we ought to "discount" the value we place on costs and benefits for future generations much in the way an economist discounts the value of future returns on an investment.[15]

The universalistic approach to intergenerational justice was developed, in part, as a response to dissatisfaction with the relational model, and specifically with the endorsement of discounting associated

---

[13]Martin P. Golding, "Obligations to Future Generations," 69.

[14]Terence Ball, *Transforming Political Discourse*, (New York: Basil Blackwell, 1988), 150.

[15]The term discounting is derived from economics and refers to the theory that proximate benefits are more valuable than remote benefits, and therefore, the value of future benefits and costs ought to be discounted in proportion to the remoteness of those benefits or costs. Advocates of discounting argue that we ought to be more concerned with the costs and benefits of actions that will affect proximate generations than with actions that will affect remote generations.

Not all relational theorists accept that future generations stand as strangers to us, and not all relational theorists who accept that future generations will be strangers accept the idea of discounting. Terence Ball, for example, does not seem to accept the argument that we ought to discount the value we place on actions that affect remote generations.

with that model. The dissatisfaction with discounting is expressed most clearly by Richard and Val Routley, who argue that moral responsibility applies to actions that affect future persons just as it does to actions that affect the present and immediate future. "...[R]esponsibility arises as a result of being a causal agent aware of the consequences or probable consequences of his action, and thus does not have to be especially acquired or assumed. ...[Moral constraints] apply as a result of the ability to produce causal effects on the distant future of a reasonably predictable nature."[16] In contemporary thought, the universalistic approach is associated with a more expansive understanding of our obligations to posterity than is the relational approach.

THE RELATIONIST CHALLENGE OF MARTIN GOLDING

Martin Golding's "Obligations to Future Generations" arguably has had a greater influence on the contemporary literature on intergenerational justice than any other article. Not only is Golding's article one of the earliest of the contemporary pieces on intergenerational justice, it continues to be one of the most frequently cited works in this field.

An important reason for the prominence of Golding's article is that he poses a fundamental challenge to those concerned about intergenerational justice. Golding asserts that because distant future generations lie outside our moral community, we have only very limited obligations to those generations. Instead, our principal obligations are to our contemporaries and our immediate descendants.

Few contemporary thinkers have embraced Golding's conclusions. But the best measure of the influence of Golding's argument is not the number of thinkers who agree with his conclusions, but the number who have framed their arguments as responses to the challenge he presents. By this standard, Golding's article is among the most influential contemporary writings on intergenerational justice.

---

[16]Richard Routley and Val Routley, 284–5.

Golding focuses on the question of what one generation owes to those future generations with whom it will not share a "common life." By this term, Golding seeks to distinguish our obligations to our immediate descendants from our obligations to our distant descendants. We share a common life with our immediate descendants. From this common life arise many obligations which do not arise in the case of our distant descendants.

Golding distinguishes between *obligations* to future generations and *duties* to perform acts which are intrinsically right. Unlike general duties, obligations to future generations are performed in an attempt to produce a desirable state for the community of the future, to promote conditions of good living for future generations.[17] Whether we actually have an obligation to promote the good of any given future generation (as distinguished from a general duty to act in a manner which may incidentally benefit future generations) depends on our moral relation to that future generation, on whether that generation is a member of our moral community.

Golding argues that there are at least three ways moral communities may be generated. The first is by an explicit contract among the members. When persons agree to a contract, they incur obligations to each other. The second arises "out of social arrangements in which each member derives benefits from the efforts of other members. As a result a member acquires an obligation to share the burden of sustaining the social arrangement."[18] In contrast to Edmund Burke, Golding argues that "a moral community comprised of present and future generations cannot arise from either of these sources. We cannot enter into an explicit contract with the community of the future. And although future generations might derive benefits from us, these benefits cannot be reciprocated."[19]

---

[17]Golding, "Obligations to Future Generations," 62.
[18]Ibid., 65.
[19]Ibid.

A third possible source of a moral community is altruistic impulses. Altruistic impulses may serve as the foundation for a moral community if they lead me to acknowledge the good of others as "good-to-me." Once I have acknowledged the good of another as "good-to-me," I can no longer deny the pertinence of his demands, "although whether I should now act so as to promote his good is of course dependent on a host of factors. ... The basis of the obligation is nevertheless secured."[20]

According to Golding altruistic impulses may also serve as the basis for obligations to strangers. The fact that, initially, we have no bonds of affection towards strangers is not crucial. What is crucial is what the stranger is like and what the conditions of his life are like.

> ... [W]hat I maintain in my attempt to exclude him [the stranger] is that my conception of the good is not relevant to him, that "his kind" do not count. He, on the other hand, is in effect saying to me: Given your social ideal, you must acknowledge my claim, for it *is* relevant to me given what I am; your good is my good, also. If I should finally come to concede this, the full force of my obligation to him will be manifest to me quite independently of any fellow-feeling that might or might not be aroused. The *involuntary* character of the obligation will be clear to me, as it probably never is in the case of individuals who command one's sympathy. And once I admit him as a member of my moral community, I will also acknowledge my responsibility to secure this good for him even in the absence of any future claiming on his part.[21]

If Golding is correct in holding that future generations are members of our moral community "because, and insofar as, our social ideal is relevant to them, given what they are and their conditions of life," the critical question is whether our conception of the good life is relevant to future generations.[22] Golding's answer is that it is highly doubtful that distant generations are members of our moral community because we do not know what the conditions of life will be in the very distant future. Indeed, we do not know what we ought to desire for distant future

---

[20]Ibid., 66.
[21]Ibid., 68.
[22]Ibid.

generations, even on such matters as genetic constitution. As a result, Golding concludes that

> one might go so far as to say that if we have an obligation to distant future generations it is an obligation not to plan for them. Not only do we not know their conditions of life, we also do not know whether they will maintain the same (or a similar) conception of the good life for man as we do. ... [T]he more distant the generation we focus upon, the less likely it is that we have an obligation to promote its good.[23]

Golding goes on to argue that it would be both unwise and possibly wrong to promote the good of distant generations if this would adversely affect the rights of intervening generations. This, in Golding's view, would be "gambling in futures." Instead we should confine ourselves to removing the obstacles that stand in the way of immediate posterity's realizing the social ideal.[24]

Golding's position puts him in conflict with the assumptions that undergirded traditional understandings of intergenerational justice. As we have seen, the classical understanding of intergenerational justice was closely linked to a concern with perpetuating an intergenerational community. Our ancestors saw the existence of posterity as one of the most important blessings God could bestow upon a person or a people. Not only did our ancestors assume their descendants would be like them, insofar as they would be the types of beings who can make demands, the validity of which they were obligated to concede, they actively sought to ensure that their descendants would be members of their intergenerational community, bound by a set of common beliefs and values.

Golding's argument amounts to a repudiation of the traditional understanding of intergenerational justice. If we accept his argument, there can be no obligation to members of an extended intergenerational community because there can be no extended intergenerational community. If this is true, Burke's understanding that society is a sacred

---

[23]Ibid., 69–70.

[24]Ibid., 70.

partnership between those who are living, those who are dead, and those who are to be born, applies, at most, only to proximate generations. If remote future generations will not share our social ideals, we would not know how to promote their good, even if we were inclined to do so. In any event, we would have no obligation to promote the good of those who do not share our social ideals.

The challenge Golding's argument presents to those who are concerned about the welfare of remote generations is substantial. If we follow Golding's advice we will avoid "gambling on futures" and take no action that would benefit more remote generations at the expense of intervening generations. Instead, we will confine ourselves to removing the obstacles that stand in the way of our immediate posterity's realizing their social ideal.[25]

The problem with following Golding's advice is that the interests of our immediate descendants and those of our more remote descendants may well not coincide. For example, a case can be made that it is in the interests of our immediate descendants for us to continue to build nuclear power plants so that they might continue to enjoy abundant and relatively inexpensive energy. But it is almost certainly not in the interest of more distant generations to pay for the decommissioning of those nuclear power plants; nor is it in their interest to live with a world polluted with radioactive "hot spots."

When the interests of remote generations come into conflict with the interests of more proximate generations, how ought we decide between them? A reasonable interpretation of our general ethical principles is that it would be unjust for the present generation to require distant generations to bear the costs of our prosperity (or the costs of our immediate descendants' prosperity). However, if we accept Golding's premise that our ignorance of the conditions of life in the distant future makes it impossible for us to know what will be beneficial or harmful to remote generations, then it makes sense to "discount" the value of acting justly towards distant generations by the uncertainty we have concerning

---

[25]Ibid.

the effect of our actions on posterity. If we assume that our attempts to act justly will be dissipated by inevitable changes in conditions and culture, then Golding would be correct in holding that it is wrong to deprive our immediate descendants of material benefits for the sake of the remote possibility that our actions might enhance the lives of our distant descendants.[26]

It is not difficult to understand why many contemporary thinkers are reluctant to accept Golding's argument. His position represents a significant departure from our general understanding of what justice requires. There is something disturbing about applying the "economic" concept of discounting to the field of moral philosophy, just as there is something disturbing about trusting that time will diminish the undesirable effects of our actions. At the same time, it is not obvious how we can escape the logic of Golding's argument.

THE UNIVERSALISTIC RESPONSE

The response to Golding's challenge has come in two parts. The first part has been to redefine the nature of our obligations to remote generations. Most contemporary thinkers have abandoned the view that we have an obligation to promote the good of remote generations in favor of a narrower concern with avoiding actions that might harm remote generations. The second part of the response has been to abandon the effort to develop a relationally based understanding of our obligations to posterity in favor of an understanding of intergenerational justice based on universal duties. Both of these responses require explanation.

The first response to Golding's argument was suggested by the theologian and ethicist, Daniel Callahan.[27] Callahan argues that by

---

[26]Ibid.

[27]Daniel Callahan, "What Obligations Do We Have to Future Generations?," *Responsibilities to Future Generations*, ed. Ernest Partridge, (Buffalo, NY: Prometheus Books, 1980), 73–85. Daniel Callahan's article was first published in *The American Ecclesiastical Review* 164 April (1971), 265–280., nearly a year before Golding's "Obligations to Future Generations." Callahan's 'response' was based

defining our obligations to remote generations as promoting their good, Golding unnecessarily narrows the time frame during which we have obligations to remote generations. Callahan points out that obligations to future generations are not necessarily limited to taking actions which would promote the conditions of good living in positive ways. We also have the obligation to avoid taking actions which would harm future persons.[28]

The advantage of understanding our obligations to future generations in terms of avoiding harms to future generations is that this understanding would appear to be less vulnerable to the objection which Golding raises concerning our inability to know how future generations will comprehend the good. Thus, Callahan argues that even if our ignorance of the desires of future generations relieves us of the obligation to work for the good of future generations, we cannot claim total ignorance of what might be harmful to future generations. "[W]e could hardly excuse our nuclear weapons testing on the grounds of our ignorance of what would be relevant to the life of those generations."[29]

The validity of the assertion that we can be more certain about what might harm remote generations than about what may benefit them is an important empirical question. At least in some areas, we would seem to have a better understanding of what is likely to harm other persons than what is likely to benefit them. Except for a few universal goods, such as clean air and drinkable water, the human good tends to be a specific good. Thus, while food is a good for all people, people do not eat food, in general, but specific foods. Foods which persons in one culture consider to be beneficial may be perceived by persons in another culture as unpalatable. On the other hand, we do not need to know much about a people to know that high doses of radiation or toxic waste are harmful to them.

---

on a draft of Golding's article.

28Daniel Callahan, 78.

29Ibid., 79.

If we hold that our obligations to future persons extend no further than our ability to foresee the probable benefits and risks of our actions for those persons, the logical conclusion is that our obligations to future generations would seem to be more extensive in some areas than in others. We have relatively short-lived obligations to future generations with respect to cultural goods. Here, our obligations can extend no further than the life of our culture. On the other hand, when our actions affect aspects of human existence that are common to all persons, our obligations are likely to be of longer duration.

If Callahan is correct in arguing that persons are more alike in what causes them harm than in what they consider to be good, then our "community" extends much further into the future than Golding suggests. With the extension of our community comes a corresponding extension of our obligations to future persons. At a minimum, our obligations to future generations extend as far into the future as our capacity to harm future persons.

Callahan's revision of Golding would seem to go a long way towards overcoming one of the most serious objections to Golding's argument, namely, the imbalance between our capacity to affect future generations and our obligations to those generations. Callahan's response is particularly interesting because, in one sense, it remains true to the communitarian roots of traditional understandings of intergenerational justice. Unlike Golding, who defines our community in terms of a shared concept of the good, Callahan defines our community on the basis of a shared concept of harm. On the other hand, by defining our obligations to future generations as avoiding causing harm to future generations, we diminish the significance of the question of whether future generations are members of our community. While we may not have an obligation to promote the good of strangers, most understandings of justice require that we not cause harm to strangers. A community which is based on a shared understanding of what is harmful is a community which embraces all of humanity. In this sense Callahan's argument obliterates the distinction, so essential to traditional understandings of intergenerational justice, between members of a community and strangers. Most contemporary thinkers have followed Callahan's lead in defining our obligations to future generations as not acting in ways that are harmful to future persons, rather than as promoting their good.

The second part of the response to Golding's argument has been to abandon theories of intergenerational obligation based on our relationship to posterity in favor of theories based on universal duties. Golding distinguishes between an obligation to promote the good of future generations and a universal duty to act in ways that are intrinsically right (and which may incidentally benefit future persons). Thus, Golding distinguishes between having an obligation to transmit our cultural heritage to future generations because we believe that our cultural heritage promotes or embodies good living, and having a duty to refrain from falsifying the records of our civilization because we believe that lying is wrong. In the first instance, we would avoid falsifying the records of our civilization because it is harmful to future generations to deprive them of the opportunity to learn from history. In the second instance, we would avoid falsifying the records of our civilization because it is intrinsically wrong to falsify historical records.[30] While Golding himself recognizes the possibility of basing a theory of intergenerational justice on universal duties, it is quite clear that he considers universal duties to be less important than the obligation to promote the good of future generations.

Other contemporary thinkers, however, have a very different view of the relative importance of universal duties as compared to the obligation to promote the good of future generations.[31] The most

---

[30]Golding, "Obligations to Future Generations," 62.

[31]In fact Golding and his critics often seem to talk at cross-purposes. Much of the confusion arises from Golding's distinction between an obligation which is owed to future generations, and a general duty to perform acts which are intrinsically right. The problem with this distinction is that the category of general duties cuts a very broad path through our moral world. It includes all duties or obligations which are universal in nature, or which can be understood to be universal in nature. Quite clearly, all Kantian principles give rise to duties and not to obligations as Golding has defined these terms. Similarly, utilitarian ethics fall

obvious case in point are utilitarians, who argue that there is a universal duty (or obligation)[32] to promote the greatest happiness (or good) for the greatest number of persons. When applied to actions that affect future generations, this becomes the obligation to promote greatest total happiness, or the greatest average happiness, of future persons.[33] The utilitarian requirement that persons act to produce the greatest amount of happiness for the greatest number of future persons is a universal duty and not a specific obligation owed to future persons, because the basis for this duty is not the relationship that exists between the present generations and posterity, but a universal moral standard that governs the conduct of all persons towards all others.

The two responses to Golding's theory are not mutually exclusive. On the contrary, they combine rather easily. Most contemporary theorists argue that we have a general duty or obligation to avoid causing harm to future persons. Most commonly, this duty is based not on a special relationship we have to remote future generations, but on a universalistic ethical imperative to avoid acting in ways which are harmful to other persons.[34]

---

into the category of duties and not obligations to future generations.

[32]Unlike Golding, most contemporary thinkers do not distinguish between a duty and an obligation. While it is necessary to distinguish between obligations and duties when discussing Golding's theory, it is neither necessary nor helpful to make this distinction when discussing other thinkers.

[33]There are two variants of utilitarianism, total and average. These two variants of utilitarianism are derived from two different interpretations of how the utility principle ought to be applied to future generations. In general, utilitarianism requires that persons act to produce the greatest amount of happiness for the greatest number of persons. When this duty is applied to actions that affect future generations it is possible to produce an increase in the total amount of happiness of future persons either by increasing the average happiness of those persons who will live in the future (while holding the size of the population constant) or by increasing the size of the population (while holding the average happiness constant). Some utilitarians hold that only the first method of increasing the total amount of happiness ought to count. These utilitarians are known as "average utilitarians." Other utilitarians hold that our concern ought to be with producing the greatest amount of happiness for future generations by seeking simultaneously to increase the size and the average happiness of the future population. Utilitarians who hold this position are known as total utilitarians.

[34]Most contemporary moral theories take the form of a duty to "refrain from doing

This is perhaps the dominant contemporary understanding of intergenerational justice. Its focus is not so much on acting justly to future generations as it is on *not acting unjustly* to future generations. Another way of saying this is that we understand intergenerational justice to consist of avoiding acting in ways that are harmful to future generations.

To say that the contemporary understanding of intergenerational justice is that we have a duty to avoid harming remote generations does not tell us what specific obligations we have to remote generations. In view of the fact that we cannot agree about what we owe to our contemporaries, it should come as no surprise that contemporary thinkers disagree about what we owe to posterity. On the other hand, the fact that there is disagreement about the specifics does not diminish the significance of the fact that there is broad agreement, at least among nonutilitarian thinkers, about the basic form of our obligations to other generations.

THE UNIVERSALISTIC RESPONSE ILLUSTRATED

Among the best illustrations of the universalistic position is an article by Richard and Val Routley entitled "Nuclear Energy and Obligations to the Future."[35] The issue they seek to address is the nature of our obligations to the future with respect to our decision to produce energy by nuclear fission. An important problem arising from our use of nuclear energy is that the benefits of abundant and relatively inexpensive energy accrue to the present generation and to our immediate descendants, while the burden of dealing with the radioactive byproducts of nuclear energy falls not only on the present generation and our immediate descendants, but also on more remote generations

---

to others that which you would not have others do to you." Utilitarianism, departs from this pattern by framing their imperative in positive form: "do unto others what you would have them do unto you."

[35]Routley and Routley, 277–301.

who will not share in its benefits.[36] The question the Routleys raise is whether it is just for us to pass on to future generations the risks and costs associated with the disposal of nuclear wastes.

If we accept Golding's position that we should focus our energies on promoting the good of our immediate descendants rather than those of distant generations, we might conclude that it is just for us to continue to produce energy by nuclear fission. After all, if we were to cease producing energy by nuclear fission, the present generation and our immediate descendants would face the possibility of energy shortages and potentially severe economic hardships. If our primary obligations are to the present generation and our immediate descendants, it would be unjust to sacrifice their interests for the sake of those of distant generations who might or might not be harmed by nuclear waste.

On the other hand, Richard and Val Routley point out that our reliance on energy produced by nuclear fission makes it likely that some future generation will suffer seriously from exposure to nuclear waste. We do not have the technology to ensure the safe storage of nuclear waste for the nearly million years that it would take for that waste to decay.[37] They argue that this situation is analogous to a person who knowingly ships a consignment of lethal gas in a fragile container. While it is theoretically possible that the container may arrive undamaged, the shipper is aware that there is a substantial risk that the container will rupture in transit. If the container does rupture, it is almost certain that many people will be injured or killed. However, the shipper cannot know whether the container will actually rupture; nor can he know the identity of those who may be injured. Nonetheless, we have no difficulty recognizing that the shipper acts wrongly.[38]

The Routleys argue, contra Golding, that the fact that we have no feelings of affection for those who may be injured, and therefore no

---

[36]The plutonium waste which results from the production of energy by nuclear fission is highly toxic to human life and will remain so for a half-million to a million years. Routley and Routley, 279.

[37]Ibid.

[38]Ibid., 277–8.

special obligation to promote the good of those persons is not relevant for determining the justice of actions which put others in peril.[39] Rather, those who maintain that we do not have obligations to remote generations fail to distinguish between

> acquired or assumed obligations towards somebody, for which some act of acquisition or assumption is required as a qualifying condition, and ... moral constraints, which require, for example, that one should not act so as to damage or harm someone, and for which no act of acquisition is required. ... In the first case one must do something or be something which one can fail to do or be, e.g. have loves, sympathy, be contracted. In the second case responsibility arises as a result of being a causal agent aware of the consequences or probable consequences of his action, and thus does not have to be especially acquired or assumed. Thus there is no problem about how the later class, moral constraints, can apply to the distant future in cases where it may be difficult or impossible for acquisition or assumption conditions to be satisfied.[40]

An essential characteristic of the Routleys' understanding of moral constraints is that they can be universalized and are law-like. They apply independently of a person's position in space or time.[41] In principle, there are no relevant differences between future and present persons which would disqualify future persons from moral consideration or reduce their claims below those of present persons.[42] On the other hand, practical considerations, such as our inability to foresee how our actions will affect future persons, may diminish our obligations to the future. But the problem of uncertainty is not unique to actions that affect distant future generations. Nor do we require certainty with respect to actions that affect contemporaries before applying moral principles.[43] Thus, actions which create an unreasonable or unjustifiable

---

[39]Ibid., 284.

[40]Ibid., 284–5.

[41]Ibid., 293.

[42]For an opposing point of view see George L. Kline, "'Past', 'Present', and 'Future' as Categorical Terms, And the 'Fallacy of the Actual Future.'," *Review of Metaphysics* 40 December (1986), 215–235.

[43]Richard Routley and Val Routley, 293–4.

risk of harm to others may be subjected to criminal penalties, even though the risk of harm is slight, and even where no person actually suffers harm as a result of the actions. For example, it is illegal to fire a gun in the air in celebration, even though the chances of a person being injured by a specific falling bullet are quite low. In this case, the risk is unjustifiable because the potential benefits of firing a gun in the air are extremely low and can be obtained in other ways that do not involve risk of harm to others.

As a result of the universalizability of moral principles,

> *there is the same obligation to future persons as to the present*; and thus there is the same obligation to take account of them and their interests in what we do .... Uncertainty and indeterminacy do not free us of these obligations. If, in a closely comparable case concerning the present, the creation of a significant risk is enough to rule out an action as immoral, and there are no independent grounds for requiring greater certainty of harm in the future case under consideration, then futurity alone will not provide adequate grounds for proceeding with the action, thus discriminating against future people.[44]

The appeal of the universalistic position is obvious. The heart of the universalistic position is the willingness to recognize that future persons are our moral equals and that they are entitled to treatment as such. A corollary of the universalistic position is the recognition that future persons are part of a universal community which embraces all of humanity. By redefining intergenerational justice as the obligation not to harm remote persons, and by extending this obligation equally to all generations regardless of the time of their existence, the universalistic position seeks to restore the balance between our capacity to affect future generations and our obligations to those generations.

The question we need to ask is whether the universalistic position represents a satisfactory response to the relationist position as illustrated by Golding's argument. Perhaps the best way to answer this question is by looking at the argument of one thinker, Terence Ball, who has examined the universalistic response and found it wanting.

---

[44]Ibid., 294.

THE RELATIONIST POSITION REVISITED

The question Terence Ball sets out to answer is whether it is possible to act justly towards distant future generations if those generations do not share our understanding of justice. This problem arises because the concepts by which we frame our moral world change over time. Actions that appear just in one era and under one set of conditions, such as the cutting off of the hand of a thief, may seem unjust or even barbaric to another people in another era.[45] If future generations have a very different understanding from our own of what justice requires, is it possible for us to act justly towards them?

Ball argues that all moral concepts including the concept of justice have "historically mutable meanings." By this Ball means that "[t]he meaning of justice—not only what the word means but what it means to act justly, the criteria used to identify and appraise (un)just actions, etc.—changes from one age and generation to another."[46] If our understanding of justice differs markedly from those[47] of our distant descendants, we cannot expect our attempts to act justly towards our descendants to be seen as just by those persons. On the contrary, we can expect our efforts to produce very different results. Ball writes that

> [w]e have no way of knowing whether, or to what extent, well-meant actions and politics [sic] in the present will be adjudged just or unjust by future generations. We act, unavoidably, into an unknown future. It is entirely possible—and over the long haul likely—that our present practices, policies, institutions and way of life will strike members of future generations as barbaric and unjust. Having a very different understanding of justice, our children's great-grandchildren are more likely to curse our injustice (as they see it) than to praise us for our far-sightedness, much less our love of justice.[48]

---

[45]Ball, *Transforming Political Discourse*, p. 158.

[46]Ibid., p. 145.

[47]"*Those* of our distant descendants" rather than "*that* of our distant descendants," because, if our species survives long enough, we can expect concepts to change many times.

[48]Ball, *Transforming Political Discourse*, 158.

In order to act in ways that future generations will recognize as just, our actions would have to conform, not to our own standards of justice, but to the standards of justice of future generations.[49] To do so, we would have to be able to predict what those standards will be. However, as Ball points out, we are inherently incapable of predicting "the direction or destination(s)" of conceptual change and theoretical innovation.[50] The problem this raises is that

> [i]f their [distant generations'] understanding of justice differs markedly from ours, and if we have no way of knowing what that understanding will be, then we are in no position to act toward them in ways that we would both recognize as just. One generation can act justly toward another only if they share the same (or at any rate similar or commensurable) conceptions of justice. The more distant the generations, the greater the likelihood that their moral concepts and ours will be at least partially or even perhaps wholly incommensurable. ... The upshot of my several arguments ... is that the very idea of intergenerational justice is incoherent.[51]

One might suppose that the inescapable conclusion of this line of argument would be that we have no obligation to act justly towards distant future generations. After all, if our actions (including, presumably, our attempts to act justly towards future generations) are *more likely* to be cursed by future generations as unjust than to be praised as far-sighted or just, there would seem to be no reason for the present generations to make the effort to act justly towards its distant descendants. Indeed, one might even argue, as Martin Golding does, that under such circumstances one ought not to make the effort to act justly. Ball, however, comes to the opposite conclusion: "From the fact that distant generations are unlikely to share our concept of justice, it does not follow—*pace* Golding—that we are thereby absolved of any responsibility to attempt to act justly toward them."[52] Instead, Ball

[49]Ibid., 151–2.
[50]Ibid., 145.
[51]Ibid.
[52]Ibid., 159.

claims that two very different conclusions follow from his argument. "The first is that we have no obligation to act towards our distant descendants in ways that *they* will recognize as just but that our own theory or framework forbids us from seeing as just."[53] We have no obligation to do this because "[w]e can have no moral obligations to think thoughts or to perform actions for which we do not (yet) possess—and cannot predict the emergence of—the required concepts or moral language."[54] The second conclusion is that even though we are unable to treat future generations justly by their lights, we are not entitled to treat them unjustly by our lights. "We ought only do what we can do; and all we can do is to try to treat them justly, given our standards and our understanding of justice. And this we have so far clearly failed to do."[55]

Ball's position represents an interesting hybrid of the relationist and universalistic positions. On the one hand, Ball can be classified as a relationist insofar as he holds that we are capable of acting in ways that are intergenerationally just only towards other generations belonging to our *conceptual community*[56] (i.e., who have the same or commensurate concepts of justice). On the other hand, Ball resembles many universalists insofar as he argues that conceptual change does not absolve us of our obligation to attempt to treat distant future generations justly, "given our standards and our understanding of justice."[57]

Ball is undoubtedly correct in holding that moral concepts, including the concept of justice, change over time. There is ample historical evidence to support this position. For example, concepts such as chivalry and honor which lay at the heart of the moral codes of our European ancestors have been discarded in favor of other moral concepts such as individual rights. We have no reason to believe that our own moral concepts will have a different fate. On the contrary, there is even

---

[53]Ibid.

[54]Ibid.

[55]Ibid., 159–160.

[56]The term "*conceptual community*" is mine.

reason to believe that further conceptual change may be essential to human survival. It may well be the case that in an era of weapons of mass destruction, the human species will survive only if our moral values change, so that, among other things, war is no longer seen as an acceptable way of resolving disputes among nation states.[58]

The more problematic issue is Ball's conclusion that conceptual change does not undermine our obligation to attempt to act justly towards future generations. This conclusion contrasts sharply with that of Martin Golding who argues that since we "do not know whether … [distant generations] will maintain the same (or a similar) conception of the good life for man as we do …, the more distant the generation we focus on, the less likely it is that we have an obligation to promote its good."[59]

In light of the fact that both Golding and Ball agree that the moral understandings of future generations are likely to be very different from our own, how can we explain their different conclusions? If, as a consequence of having "a very different understanding of justice, our children's great-grandchildren are more likely to curse our injustice (as they see it) than to praise us for our far-sightedness, much less our love of justice,"[60] would we still have an obligation to attempt to act justly towards remote future generations?

The obvious place to begin is with Ball's own justification for his conclusion. Ball argues that while

> we have no obligation to act towards our distant descendants in ways that *they* will recognize as just but that our own theory or framework forbids us from seeing as just …[,] it does *not* follow that we need not worry about

---

[57]Ball, *Transforming Political Discourse*, 160.

[58]The necessity of such a change, of course, does not guarantee that it will take place. But there is also no guarantee the human species will survive to see the twenty-second century.

[59]Golding, "Obligations to Future Generations," 69–70.

[60]Ibid., 158.

> their welfare. Still less does it follow that we are entitled to treat future generations in ways that are unfair or unjust by *our* lights.[61]

Our inability to act justly by the standards of distant future generations does not prevent us from doing what we are capable of doing, namely trying to treat future generations justly, "given our standards and our understanding of justice."[62] One way of interpreting these statements is to understand Ball to be making the classical argument that our inability to act in the manner which is ideally just (i.e., just by the standards of remote generations) does not absolve us of the obligation to act justly by the best practically possible standard (i.e., our own standard of justice).

However, we need to raise at least two questions concerning this interpretation of Ball's conclusions. The first is whether it is true that the ideal would be to act justly by the standards of future generations (were we capable of doing so). How we answer this question may well speak to the priority with which we view our obligations to posterity. If acting justly by our own standards is simply the best we can do for future generations, then it is plausible that we may prefer to discount the value we place on justice to future generations in order to place greater emphasis on justice to our immediate descendants (for whom our conception of the good life is more likely to be relevant).[63] The second, more general question is whether Ball's justification of his conclusion is sufficient in light of the fact that Martin Golding comes to the opposite conclusion, based on similar premises.

Ball is correct in arguing that our inability to anticipate the "direction and destination(s) of conceptual change and theoretical innovation,"[64] prevents us from acting justly by standards of remote generations. On the other hand, even if we could anticipate the direction of conceptual change, it is not clear that we would have an obligation to take actions that future generations will see as just, but that

---

61Ibid., 160.

62Ibid., 159–160.

63See Golding, "Obligations to Future Generations," 70.

64Ball, *Transforming Political Discourse*, 145.

our moral framework forbids us from seeing as just.[65] An essential part of what it means to be a moral being is to be bound by one's own standards of justice. The moral framework of another cannot be binding on us unless we *first* come to accept that framework as just. Thus, even if we were capable of anticipating the values of future generations, we would not be obligated to take actions that future generations will see as just, but that our own moral framework forbids us from seeing as just.

On the other hand, if we could anticipate how future generations will be affected by our actions, our own moral theories would require us to take this information into account before framing our actions. A concern with justice to future generations necessarily includes a concern with the consequences of our actions for future persons. There is a *prima facie* obligation not to act in ways that cause harm to other persons. Unless there are other, overriding reasons for doing so, we would have an obligation to avoid taking actions that are harmful to future generations.

A consequence of conceptual change, and our inability to anticipate the direction of that change, is that our efforts to act justly towards remote future generations are less likely to be successful than comparable efforts towards more proximate generations. One reason this is the case is that how persons are affected by actions is determined, in part, by how those persons perceive the world. Actions intended to produce results which are just to future generations may be eroded or undermined by changes in people's conceptual framework.[66] The extent of this erosion, is largely a function of the extent of conceptual change. If we assume, as Golding does, that the conditions and the conception of the good life of future generations are likely to be so different from our own that we do not know what to desire for them,[67] then we would lack the capacity to act justly towards future generations both by the

[65]Ibid., 159.

[66]Other sources of erosion of our efforts to act justly include intervening events and actions and changes in the conditions of life of future generations.

[67]Golding, "Obligations to Future Generations," 69–70.

standards of remote generations and, more importantly, by our own standards.

Our own standards of justice require that we attempt to act justly towards others *only if* there is reason to believe that our actions are likely to produce results which are just. For example, we have an obligation to avoid depleting the ozone layer *because* we believe that doing so will cause harm to future generations.[68] If we had reason to believe that distant generations would find a depleted ozone layer a favorable condition for life, we would have no reason to attempt to preserve the ozone layer for them, and, therefore, no obligation to do so.[69]

This is a familiar problem. It is strikingly similar to the disagreement between Golding and thinkers such as Daniel Callahan and Richard and Val Routley, who argue that future generations will be very much like us in those things that are harmful to them. Significantly, it is also a pivotal issue for Terence Ball's argument. If we interpret passages such as Ball's statement that "[h]aving a very different understanding of justice, our children's great-grandchildren are more likely to curse our injustice (as they see it) than to praise us for our far-sightedness, much less our love of justice ..."[70] as indicating that our attempts to act justly towards remote generations are as (or more) likely to produce consequences that future generations will see as harmful as to produce consequences that future generations will see as beneficial, then the conclusion that we have no obligation to attempt to act justly (by our standards) towards remote generations would seem inescapable, unless we had reason to believe that the moral standards of future generations will be so perverse that we ought to ignore their judgments. Because there is no reason to make the later assumption, we can have no reason

---

[68] Other necessary preconditions for our having the obligation to preserve the ozone layer include the belief that future persons are entitled to a safe environment in which to live, and that future generations are the types of beings to whom we can have obligations.

[69] Even under these assumptions we would still have an obligation to preserve the ozone layer for our immediate descendants, and we might have an obligation to preserve the ozone layer for the sake of other species.

[70] Ball, *Transforming Political Discourse*, 158.

to attempt to act justly towards future generations, if we are convinced that doing so is no more likely to produce consequences remote generations would find beneficial than to produce consequences they would find harmful.

The fact that our standards of justice are the only ones available to us is very largely beside the point. Our own standards of justice do not require us to take futile actions. If we have every reason to believe that our attempts to act justly towards distant generations will fail to produce consequences that *we* would recognize as just, we would have no reason to devote our energy and our resources to the attempt.[71] On the other hand, if we make the opposite assumption, namely that future generations are sufficiently like us that we have the capacity to foresee the probable benefits and harms of different courses of action, and if we further assume that we have the ability to act in ways that reduce the likelihood of harm to future generations, then the conditions exist for us to speak coherently about intergenerational justice.

How, then, can we understand Ball's conclusion that we have an obligation to try to treat future generations justly "given our standards and our understanding of justice"?[72] This conclusion makes sense only if we believe that our efforts to act justly will actually make a positive difference to the lives of distant future persons, despite conceptual change. Significantly, there is textual evidence from an earlier published version of his article that Ball believes that such conditions do exist even with respect to distant future generations. In the conclusion to this article Ball writes:

> it seems a safe bet (though nothing more than that) that our distant descendants are unlikely to subscribe to some theory of justice and the human good such that they would respect, revere, or even excuse us for

---

[71]As I argued earlier in this chapter, an important condition for talking about intergenerational justice is the ability to choose a morally preferable course of action. To the extent that our best efforts are no more likely to be seen by future generations as beneficial than they are to be cursed by future generations, this precondition for speaking of justice would not be met.

[72]Ball, *Transforming Political Discourse*, 160.

> having bequeathed to them an eroded, poisoned, polluted and overpopulated planet whose inhabitants experience increased rates of skin and other cancers, of infant mortality, birth defects, mental retardation, radiation sickness, and other preventable ills.[73]

If my analysis is correct, a great deal depends on whether this last statement is true. If future generations are likely to be so different from us that we are unable to foresee what risks our actions may create for them, then the preconditions for having obligations to future generations are not met. Moreover, to the extent that we know so little about the conditions of life in the future save that "we do not know what we ought to desire for them ...,"[74] we have every reason to devote our resources to endeavors other than the attempt to act justly towards our remote descendants. On the other hand, if we believe that future generations are "unlikely to subscribe to some theory of justice and the human good such that they would respect, revere, or even excuse us for having bequeathed to them an eroded, poisoned, polluted and overpopulated planet ...,"[75] then it is reasonable to hold that justice *requires* that we devote resources to preventing harms to distant generations.

Does our uncertainty regarding the direction of conceptual change or the effects of our actions on future generations render the concept of intergenerational justice incoherent? I am convinced that it does not. Even if we accept that there can be no "intergenerationally valid theory of justice" it does not follow that there can be no "valid theory of intergenerational justice." The validity of a theory of intergenerational justice is determined not by whether future generations will share that theory, but by whether the actions our theory requires us to take are likely to produce consequences that will be just (to other generations) by our own standards (despite conceptual and other changes). It is not necessary that future generations find our actions just in order for us to

---

73Terence Ball, "The Incoherence of Intergenerational Justice," *Inquiry* 28 (1985), 334.

74Golding, "Obligations to Future Generations," 70.

75Ball, "The Incoherence of Intergenerational Justice," 334.

have the obligation to act justly towards them. Not only may remote generations have a different understanding of justice from us, it is entirely possible that their moral vocabulary may include no concept that corresponds to our concept of justice.[76] Thus, Ball is correct in arguing that the inability to act justly by the standards of future generations does not absolve us of the obligation to act justly by our own lights.[77] Even if future generations are composed of persons who have different moral concepts from ours, we must assume that they, no less than we, are the types of beings who count morally and to whom it is possible to have obligations.[78] Given this understanding, it is sufficient to sustain the obligation to attempt to act justly towards future generations if our efforts are more likely to produce consequences that are just (by our own standards) than consequences that are unjust. If this condition applies with respect to any given future generation, then, if the other conditions of justice prevail, it is coherent to speak about the obligation to act justly towards that generation. There is every reason to believe that this condition applies to remote generations into the far distant future.[79]

---

[76]It is more accurate, and less confusing, to say that remote future generations are likely to have "no concept of justice" than to say, as Ball does, that they are likely to have a "different concept of justice." For if future generations truly have a different concept of "justice," (as opposed to a different "conception of justice"), then we must ask why it would be correct to describe this different concept as a concept of "justice" at all.

[77]Ball, *Transforming Political Discourse*, 159–160.

[78]It is possible that future generations will be composed of "monsters" who are incapable of moral action, and who, thereby, do not count, morally. But (1) we have no right to make this assumption and (2) our making this assumption about our own descendants would speak volumes about our own moral worth!

[79]To the extent that we cannot foresee the pace and direction of conceptual change, no empirical evidence can be given to support this statement. On the other hand, there is no reason to think that this is not true. Moreover, it seems reasonable to hold that the burden of proof ought to fall on those who argue that we have no obligations to remote generations. They ought to have the burden of proof because the normal presumption is that we are accountable for the effects of our actions on others. To argue that the inability to foresee the direction and pace of conceptual change makes it impossible to act justly towards posterity is to offer a justification or excuse for failing to act justly. We generally place the burden of proof on those who seek an exemption for general standards of conduct rather than on those who hold that we must adhere to those standards.

CONCLUSION

If my argument is sound, the contemporary universalistic position represents a logically coherent understanding of intergenerational justice. Even if we considered remote generations to be strangers, whose welfare we have no special obligation to promote, we would still have a duty to avoid causing them harm. Even if we also believed that remote generations will have very different moral concepts from our own, we would still have an obligation to attempt to act justly towards them, as long as there was reason to believe that our attempts to do so were more likely to produce consequences we would recognize as just than to produce consequences we would recognize as unjust. While we act with no guarantee of the gratitude of our remote descendants, it is likely that future generations will find our attempts to act justly preferable to inaction or unjust action on our part. This is all that is required to sustain a "universalistic" obligation to act justly towards posterity.

On the other hand, it is important to recognize the limitations of this universalistic position. At its best, a universalistic understanding of intergenerational justice sustains an obligation subject to erosion from many sources. Among the sources of erosion are the likelihood that changes in the conditions of life[80] and the moral understandings[81] of future generations may make our efforts to act justly towards future generations less likely to succeed than comparable efforts to act justly towards more proximate generations.

Nor are these the only sources of erosion. Our attempts to act justly can also be undermined (or rendered meaningless) by intervening events and actions. For example, a policy of conservation of petroleum resources could be rendered meaningless by a scientific breakthrough which allows us to tap alternate energy resources less expensively and with less destruction to the environment. Although it is not permissible for us to *count* on such a breakthrough, the *possibility* that our sacrifices

---

[80]Golding, "Obligations to Future Generations," 70.

[81]Ball, *Transforming Political Discourse*, 145, 155, 158.

will be for naught inevitably may influence our thinking when calculating what proportion of our resources we ought to devote to conservation for future generations.

None of these considerations makes it permissible to ignore the interests and rights of remote generations. The universalistic thinkers are surely correct in arguing that justice requires that we treat future persons as equals. But, as Ronald Dworkin points out, treatment as equals is not the same as equal treatment.[82] "The right to equal treatment is the right to an equal distribution of some opportunity or resource or burden."[83] The right to treatment as an equal is "the right, not to receive the same distribution of some burden or benefit, but to be treated with the same respect and concern as anyone else."[84] To the extent that our resources are used more efficiently when devoted to acting justly towards our contemporaries (and our proximate descendants) than when they are used to seek justice for remote generations, an argument can be made that it is not inconsistent with our obligation to treat future persons as equals for us to place greater emphasis on meeting the needs of our contemporaries and our immediate descendants than on meeting the needs of remote generations. Another way of saying this is that the obligation to treat remote future generations as equals may not be inconsistent with "discounting" the amount we invest in seeking to advance the interests of remote generations by the uncertainty we have concerning our capacity to do so successfully. As J. R. Cameron argues, our responsibility to the future is not limitless. "It extends indefinitely into the future, but the further it extends, the smaller is our share in it."[85]

At the same time there are good reasons for feeling uncomfortable about applying the concept of discounting to questions of intergenerational justice. Because future generations cannot advance their own

---

[82]Dworkin, 227.

[83]Ibid.

[84]Ibid.

[85] J. R. Cameron, "Do Future Generations Matter?," *Ethics and the Environmental Responsibility*, ed. Nigel Dower, (Aldershot: Avenbury, 1989), 72.

interests, there is the very real danger that "discounting" will result in systematically and illegitimately favoring the interests of proximate generations over those of remote generations.[86] A strong case can be made that a thinker such as Martin Golding goes too far in discounting the value of acting justly towards remote generations.[87]

As we have seen, one way of minimizing the need for discounting is to define our obligations to future generations in terms of those human characteristics that are most enduring. This approach is favored by Daniel Callahan,[88] and has been adopted by many other universalistic thinkers. To the extent that human beings are more alike in what is harmful to them than in what they consider to be beneficial, it follows that we can have greater confidence in our ability to foresee the probable effects of policies that pose a risk of harm to future generations than we can in policies that offer to confer benefits.

One difficulty with this approach is that the distinction between a harm and the absence of a benefit is far from absolute. Harms can often be defined as the absence of a benefit and benefits as the absence of a harm. For example, if environmental pollution is harmful to future generations, then a policy of cleaning up the environment can be said to be a benefit to future generations. If we can have confidence in our

---

[86]For excellent critiques of the concept of discounting as it applies to intergenerational justice, see Derek Parfit, "Energy Policy and the Further Future: The Social Discount Rate," *Energy and the Future*, ed. Douglas MacLean and Peter G. Brown. (Totowa, NJ: Rowman and Littlefield, 1983), 31–37; and Tyler Cowen and Derek Parfit, "Against the Social Discount Rate," *Justice between Age Groups and Generations*, ed. Peter Laslett and James S. Fishkin. (New Haven: Yale University Press, 1992), 144–161. Cowen and Parfit point out that there is a fundamental difference between (legitimately) discounting remote effects because they are less likely to occur and (illegitimately) discounting remote effects because we give less weight to the value of future lives. Tyler Cowen and Derek Parfit, 146–147.

[87]Not all relational thinkers espouse discounting enthusiastically. Terence Ball, for example, seems to be every bit as uncomfortable with the notion of discounting as any universalist thinker. On the other hand, George Kline endorses Golding's position. George L. Kline, "'Past', 'Present', and 'Future' as Categorical Terms, And the 'Fallacy of the Actual Future'," *Review of Metaphysics* 40 December (1986), 233.

[88]Daniel Callahan, 78–79.

belief that environmental pollution is likely to be harmful to remote generations, there is no reason not to have similar confidence in our belief that cleaning up the environment will be beneficial to remote generations.

Our ability to foresee the effects of our policies on remote generations varies greatly from situation to situation and is undoubtedly more complex than the dichotomy between benefits and harms suggests. In specific cases, such as nuclear war and the storage of radioactive waste, we can have great confidence in our conclusions concerning the long-term effects of our actions. In other cases, such as the depletion of the earth's fossil fuel reserves, we can have a lower degree of confidence. In some cases, our ability to foresee the long-term risks of public policies may even be greater than our ability to foresee the short-term risks of those policies. For example, it is easier to forecast the long-term effects of acid rain, the depletion of the ozone layer, and global warming than to foresee their short-term effects.[89] Similarly, it is easier to foresee the long-term dangers associated with the storage of nuclear and other hazardous wastes in metal containers subject to corrosion than it is to predict which future generation will be exposed to lethal doses of radiation.

Despite these arguments, there seems to be no escaping the conclusion that we are generally in a better position to estimate the effects of our actions on our contemporaries and our proximate descendants than on our remote descendants. This means that we are also in a better position to act justly towards our proximate descendants than towards our remote descendants. From this it follows that, other things being equal, we may be justified in devoting fewer resources to remote generations than to our contemporaries and to our immediate descendants. Of course, other things rarely are equal. We need to consider the nature of the threat to future generations as well as the

---

[89] To give but one illustration: from the fact of global warming, we cannot predict that next winter will be milder than average, but we can predict that winters in the distant future will be milder in most parts of the country.

probability of success when allocating resources. The principle of treatment as equals requires that we devote greater resources to avoiding a calamity to remote future generations than to avoiding an inconvenience to the present generation or to our immediate descendants. These types of considerations may counteract the greater uncertainty we have concerning the effects of our actions on remote future generations.

Nonetheless, the inability to dismiss the legitimacy of arguments supporting the concept of discounting is disturbing. It is disturbing because discounting seems to reinforce and justify policies which shortchange remote generations. It hardly seems to be moving in the right direction to add one more reason to be unconcerned with the effects of our actions on remote generations. Nor are the effects of discounting eliminated by focusing on our immediate descendants, as Golding and Ball would have us do. While it would undoubtedly be a step in the right direction for us to do more for our immediate descendants, we should not equate a concern with the welfare of our immediate descendants with justice to remote generations. The interests of remote generations and those of our immediate descendants may diverge significantly over policies such as industrial economic development and the use of nuclear energy (as, indeed do the interests of contemporaries living in different regions of this planet). In situations such as these, focusing on the interests of our immediate descendants may prove to be a disservice and not an advantage to remote generations.

The question we need to pose is whether there is any theoretical basis for arguing that we ought to place a higher priority on acting justly toward remote generations than would follow from the universalistic understanding which dominates contemporary thought. In Chapter VIII, I argue that it is possible to develop such a theory. For the moment, it is sufficient to conclude that such a theory is needed if we are to avoid the erosive effects of discounting and to account for our intuitive judgment that we are shortchanging posterity.

IV

The Limitations of Contemporary Approaches to Intergenerational Justice

PERHAPS THE MOST FUNDAMENTAL DIFFERENCE between *inter*generational and *intra*generational action is that when we act intergenerationally our actions affect not only the conditions in which future persons will live, but also the identity and size of the future population. The power to determine simultaneously several dimensions of the future not only distinguishes *inter*generational action from *intra*generational action, it also makes the task of determining the appropriate standards by which to judge intergenerational actions immensely more complex.

When we act intragenerationally, the focus of public policy is on the conditions in which persons live rather than on the size or the identity of the population, which are treated as "given." By contrast, when we act intergenerationally, the size and identity of the population are variables, which may be altered legitimately by public policies. Although it is possible to alter the size and even the identity of the existing population, our moral theories treat the size and identity of the existing population as a standard against which the effects of our actions and policies are measured. Thus, a policy which sought to increase per capita resources by exterminating a large percentage of the existing population would be condemned by decent people everywhere as an immoral policy. Similarly, efforts to alter the identity of the existing population by forced religious conversion or by pogrom, although tolerated by some, would also be widely condemned as violations of fundamental human rights. By contrast, when we act intergenerationally, our actions affect the size and identity of the future population before that population comes into existence. Consequently, we allow much greater moral latitude to policies which seek to alter the size or the identity of future generations.

There is nothing terribly mysterious or surprising about the fact that our actions can affect simultaneously the size of the future population, the conditions in which future generations will live and the identity of those who will comprise that population. On the contrary, we recognize that we make multidimensional choices in both our daily lives and our public policies. For example, a couple considering whether to have another child may weigh the benefits of adding to their family circle against the added burden an additional child would place on family resources. Or, persons with a family or ethnic group history of certain genetic diseases, such as Tay-Sachs or Sickle Cell Anemia, may undergo genetic screening and counseling to avoid giving birth to a child with one of those diseases. Nations, too, make decisions with the awareness that any given public policy may affect the future in a variety of different and interrelated ways. Thus anti-natalist policies have been instituted in some nations in order to control population growth which threatens to undermine the nation's ability to provide a decent living standard for its citizens in the future.

Even though we have little difficulty recognizing that our actions shape the future in several ways simultaneously, we still have considerable difficulty determining the appropriate standards by which to judge intergenerational actions. It is my thesis that an important source of the difficulty we have in developing adequate theories of intergenerational obligations is that our philosophical and moral concepts are finely tuned to the problems of *intra*generational action. Because most contemporary moral theories (including both individual rights-based theories and utilitarianism) developed in an era largely unconcerned with intergenerational justice, we encounter a series of paradoxes and contradictions when we apply those theories to the problems of intergenerational action. Derek Parfit has compared this to the problem of attempting to understand the universe only with the Newtonian Laws of physics.[1]

---

[1]Derek Parfit, "Energy Policy and the Further Future: The Identity Problem," *Energy and the Future*, ed. Douglas MacLean and Peter G. Brown. (Totowa, NJ:

Even among those who agree that our theories need to be revised or extended to guide intergenerational action better, there is no consensus on whether we can do this, and if we can, on what direction these efforts should take. There is no consensus on these questions, in part, because there is no agreement on which failures of our moral theories are critical. Only when we have a better understanding of why and where our moral theories fail will we be in a position to understand how to reformulate those theories.

In this and subsequent chapters, I focus on three issues generally not addressed, or not addressed adequately by contemporary theories of intergenerational justice. The first is the ethical questions raised by our capacity to determine the size of the future population. Included within the question of population size is the question of the survival of the human species. The second issue concerns our power to affect the identity of future persons. Questions of identity are raised by a variety of policies and actions including genetic engineering, genocide, eugenic breeding, and population control. The third issue is the nature of our obligations to past generations. Do we have obligations to past generations, or should we be concerned exclusively with the welfare of future generations?

It is clear that our actions can have a dramatic impact on the size and identity of the future population, just as they can on the conditions in which future persons will live. For example, a worldwide policy of encouraging family planning could reduce the size of the Earth's population by several billion persons over the course of the next two centuries (as compared with projections based on the assumption of uncontrolled population growth). Environmental pollution and soil

---

Rowman and Littlefield, 1983), 178–179. See also Hans Jonas, "Technology and Responsibility: The Ethics of an Endangered Future," *Responsibilities to Future Generations*, ed. Ernest Partridge. (Buffalo, NY: Prometheus Books, 1980), 23–36, for a discussion of the inability of traditional moral understandings to address the new problems of intergenerational justice.

erosion also could have a significant impact on population size.[2] Still more disastrous consequences would result from a nuclear war. Even a "limited" nuclear war could extinguish all human life, thereby preventing the existence of all future generations.[3]

Our actions can also have a significant effect on the identity of those who will live in the future. Policies such as genocide, eugenic breeding, the emerging science of genetic engineering and even widespread family planning could have a dramatic impact on the identity of future generations. The identity of the future population can be altered deliberately through genocide, eugenic breeding, or even screening for genetic diseases (if followed by abortion). It also can be altered inadvertently by policies such as public support for family planning, if this policy results in lower birth rates among some segments of the population than among others.

Deliberate attempts to alter the identity of future generations raise serious ethical questions. This is most obviously the case with respect to the genocidal and eugenic breeding policies of the Nazis. It is also true with respect to benign attempts to alter the characteristics of the future population such as medical efforts to control genetic diseases including Tay-Sachs and hemophilia. The use of genetic screening, amniocentesis and "therapeutic" abortion to control such diseases has a nonrandom, and potentially nontrivial effect on the identity of the persons who will exist in the future. To the extent that these policies represent conscious efforts to alter the characteristics if not the identity of the future population, it is essential to examine their ethical justifiability. To raise ethical questions about efforts to eliminate or control genetic diseases does not imply, of course, that these policies are wrong. On the

---

[2]The reduction of the size of the human population as a consequence of a decrease in the capacity of the Earth to support life would almost certainly entail great suffering due to starvation and the dislocation of existing communities.

[3]Carl Sagan, "Nuclear War and Climatic Catastrophe: Some Policy Implications," *Foreign Affairs* 62 Winter (1983), 291–292. Carl Sagan, *Nuclear Winter and Its Implications*, Senate Armed Services Committee, Hearings 99–478, 99th Congress, 1st Session, Washington: G.P.O., 1986.

contrary, a strong case can be made that it is desirable to eliminate debilitating genetic diseases. Nonetheless, it is important to differentiate between those policies which are ethically proper and those which ought to be condemned; and to do this we need to ask hard questions of any policy that deliberately seeks to alter the identity of future generations. In an era in which genetic engineering is becoming a major growth industry, it is vital that our theories of intergenerational justice (or of intergenerational ethics) allow us to distinguish clearly between ethically proper and ethically improper efforts to alter the identity of the future population.

Policies which inadvertently alter the identity of future generations may also raise serious ethical issues. For example, in the 1970s the policy of encouraging the use of birth control by the poor was criticized by some black leaders as a racist and genocidal policy designed to limit the size of the black population. Regardless of whether this policy was actually motivated by racism, it is important to recognize that a policy of encouraging family planning can cause one segment of the population to grow more slowly than another. To the extent that this is the case, it is legitimate to ask whether the effects of family planning (and other public policies) on population identity raise ethical concerns, distinct from a concern with the welfare of those who will exist in the future.

Unfortunately, most contemporary understandings of intergenerational justice do not lend themselves to addressing the issues which arise from our capacity to affect the size and the identity of the future population. One source of difficulty is that often it is not possible to describe the effects of our actions on population size and identity in terms of harms or benefits to future persons. The most dramatic example of this is that a nuclear war which exterminates the human species cannot be said to harm future persons, since no future persons would exist if such a war occurred. If we hold that the sole criterion by which we ought to judge *intergenerational* actions is the effect of those actions on *actual future persons*, then, by definition, such a nuclear war could not be intergenerationally unjust.[4]

For similar reasons, it is not possible to understand the significance of actions which affect the identity of the future population exclusively in terms of benefits or harms to future persons. For example, we cannot explain why the Holocaust was intergenerationally unjust by focusing exclusively on the children of the survivors of the Nazi death camps or on the impoverishment of European culture which resulted from the destruction of the Jewish community in many parts of Europe. While the children of the survivors were affected by the experiences of their parents, and while European culture has been impoverished by the absence of a thriving Jewish community, neither is an adequate measure of the intergenerational impact of the Holocaust.

It is also possible to argue that genocide harms future generations by reducing the diversity of the gene pool. Diversity of genetic material is associated with hybrid vigor in plants and improved health, better physique, and longer life in animals. Lack of genetic diversity is directly associated with recessive trait diseases such as hemophilia.[5] Although these effects are real, they are likely to be noticeable only when the numbers of people exterminated is very large. In any event, harm to the gene pool constitutes a secondary rather than a primary reason to condemn genocide.

We also cannot explain why the Holocaust was *inter*generationally unjust by focusing on the harm done to the those who were exterminated in the Nazi death camps. While we can measure the *intra*generational injustice of the Holocaust in terms of what the Nazis did to its immediate victims, if we focus exclusively on the harm done to those who perished, we ignore the most important *inter*generational effect of the Holocaust. The purpose of the Nazis was not simply to kill

---

[4]Needless to say, the judgment that nuclear war is not *inter*generationally unjust does not imply that it is not *intra*generationally unjust. The deaths of billions of noncombatants in a war that cannot be won is properly condemned as unjust.

[5]This argument was suggested in written comments on a draft of this work by Professor Theresa Smith.

individual Jews and other targeted peoples; it was to alter the *identity* of future generations by exterminating the Jewish people and other peoples. Unless we recognize this intergenerational dimension, we distort the meaning of the Holocaust. To the extent that our moral understandings preclude us from assigning moral weight to such "missing victims,"[6] those understandings represent a poignantly inadequate foundation for a twentieth-century theory of intergenerational justice.

The last question we need to examine is the nature and extent of our obligations to past generations. As I indicated in my opening chapter, this question was largely ignored in the contemporary literature on intergenerational justice until very recently. The principal obstacle to recognizing obligations to past generations is that our secular world view holds that once a person is dead, she or he can no longer be affected by the actions of the living. To the extent that we adhere to this view, it seems to follow that we can have no obligations to the dead, at least none based on consequentialist ethical principles. On the other hand, the fact that there can be no consequentialist obligations to past generations does not preclude our having obligations to past generations based on nonconsequentialist ethical principles. Thus, even though it may not cause actual harm to a person who has died if we fail to execute her or his will faithfully, under most circumstances we would not hesitate to say that the failure to execute a will faithfully breaches our obligation to the person who entrusted us with the execution of her or his will.

In order for a theory of intergenerational justice to be sufficient, it must do more than focus only on our obligations to future persons. A

[6]While the term "missing victim" lacks analytic rigor, in the sense that those who are never born cannot be *actual* victims, the concept of a "missing victim" does have the heuristic value of calling our attention to the fact that some actions wrongfully prevent the existence of future persons, thereby creating a real "demographic deficit." It is true that the term "missing victims" cannot refer to identifiable hypothetical individuals, but it is also important to differentiate between actions which affect the identity of the future population randomly or in a nondiscriminatory manner and actions which effectively and wrongfully prevent the existence of future people in a specific demographic category.

theory of intergenerational justice must also address the moral dimensions of policies which affect the survival of the human species, the size and the identity of the future population and the nature of our obligations to our ancestors. As we will see, the extension of our understanding of intergenerational justice to cover these questions does not mean that we must abandon person-affecting principles[7] altogether. It may well be possible to overcome the deficiencies of person-affecting principles by supplementing those principles with others drawn from our cultural heritage. The examples we have examined to this point suggest a need to reexamine the sufficiency of contemporary approaches to intergenerational justice. Such a reexamination is the principal task of the remainder of this book.

THE NEW ORTHODOXY

The argument that person-affecting principles do not represent an adequate foundation for a theory of intergenerational justice is intensely controversial. The dispute does not center on whether the actions of the present generation can have a substantial effect on the size and the identity of the future population, for it is obvious that they can. Nor does it center on whether our capacity to affect the size and identity of the future population is different, both in kind and in extent, from our capacity to affect that of the present population, for it is clear that it is. Rather, the focus of the dispute is on the moral significance of our capacity to affect the size and identity of the future population.

Perhaps the dominant position in the contemporary literature is that our principal ethical concern ought to be with how our actions will affect those who actually will exist in the future. Most thinkers seem to arrive at this position by default. They simply do not examine the moral issues which arise from our capacity to affect the size and identity of the future population. Some thinkers go even further and argue that questions of intergenerational justice or intergenerational ethics cannot arise from

---

[7]By "person-affecting principles," I understand that moral theory which holds that actions are morally significant only to the extent that they affect persons.

our capacity to affect the size and the identity of the future population, because justice (or ethics) deals only with how our actions affect those persons who actually exist, whether now or in the future.[8] I call this the neo-orthodox position because those who defend this view are in the position of defending the dominant moral understanding of our culture against attempts to extend that understanding.

Those who hold the opposing view argue that our moral traditions require us to be concerned not only with how our actions will affect persons in the future, but, more broadly, with how our actions shape the future of humanity.[9] Some add a more traditional concern with our obligations to past generations.[10] This broader understanding of our moral tradition includes (but is not necessarily limited to) a concern with the effects of our actions on the size and identity of the future population.

The debate over the scope of intergenerational justice cuts across philosophical traditions. Those who defend the dominant contemporary understanding that our only intergenerational obligations are to those individuals who actually will exist in the future include not only adherents to rights-based understandings of justice but also utilitarians. Those who argue that this position represents too narrow an understanding of our intergenerational responsibilities likewise include both utilitarians and non-utilitarians.

The more expansive understandings of intergenerational justice are controversial because they challenge the assumptions which underlie many contemporary understandings of justice, and by extension, many

---

[8]For example, Mary Warren, "Do Potential People Have Moral Rights?," *Obligations to Future Generations*, ed. R. I. Sikora and Brian Barry, (Philadelphia: Temple University Press, 1978), 14–30.

[9]See for example Part Four of Derek Parfit's *Reasons and Persons*, Hans Jonas's "Technology and Responsibility: The Ethics of an Endangered Species," and Joel Feinberg's, "The Rights of Animals and Unborn Generations."

[10]See for example Barbara Baum Levenbook, "Harming Someone after His Death," 407–419, Joel Feinberg, *Harm to Others*, and "The Rights of Animals and Unborn Generations," 139–150 and George Pitcher, "The Misfortunes of the Dead," 183–188.

contemporary understandings of intergenerational justice. Specifically, they challenge the assumption that only the effects of our actions on those who actually exist now or who will actually exist in the future are morally significant.

In order to understand why a more expansive understanding of intergenerational justice is controversial, it is helpful to recall that most contemporary understandings of ethics and justice are based on person-affecting principles. The fundamental premise of person-affecting principles is that actions are morally significant only to the extent that they affect persons or by extension, other living beings. Thus, actions are good to the extent that they benefit persons. They are wrong to the extent that they harm persons. Actions which benefit and harm persons in equal measure are considered morally neutral, while actions which neither benefit nor harm persons are considered morally insignificant.

Person-affecting principles thus recognize as morally significant only the effects of our actions on those persons who exist at present or will actually exist in the future. They place no value on the interests of merely potential persons, nor do they place a value on bringing persons into existence.

This position is stated clearly by Mary Warren who argues that "the prima facie aim of morality should be to maximize the extent to which each *actual*—present or future—person's interests are promoted."[11] This means that "we have many obligations towards the people who will exist after us ... [but if] the human race were suddenly and deliberately to stop reproducing altogether no wrong would have been done to merely potential people, who cannot be wronged, or to people of future generations, since there would not be any."[12]

Another way of saying this is that our obligations to future generations are contingent in nature. Before we can say that an intergenerational action is morally significant, we must first *assume* that there will exist some future person(s) who will be affected by that action.

---

[11]Warren, 24.
[12]Ibid., 28.

If we have good reason to believe that this assumption is false, and that no future person(s) will be affected by an action, then it follows from the premises of person-affecting principles that the action in question is not morally significant *as an intergenerational action*.

On its face, the need to assume that future persons will exist and will be affected by our actions seems unremarkable. For example, if scientific studies produced convincing evidence that our sun will explode within a century, the question of whether it would be just to our distant descendants to pollute the lakes and rivers of this planet would have no meaning, because we would have no distant descendants. Under these assumptions, we would not be acting in an intergenerationally unjust manner if we failed to take into account the effects our actions *might have had* on distant future generations had circumstances been different.

However, to say that obligations to future generations are contingent on the assumption that future generations will exist is very different from saying that we can have obligations only to persons who exist at present. The later position would make obligations to future generations impossible, by definition. By contrast, the need to assume that future persons will be affected by our actions absolves us of the responsibility to attempt to consider the interests of future generations only if we are in a position to foresee that no future persons will be affected by a particular course of action.

While most people believe the human species will continue to exist far into the future, not everyone is convinced this will be the case. Former Secretary of the Interior, James Watt, for example, seems to have believed that it would not be too many generations "before the Lord returns" and the Apocalypse occurs.[13] If Watt had been (were) correct in this belief, then his policy of encouraging the "development" of the remaining American wilderness would not have been unjust to distant future generations, since there would be no distant future generations to be harmed by our actions.

[13] J. Adler, et al., "James Watt's Gold Rush," *Newsweek*, (June 29, 1981) 97, 29.

On the other hand, whether we see the end of human life on this planet as excusing the destruction of the wilderness depends, largely, on the cause of the Apocalypse. If the extinction of life on Earth is not the result of a natural disaster (or the "will of God"), but our own pollution of the natural environment (or God's punishment for our having despoiled the planet), then the question of whether it is intergenerationally just to pollute the Earth would not be rendered moot by the absence of future generations. Similarly, if the ultimate consequence of building larger and larger nuclear arsenals is the extinction of our species, then it is entirely appropriate to ask whether the nuclear arms race is (was) intergenerationally just. Even though we would have no obligation to set resources aside for future generations if the end of the world were at hand, we most definitely have an obligation to be certain that our own actions do not cause the Apocalypse and that our prophesies of the end of the world are not self-fulfilling.

While it may be appropriate to raise questions of intergenerational justice in these circumstances, if we accept the premises of person-affecting principles, we may well conclude that such questions are incoherent. According to person-affecting principles, whatever injustice results from pollution, nuclear war, or any other public policy must arise from the effects of those policies on *actual persons*. If a nuclear war extinguishes all human life on this planet, the entire harm of such a holocaust must be accounted for in terms of the death of those alive at the time of the war. Person-affecting principles place no value either on the interests of merely potential persons or on bringing future persons into existence. To paraphrase Mary Warren: if the human race were suddenly and deliberately to put an end to itself in a nuclear war, altogether no wrong would have been done to merely potential people, who cannot be wronged, or to people of future generations, since there would not be any.[14]

The possibility that the human species may destroy itself in a nuclear war raises a number of important moral questions which must be

---

[14]Paraphrased from a statement cited earlier, Warren, 28.

addressed by any contemporary theory of intergenerational justice. The most fundamental of these questions is what value should be placed on the continued existence of the human species. The only response person-affecting principles allow one to give is that the extinction of the human species has no moral significance apart from the deaths of those individuals alive at the time of the holocaust. This is a myopic and profoundly disturbing response. In the chapters which follow, I argue that this response is also quite wrong.

V

The Population Problem

IN THE CONTEXT OF INTERGENERATIONAL JUSTICE, the population problem consists of two distinct but related issues. The first is the survival of the human species. Do we have an obligation to ensure the survival of the human species, or is the continued existence of the human species merely a precondition for our having obligations to future generations? The second issue concerns population. Is there an ethical basis for preferring a larger population to a smaller one, or ought we be concerned only with the effects of population size on those persons who will actually exist in the future?

The power to determine the size of the population serves to distinguish intragenerational action from intergenerational action. When we act intragenerationally, population size is a given against which we measure the effects of our actions. By contrast, when we act intergenerationally, population size is as much as a variable as are the effects of our actions on future persons. Indeed, our power to determine the size of future generations helps determine the extent of our obligations to the future. If we have more children, we may need to set aside greater resources to ensure their welfare.

Our capacity to determine the size of the future population also raises important ethical questions in its own right. While these questions are not necessarily definable as questions of justice, the intimate connection between population size and obligations to the future makes it important to examine broadly the ethical constraints on actions that affect population size.

This chapter is primarily concerned with examining the intrinsic value we place, or ought to place, on the continued existence of the human species and on the existence of larger numbers of human beings. By "intrinsic value," I mean that value we place *directly* on the existence of the human species and on the existence of larger numbers of persons, excluding any secondary benefits that may be derived by others from the existence of larger numbers of persons.

The questions of the survival of the species and the size of the human population are obviously related. Those who hold that there is a moral basis for preferring a larger population to a smaller one necessarily hold that there is a moral reason to perpetuate the human species. The contrapositive is also true. Those who hold that we have no moral obligation to perpetuate the human species also must hold that there is no intrinsic reason to prefer a larger population to a smaller one, though they may recognize other reasons for preferring a larger population to a smaller one.

On the other hand, the questions of the survival of the species and population size are not interchangeable. It is coherent to hold that we have a moral obligation to perpetuate the human species, but that there is no reason to prefer a larger population to a smaller one, so long as the survival of the human species is assured.

THE SURVIVAL OF THE SPECIES

Do we place a positive value on the existence of the human species, distinct from the value we place on the continued existence of specific individuals? Methodological individualists argue that we do not and should not place a value on the existence of the human species apart from the value we place on the existence of discrete individuals. Indeed, they argue that the species is neither more nor less than the sum of those individuals who exist now, or who will exist in the future. More communitarian thinkers argue that the value we place (or ought to place) on the human species transcends the value we place on the "sum of the individuals."

How we answer this question has a direct bearing on the types of theories of intergenerational justice we can construct. If we hold, with the methodological individualists, that only the effects of our actions on actual persons are morally relevant, then the goal of intergenerational policies ought to be to improve the conditions in which future persons will live. On the other hand, if we accept the more communitarian understanding that the value we place (or ought to place) on the human species transcends the value we place on the "sum of the individuals," it may be necessary to give a different focus to our intergenerational policies.

Because the existence of the human species entails the existence of individual members of the species and vice versa, it is not a simple matter to differentiate between the value we place on the survival of the species and the value we place on the survival of individuals. In an effort to place our moral judgments in sharper focus, I have constructed three imaginary but theoretically possible scenarios involving nuclear war. My purpose in constructing these scenarios is to help us differentiate between our concern for individuals and our concern for the human species and at the same time to help us differentiate between injustices done to contemporaries and intergenerational injustices. My goal is to demonstrate that, at least under some circumstances, the extinction of the human species raises ethical concerns distinct from the ethical concerns raised when actions cause suffering and death to individuals. Because person-affecting principles define as morally significant only those actions which benefit or harm actual persons, if it is possible to demonstrate that we place a value on the existence of the human species, apart from the value we place on the continued existence of specific individuals, we must conclude that person-affecting principles represent an incomplete description of our actual moral judgments. By itself, this will not tell us what we need to do in order to develop a sufficient explanation of our moral judgments. However, it should demonstrate the need to move beyond person-affecting principles in the search for a more adequate theory of intergenerational justice.

The following set of scenarios requires us to differentiate between the effects of a nuclear war on those persons alive at the time of the war and the effects of such a war on posterity. Specifically, I want to differentiate between three possible outcomes of a nuclear war.

1. In the first scenario, a nuclear war kills every human being either immediately, from the direct impact of the nuclear weapons, or within a few weeks, from exposure to radioactive fallout.

2. In the second scenario, a nuclear war kills 99% of the persons alive at the time of the war, either immediately or within a few weeks. The remaining 1% survive, despite severe physical and psychological injuries. Gradually, over the centuries, the human population is replenished and a new civilization built.

3. In the third scenario, a more limited nuclear war is fought. 80% of the existing population survives both the immediate impact of the war and its radioactive fallout. While many of the survivors are injured, the majority is able to resume relatively normal lives, with one notable exception. This exception is that as a result of exposure to radioactive fallout, the entire surviving population is rendered sterile. Most of the war's survivors live out their normal years, but none is able to reproduce. Within 100 years humanity is extinct.

If our moral judgments conformed strictly to the precepts of person-affecting principles, we would judge the three nuclear war scenarios solely on the basis of their effects on actual persons. If we accepted this standard, then the worst of the three outcomes clearly would be the first scenario, since this scenario envisions the greatest amount of harm to actual persons.

Based solely on the criterion of harm to actual persons, the second scenario is nearly as bad as the first. A mere one percent of the population survives the war and those who do survive suffer physically and psychologically from the effects of the war.

By comparison the population in the third scenario is less severely injured than the population in the second. Eighty percent of the population survives the war, and except for the inability to procreate, the majority of the surviving population live out their full years in relatively good health.

If we place no value on bringing into existence "merely potential persons," then the third scenario is preferable to the second. Fewer persons are killed, and the physical injuries to the surviving population are less severe than those in the second scenario. But would we find the third scenario preferable to the second? I am convinced we would not. It is my sense that the third scenario is indistinguishable from the first scenario in all respects except the details of how the human species becomes extinct. In both cases the single most important effect of the nuclear war is the extermination of the species. The fact that several billion persons survive the war to live out their "normal years" may make the third scenario marginally preferable to the first, but this difference fades in light of the overwhelming fact that in both scenarios the species is exterminated.

By contrast, as horrible as the second scenario is, it seems less odious than the other two. Certainly, the difference is not to be found in the amount of harm done to actual persons. By this measure the second scenario is nearly as bad as the first and is decidedly worse than the third. What makes this scenario less horrible than the other two is the fact that the human species survives.

It might even be argued that scenario three is actually the worst of the three scenarios if we take into account not merely physical harm but also the psychological harm of living with the awareness that we are a doomed species.[1] This is a plausible interpretation. However, not everyone may share this understanding. Some people may think that death is so much worse than sterility that scenario three would be decidedly preferable to scenario one. Although sterility is generally considered a serious injury, under normal circumstances we do not consider sterility to be tantamount to death. Indeed, some persons voluntarily undergo surgical sterilization in order to avoid giving birth to (additional) children. In order to hold that scenario three is the worst of the three scenarios, we must believe that people place so much value on the existence of posterity that they would prefer death to an existence without the possibility of a posterity. Such an understanding of the importance of posterity cannot be based on strictly person-affecting principles.

---

[1]This argument was suggested in written comments on a draft of this work by Professor Terence Ball.

To verify that this is the case, imagine that in the second scenario radiation does not cause the sterility of every person, but only the sterility the entire male population (and the destruction of all sperm stored in sperm banks). In this revised scenario, we can imagine that 25% or more of the prewar population suffers no physical injury whatsoever. If we based our judgment solely on person-affecting principles, this change in assumptions ought to make a difference in how we view the effects of the war. However, if we are concerned with the species and not just with individuals, this change in assumptions would make no difference in our overall assessment of the war (except perhaps to make the fate of humanity seem all the more ironic). It is my sense that the change in assumptions makes no difference.

An alternate explanation for our judgment that the survival of the species (in scenario two) is preferable to the survival of larger numbers of individual persons (in scenario three), is that it is possible to count as survivors (in scenario two) not only the 1% of the population who are not killed by the war, but also the (billions of) persons who will be born in subsequent generations. If we perform such a recalculation, the survival rates of the second and third scenarios begin to look very different. It would not take too many millennia before the 80% survival rate of the third scenario is surpassed by the enhanced survival rate of the second scenario.

It is most uncertain that this method of calculating the survival rate is legitimate. However, even if we grant, for the sake of argument, that it is legitimate to recalculate the survival rate of scenario two, for such a recalculation to alter our judgment we must place a positive value on bringing future persons into existence. The harm done to actual persons (in scenario two) can be mitigated by the births of larger numbers of future persons only if we place an intrinsic value on the existence of persons who do not now exist. For Warren and other methodological individualists who hold that there is no intrinsic value to bringing merely potential persons into existence, such a recalculation would have to be considered illegitimate.

More importantly, we do not need to appeal to such a recalculation of the survival rate in order to explain why we prefer scenario two to scenario three. A far simpler explanation is that we place a value directly on the continued existence of the human species, quite apart from the value we place on the survival of individual members of the human species.

It is true, of course, that for the species to survive, individual members of the species must continue to exist. But, as we have seen, a concern with the survival of the species is not equivalent to a concern with the survival of particular members of the species. This is true not only with respect of human beings, but also with respect to animals. We are willing to make significant sacrifices to preserve endangered species of animals, even as we tolerate the killing for sport and food of individual members of closely related, but nonendangered species. The fact that we accept the hunting and slaughter of animals for food indicates that while we place a value on the preservation of entire species of animals, we do not value individual members of those (and other) species as ends in themselves, rather than as a means to our pleasure.[2]

Our relationship to our own species requires that we treat our fellow humans as ends rather than as means to an end. Nonetheless, it is important to distinguish between a concern with the survival of the human species and a concern with the survival of individuals. Our preference for scenario two, which envisions the survival of the species, rather than scenario three, which envisions less harm to actual persons, cannot be explained on the basis of a concern with actual persons; nor can it be explained on the basis of person-affecting principles. The fact that we see the perpetuation of the species as more important than the numbers of individuals who might survive a nuclear holocaust supports two conclusions. The first is that we place a value on the survival of the species distinct from and in addition to the value we place on the survival

[2]Martin Buber would describe our relationship to animals as an I-It relationship rather than an I-You relationship. Martin Buber, *I and Thou*, (New York: Charles Scribner's Sons, 1970), 53–59.

of discrete individuals. The second is that a narrow understanding of intergenerational justice, based on person-affecting principles, cannot explain our intuitive judgments concerning some types of actions that affect the survival of the human species.

IS THERE AN OBLIGATION TO PROCREATE?

Although most contemporary concern with intergenerational justice has focused on our obligations to actual but future persons, some contemporary thinkers have attempted to address the more difficult questions arising from our capacity to affect the size and the identity of future generations. The principal focus of these efforts has been on the obligation to procreate. At one extreme we find those who argue that the present generation has an obligation to bring "potential persons" into existence. At the other extreme we find those who argue that there is no obligation to reproduce the species. Between these poles lies a variety of positions representing the efforts of thinkers of different schools to address the problem of "potentiality."[3]

The question of what value we ought to place on procreation is important for a theory of intergenerational justice. Depending on the value we assign to procreation, we may have more or less difficulty, and more or less success, addressing the questions arising from nuclear war, genocide, genetic engineering, and other public policy issues.[4] For example, if we recognize the right to existence of "potential persons," it becomes relatively easy to explain why it is intergenerationally unjust to exterminate the human species in a nuclear war or to commit genocide: both would be intergenerationally unjust insofar as they would violate our obligation to "potential persons." By contrast, if we recognize no

[3]The term "potentiality" refers to the fact that we have the capacity to bring into existence persons who do not exist at present.

[4]It should be kept in mind that the fact that a particular theory allows us to address these types of intergenerational questions with relative ease does not necessarily mean that the theory allows us to address these questions well. As with other philosophical questions easy answers may very well be poor answers.

obligation to procreate, we have to look to other principles to explain why nuclear war and genocide are intergenerationally unjust.

The question of whether there is an obligation to procreate is as old as the Bible and as recent as today's headlines. Rabbinical scholars interpreted God's commandment to Adam and Eve to "Be fruitful and multiply and fill the Earth"[5] as commanding that couples have at least one male child (be fruitful) and one female child (multiply).[6] Other religions have interpreted their sacred writings as requiring (or at least prescribing) procreation. Perhaps the most controversial of these interpretations is the Roman Catholic Church's prohibition on the use of "artificial" methods of contraception.

Although there are some advantages to recognizing an obligation to procreate, such a position is fraught with peril. In an effort to explore this question more systematically, I have identified six different positions regarding the issue of "potentiality." Five of these positions are presented roughly in order from the greatest acceptance of the obligation to bring "potential persons" into existence, to the sharpest rejection of this principle. I look at the most important advantages and shortcomings of each position. Finally, I look at a sixth position which overcomes many of the difficulties associated with the other five, and examine some of the implications of this sixth position.

The five positions on the question of potentiality identifiable in the contemporary literature on intergenerational justice are:

1. There is an obligation to bring "potential persons" into existence. This obligation is rooted in the right of "potential persons" to exist.

2. While "potential persons" do not have a right to existence, there is a general duty to bring "potential persons" into existence. More specifically, there is a duty to bring "potential persons" into existence if doing so would increase the total happiness of the population. If bringing a "potential person" into existence would cause a decrease in the total happiness of the population, there is a duty not to do so.

---

[5]Genesis 1, 28.

[6]Michna Yevamot 6:6.

> 3. We have an obligation to bring "potential persons" into existence if, and only if, doing so will increase the average happiness of future generations.
>
> 4. There is no general obligation to procreate because one can have obligations only to persons who exist now or who will exist in the future. The act of procreation *or* the failure to procreate can be wrong only if those who exist now or others who will exist in the future would be affected adversely.
>
> 5. There is no general obligation to procreate because one can have obligations only to persons who exist now or who will exist in the future. The act of procreation *or* the failure to procreate can be wrong only if those who exist now or others who will exist in the future would be affected adversely. The act of procreation can also be wrong if the resulting child would be condemned to a life not worth living.

The sixth position is that

> 6. There is no specific obligation to procreate, but there is a general duty to do good with one's life. To bring children into the world and to raise them so that they may lead happy and fruitful lives is one way of fulfilling this duty. Whether it is desirable to bring a child into existence in any given situation depends both on the expected quality of life of the child and on the effects the child's existence will have on others.

The first two positions represent attempts to move beyond person-affecting principles by recognizing an obligation to procreate. The third position represents a retreat by average utilitarians from the total utilitarians' preference for increasing the size of the human population. The next two positions represent rejections of the idea that we can have an obligation to procreate. Both are rooted in person-affecting principles. The sixth and final position represents a moderate attempt to move beyond person-affecting principles without falling into the quagmires associated with the first two positions.

The rights of "potential persons"

The first, and most extreme, position is that

> There is an obligation to bring "potential persons" into existence. This obligation is rooted in the right of "potential persons" to exist.

The argument that we have an obligation to procreate because "potential persons" have the right to exist is not made explicitly in the literature. However, a number of thinkers frame their arguments as refutations of this position. Among these are Mary Warren, Jan Narveson, and Joel Feinberg. Warren interprets R. M. Hare as making this argument when he argues for extending the "Golden Rule" to say that we should "do to others what *we are glad was* done to us."[7] Based on this extension of the Golden Rule, Hare argues there is *prima facie* obligation not to abort a pregnancy, nor to use contraceptives, nor to refrain entirely from procreating.[8]

It is important to distinguish between saying there is a duty or obligation to procreate, based on the Golden Rule, and saying there is an obligation to procreate because a "potential person" has a right to be brought into existence. The duties associated with the Golden Rule are general moral duties that are more easily overridden by practical considerations than are the rights of persons. As I read Hare's argument, he does not assert that "potential persons" are bearers of rights.

If we did accept that "potential persons" have a *prima facie* right to exist, we would be able to address some of the important shortcomings previously identified in contemporary understandings of intergenerational justice. For example, if we accepted that "potential persons" have a right to exist, we would have no difficulty explaining why nuclear war and genocide are intergenerationally unjust, even though no remote future person suffers an actual harm if the species is exterminated, and no direct descendant of an exterminated people is harmed by genocide. The fact that recognizing the right of "potential persons" to exist would give direct expression to our moral intuitions and

---

[7]Warren, 17–18.

[8]R. M. Hare, "Abortion and the Golden Rule," *Philosophy and Public Affairs* 4 Spring (1975), 212.

judgments concerning nuclear war and genocide constitutes an argument in favor of this understanding.

Unfortunately, the concept of the rights of "potential persons" is nothing short of an analytic nightmare. The crux of the problem is that this concept is far too inclusive. If we understand a "potential person" to be *any* individual who potentially might exist in the future, then there are far more "potential persons" than could ever exist in actuality. This is so because every unique genetic combination results in a unique individual, and for every male gamete that fertilizes an ovum there are billions of other male gametes which are capable of doing so. It follows that for every individual who is actually conceived, there are billions of "potential persons" who cannot be conceived. In order to honor the right of any one "potential person" to exist, we must deny that same right to billions of other "potential persons." In theory, it might be possible to balance the claims of each "potential person" against those of all other "potential persons." However, it would require nothing short of Divine omniscience to sort through the indefinitely large number of possible futures. No ethical system reasonably could require that human beings undertake such a task.

Even if we leave aside these not inconsiderable difficulties, there are other practical reasons for rejecting the argument that "potential persons" have a right to exist. One good and sufficient reason is that if we recognized this right, women would have a corresponding duty to bear as many children as possible. If we take seriously the right to exist of "potential children," women might well be obligated to bear children, even when they do not want children, and even when they had already borne several other children. This argument treats women instrumentally and is inconsistent with our understanding of individual autonomy and dignity. The fact that the "rights of 'potential persons'" has such oppressive implications is a sufficient reason to reject this concept.

The approach of total utilitarianism

A milder version of the argument that we have an obligation to bring "potential persons" into existence is that

> While "potential persons" do not have a right to existence, there is a general duty to bring "potential persons" into existence. More specifically, there is a duty to bring "potential persons" into existence if doing so would increase the total happiness of the population. If bringing a "potential person" into existence would cause a decrease in the total happiness of the population, there is a duty not to do so.

This argument is based on the total utilitarian understanding that there is an obligation to act to bring about "the greatest happiness for the greatest number" of (future) persons.[9]

The application of utilitarian principles to intergenerational actions results in an ambiguity. It is possible to bring about the greatest happiness for the greatest number either by acting to make future persons happier (presumably by improving the conditions in which future persons will live), or by increasing the size of the future population (if doing so does not cause a significant decrease in the *average* happiness of future persons), or, of course, by doing both.

Utilitarians, themselves, are sharply divided over how the happiness principle should be applied to actions that affect future generations. The two utilitarian approaches bear the names "total" utilitarianism and "average" utilitarianism. "Total" utilitarians argue that our goal should be to maximize the *total* amount of happiness either by making future persons happier or by increasing population size (or both). "Average" utilitarians argue that only increases in the "average" happiness of future persons are morally relevant. While this debate is of interest principally to other utilitarians, the principles which underlie this debate are significant for nonutilitarians as well.

---

[9]Among those who defend this position are R. I. Sikora, "Is it Wrong to Prevent the Existence of Future Generations?" *Obligations to Future Generations*, ed. R. I. Sikora and Brian Barry, (Philadelphia: Temple University Press, 1978), 112–166.

Total utilitarianism contains two different value preferences. The first is the traditional utilitarian preference for increasing the happiness of (future) persons. The second is the preference for bringing additional (happy) persons into existence. Total utilitarianism places the same value on actions that increase happiness by making future persons happier as on actions that increase happiness by increasing the size of the future population. For example, if we start with a population of 10,000 persons with an "average happiness level" of 100, it is possible to increase the total "utility" (happiness) of that population either by increasing the average happiness of the population to 101, or by increasing the size of the population to 10,100. In both cases the total "utility" of the new population would be 1,010,000. Total utilitarians are indifferent as to how this new total is achieved.

On its face, the total utilitarian preference for a larger population is unobjectionable. Indeed, it is a quite conventional preference in some cultures and traditions.[10] A distinct advantage of total utilitarianism is that it provides an unambiguous explanation for why we ought to act to preserve the human species. We can only maximize total "utility" if we first ensure the existence of future generations. On the other hand, total utilitarianism achieves this clarity of explanation at the cost of permitting, and in some cases requiring, tradeoffs between the size of the future population and the happiness of that population.

The most serious problem facing total utilitarianism is that policies which encourage population growth may have the effect of decreasing the average happiness of the future population. For example, if we assume that increasing an island's population from 10,000 to 12,000 would result in a decrease in the average happiness of the population from 100 to 90 (perhaps due to competition for scarce resources), the net effect of the increasing population size would be to increase the "total amount" of happiness of the population from 1,000,000 to 1,08,000. In

[10]For example God promises Abraham that He will multiply Abraham's descendants "as the stars of heaven and as the sand which is on the seashore." Genesis 22:17. Traditionally, a man (but not necessarily a woman) was described as being blessed with many children (particularly sons).

this case, the loss of happiness of the average person would be more than "offset" by the increase in total utility or happiness resulting from the larger population size. Under such circumstances, a total utilitarian would hold that it is not only desirable to increase the size of the population, but it is actually mandatory to act to do so.

An even more dramatic example of the counterintuitive conclusions which follow from total utilitarianism can be seen by imagining a couple who sought to base their decision as to whether to have a third child on total utilitarian principles. Let us assume that each member of the family presently has an "average happiness level" of 10, resulting in a "total utility" of 40. Let us further assume that the family is not financially well off. Because both parents work, they spend less time with the children than they would like. The couple estimates that having an additional child would further strain the family's resources, resulting in a decrease in the average happiness level of all members of the family to 8.5. If we assume that the additional child has the same level of happiness as the rest of the family, the "total utility" of the family after the birth of the child would be 5 x 8.5, or 42.5. Being good total utilitarians, the couple has the child, causing everyone (except the new child) to be less happy than they had been.

There are few notions which seem more antithetical to either common sense or the spirit of Bentham than that we should make the average future person less happy in order to increase total happiness of the future population. Indeed, this has been termed "the repugnant conclusion" and is seen by many as a sufficient reason to reject the total utilitarian premises which lead to this conclusion.[11]

---

[11]Derek Parfit, *Reasons and Persons*, 381–390. This feature of total utilitarianism has been examined and criticized by a number of other thinkers including John Rawls in *A Theory of Justice*, (Cambridge, Massachusetts: Harvard University Press, 1971), 161–163. See also Larry S. Temkin, "Intransitivity and the Mere Addition Paradox," *Philosophy and Public Affairs* 16 Spring (1987), 138–187.

The approach of average utilitarianism

One way to avoid the repugnant conclusion is to hold that we ought to be concerned only with increasing the average happiness of future generations. Those who argue for this position are known as "average utilitarians." Average utilitarianism eliminates the possibility of coming to the repugnant conclusion, by placing no value whatsoever on increasing the size of the future population.

Average utilitarianism represents a third approach to potentiality. This approach holds that

> We have an obligation to bring "potential persons" into existence if, and only if, doing so will increase the average happiness of future generations.

Average utilitarians are concerned only with the average level of happiness of the population (at any given time). From the point of view of an average utilitarian, a population of one hundred very happy persons is preferable to a population of one billion merely happy persons.

Average utilitarianism addresses satisfactorily some of the concerns examined earlier. For example, average utilitarianism places a positive value on the survival of the species since the average happiness of the human population would be zero if the species were exterminated in a nuclear war. Average utilitarianism also avoids many of the pitfalls of total utilitarianism.

On the other hand average utilitarianism has its own difficulties. Among the more disturbing implications of average utilitarianism is that a couple who did not want children might be morally required to have a child if the happiness of the child would more than offset their own loss of happiness. In this sense, average utilitarianism contains the same value preference for bringing "potential persons" into existence as does total utilitarianism. However, this value preference is unlikely to represent as serious problem for average utilitarianism as it does for total utilitarianism, since a couple who do not want a child would be unlikely to rear a child who was so happy as to more than "compensate" for their own loss of happiness. Nonetheless, the notion that the projected happiness of a "merely potential child" could outweigh the desire of the couple to remain childless raises serious questions about the acceptability of average utilitarianism.

An even more serious problem is that average utilitarianism does not adequately explain our judgments concerning genocide. If a population experiencing ethnic conflict is less happy than a population without such conflict, it would be desirable to seek to eliminate that conflict. However, there is more than one way to put an end to ethnic conflict. An all too common response to ethnic conflict is to seek to eliminate the minority population, whether by expulsion, conversion, assimilation, or extermination. We have only to look to the former Yugoslavia during the 1990s to see that these impulses have not been overcome. Only when attempts "to get rid of the 'problem'" have failed are peaceful resolutions generally attempted. Among the arguments put forth by advocates of so-called "ethnic cleansing" is that if the minority population is eliminated, future generations of their (now ethnically pure) nation will be happier because they will not experience the tensions associated with ethnic differences. Regardless of the truth of the assertion that future generations will be happier in ethnically pure nations, the desire to increase the average level of "happiness" of future generations cannot justify a policy of genocide.

Nor are these the only failings of average utilitarianism. Average utilitarianism holds that we have an obligation to bring a child into existence if the net effect of doing so would be to increase the average happiness of the population. This understanding of our moral obligations leaves open the possibility of breeding a servant or slave class if the relative unhappiness of that class would be more than offset by the increased happiness of the master class. This problem is also a basis for criticism of utilitarianism as a general theory of justice.[12]

Average utilitarianism also holds that whether it is morally permissible (or even mandatory) to bring a child into the world depends neither on the desires of the parents nor on the "absolute" quality of the child's life, but on the *relative* happiness of that potential child as

---

[12] See for example John Rawls, *A Theory of Justice*, 167–168.

compared to the average happiness of the existing population. Thus, average utilitarianism holds that it would be wrong to bring a child into the world if that child would be less happy than the average person, even if the child would be generally happy and find life desirable (unless the benefits to others more than offset impact of bringing a "below average" child into the world). On the other hand, it would be mandatory to bring the *same* child into the world if the average happiness of the existing population were lower than that of the child.[13] Average utilitarianism thus judges the worth of a child's life not by fixed standards, but by the purely relative standard of the average level of happiness of others. Such a purely relativistic standard is inconsistent with our moral traditions.[14]

Two positions based on person-affecting principles

One way contemporary thinkers have responded to the problems of both total and average utilitarianism is by asking why we should have any obligation to bring "potential persons" into existence. After all, we can have no contractual or promissory obligations to nonexistent "persons." More importantly, nonexistent "persons" cannot be harmed by our failure to bring them into existence. To some thinkers there seems to be no reason for holding that we have any obligation to bring "potential persons" into existence.[15]

A fourth position, then, is

> 4. There is no general obligation to procreate because one can have obligations only to persons who exist now or who will exist in the future.

---

[13]Derek Parfit examines the implications of this line of argument in *Reasons and Persons*, 420–425.

[14]For a persuasive argument that despite the initial appeal of average utilitarianism and despite the difficulties of the total utilitarian position, total utilitarianism is preferable to average utilitarianism, see R. I. Sikora, "Is It Wrong to Prevent the Existence of Future Generations?" 112–166. See also Thomas Hurka, "Value and Population Size," *Ethics* 93 April (1983), 496–507, for a discussion of other approaches which might avoid some of the difficulties associated with total and average utilitarianism.

[15]Warren, 14–30.

> The act of procreation *or* the failure to procreate can be wrong only if those who exist now or others who will exist in the future would be affected adversely.

This is the position on "potentiality" of many who subscribe to person-regarding ethics. It is classified as a person-regarding position because it holds that we can have moral obligations only to persons who actually exist now or will actually exist in the future. This understanding recognizes the possibility that our obligations to our contemporaries may include the obligation to procreate. Whether we actually have this obligation depends on the details of our relationships. For example, if a couple had promised their parents they would produce grandchildren for them, then the couple would have a *prima facie* obligation to try to have children. One could also base the obligation to have children on the needs of those of the next generation who already exist or whom one anticipates will exist. Thus parents might feel an obligation to have a second child in order to provide their first child with a sibling.

This fourth position places no independent value on bringing persons into existence. The act of procreation, in and of itself, is understood to be morally neutral with respect to the child brought into existence. Procreation is a precondition for having moral responsibilities to one's child rather than a person-regarding act in its own right.

One problem with this position is that the lives of some persons born with genetic diseases or into conditions of extreme privation may be so miserable that one might say of those persons "it would have been better if they had never been born." Does it make sense to say that the decision to bring a child into the world afflicted with Tay-Sachs does not affect the child? Or that one does not affect a child by bringing her into an existence made miserable by disease and foreshortened by starvation?

Questions such as these have divided contemporary thinkers. Many argue that it is wrong to conceive a child, if that child would be condemned to a life of misery.[16] Others hold that procreation can be

---

[16]Among those who adopt this position are Mary Warren, "Do Potential People Have Moral Rights?" 25; Don Locke, "The Parfit Population Problem," *Philosophy* 62 April (1987), 148; and S. I. Sikora, "Is It Wrong to Prevent the

neither a benefit nor a harm to the being brought into existence by that act. Instead, procreation is a precondition for the possibility of other benefits or harms.[17] I call the first position the "liberal" understanding of person-affecting principles and the second position the "conservative" or "purist" understanding.

To reiterate, the conservative understanding of person-affecting principles is that

> There is no general obligation to procreate because one can have obligations only to persons who exist now or who will exist in the future. The act of procreation *or* the failure to procreate can be wrong only if those who exist now or others who will exist in the future would be affected adversely. The act of procreation can also be wrong if the resulting child would be condemned to a life not worth living.

The liberal position is identical except that it also includes the following provision:

> The act of procreation can also be wrong if the resulting child would be condemned to a life not worth living.

The principal advantage of the liberal position is that it avoids some of the unacceptable conclusions of the conservative position. For example, because the conservative position recognizes as morally relevant only the effects of procreation on others, the conservative position would hold that there is nothing wrong with deliberately bringing into existence a child with a genetic defect which would limit the child to a short and painful life. If the possibility of harm or benefit begins after conception (or with birth), it would be morally permissible for a couple deliberately to produce such a child in order to use that child's organs for transplantation. However, to bring a child into the world for the sake of

---

Existence of Future Generations?" 140. See also James P. Sterba, "Explaining Asymmetry: A Problem for Parfit," *Philosophy and Public Affairs* 16 Spring (1987), 188–192; and Derek Parfit, "A Reply to Sterba," *Philosophy and Public Affairs* 16 Spring (1987), 193–194.

[17]Fewer thinkers have defended this position. Among those who have is Richard T. De George, "The Environment, Rights, and Future Generations," *Responsibilities to Future Generations*, ed. Ernest Partridge, (Buffalo, NY: Prometheus Books, 1980), 160.

her or his organs would seem to violate the most basic moral principle that humans be considered to be ends-in-themselves and not means to an end. It is difficult to see how human beings can be considered to be ends-in-themselves after their birth if there are no moral constraints which apply to their conception.

A real world example of conceiving a child for the sake of its body parts is that of the couple who conceived a baby in an effort to provide a compatible bone marrow "stem cell" donor for an older child with leukemia. While conceiving a child in order to provide a bone marrow donor for an older child is very different than conceiving a child in order to harvest a liver or heart, it is not fundamentally different from conceiving a child in order to harvest a single kidney for transplantation into a sibling. Both cases raise serious ethical concerns because a child is conceived for the sake of her body parts and primarily for the benefit of others. What makes this actual situation especially interesting is the fact that the parents of this baby did not understand or accept as valid the view of "ethics experts" that what they were doing was morally suspect. The couple was widely reported as speaking of their baby as "the miracle baby" because she might give them back their older daughter. In defense of their decision, the couple stated they would love their baby because of the special circumstances of her birth, regardless of the success of the transplant procedure.[18]

While one should not minimize the very real danger that a child conceived for the purpose of providing bone marrow to an older sibling would be rejected if the transplant failed, there is also some validity to the couple's interpretation of their own actions. No child is (or can be) conceived for her own sake, at least insofar as a child has no "sake" until she or he is conceived. In this sense, the argument of Professor Capron, of the University of Southern California, that "the ideal reason for having a child is associated with that child's own welfare—to bring a

---

[18]"Ethics Experts Question Morality of 'Bone Marrow' Baby," *The Times Leader, Wilkes-Barre, PA,* February 17, 1990, 1, 8.

child into being and to nurture it,"[19] cannot literally be true. What one can say is that the ideal reason to have a child is to fulfill the desire of the parents to bring a child into being and to nurture it. This position links the desires of the parents with the welfare of the child and is different from and ethically preferable to bringing a child into existence primarily for the sake of her bone marrow.

On balance, then, the liberal view of person-affecting principles would seem to be superior to the conservative view. The liberal view accepts that the interests of existing persons ought to be the determining factor in the decision to procreate, but holds that it is wrong to bring a child into existence if her or his life will be miserable. As Mary Warren argues persuasively, "once we do decide to have children then we are obligated to begin taking their interests into account, and this process may even lead to a reversal of that decision."[20]

The liberal person-regarding position is not without its own limitations and difficulties, however. One important limitation of the liberal position is that it presupposes a degree of knowledge and control over procreation which exists only in advanced industrial nations and then only among the middle and upper classes. A more general difficulty with this position is that it places a moral value (either positive or negative) on procreation only when two conditions are met. The first is when procreation or the failure to procreate affects others. Quite clearly, it can be either beneficial or harmful to existing persons to add to the population. The second condition is when the child is condemned to a life of misery. Under this condition, procreation has a negative value (at least for the child born into this condition). The act of procreation is understood to have neither a positive nor a negative value *for the child* if she or he is born normally healthy and happy.

The problem with this understanding, as Hermann Vetter has pointed out, is that we can never be certain a child will not be born deformed, or that the life of a child will not be one of misery. To the

---

[19]Ibid., 1, 8.
[20]Warren, 25.

extent that we place an intrinsic value on bringing a person into existence *only* if that individual is born to a miserable existence, the act of procreation has a slightly negative *net* intrinsic value. This is to say, the average value we place on the act of procreation, without counting the effect the existence of the child will have on others, is slightly negative. The liberal position on potentiality thus leads to the conclusion that we ought not to procreate.[21] Such a value preference is inconsistent with our traditional understanding that "children are a blessing" and with the widely shared judgment that the survival of the human species is an ethical priority, though evidently not with Professor Vetter's own value judgments.[22]

Finally, both the liberal and the conservative variants of person-affecting principles lead to difficulties in addressing the intergenerational questions arising from nuclear war and genocide. As we saw earlier in this chapter, person-affecting principles do not allow us to explain our moral judgment that both nuclear war and genocide are *inter*generationally unjust and not merely unjust to contemporaries. As a result, neither position, by itself, can serve as the foundation for a satisfactory theory of intergenerational justice.

An asymmetrical view of the ethics of procreation

In light of the serious shortcomings of all the positions on potentiality examined thus far, we must ask whether there is any satisfactory solution to the problem of potentiality. I believe there is at least a partially satisfactory solution. A starting point is to recognize that person-regarding principles make sense only if we accept that life itself has value. We hold that it is wrong to take a life *because* we believe life has intrinsic value. If life has intrinsic value, then it follows that to bring a life into existence is to create something of value. If this is true, we should place a generally positive value on procreation.

---

[21]Hermann Vetter, "Utilitarianism and New Generations," *Mind* 80 April (1971), 301–302.

[22]Ibid.

On the other hand, the positive value we place on procreation can be overridden when the life we bring into existence is so unpleasant that it is not worth living. Just as we should place a positive value on bringing a happy child into existence, so we should place a negative value on bringing a child into a miserable and hopeless existence. The negative value we place on procreation under these circumstances constitutes the exception that confirms the general rule that procreation is an ethically positive act.

The presumption that it is morally desirable to procreate can also be overridden when the addition of a child to a family would represent an undue burden on others. Even though it is generally morally desirable to procreate, it can be undesirable to do so, if bringing an additional child into the world would deprive others of scarce resources, or represent a significant and unwanted burden on the family or the community.

It is here that we see important differences between the status of a "potential person" and that of an actual person. A person, whether a child or an adult, is presumptively entitled to equal consideration to other persons. But a "potential person" is entitled to consideration *only* on the assumption that he or she will exist at some point in the future. *With respect to the right to exist*, a "potential person" is not entitled to the same consideration as actual persons.[23]

A more difficult dilemma exists when it would be a benefit to others to bring a child into existence, but existence would be a burden to the child herself. Here we must ask whether the right to consideration "as a person" begins with existence (or conception) or whether it exists prior to existence (or conception). If the right to consideration as a person begins only with existence, there is no such a thing as wrongful existence. Because a person's genetic makeup is determined at the

---

[23]Not surprisingly, the debate over abortion has gravitated to the question of whether a fetus is a "person" or a "merely potential person." A middle ground in this debate is that a fetus is more than a "merely potential person," but not fully a "person" in the sense that a fetus is not entitled to the same consideration as the woman who carries the fetus.

moment of conception, the view that the right to consideration begins only with existence might make it morally permissible deliberately to conceive and bring into existence a child with a painful, life-limiting disease solely for the purpose of "harvesting" that child's organs. The better view is that the right to consideration as a person begins prior to existence but is conditional until birth (or viability or, at least, until conception).[24] Although it is legitimate and even necessary to base the initial decision to procreate on the desires of others, it is not ethical to persist in this decision unless one is willing to consider the (future) child an end-in-her-own-right and not merely as a means to an end.[25]

To hold that it is a positive act to procreate does not imply, however, that to fail to procreate is morally wrong, even when there are no pressing reasons not to do so. There is no specific obligation to procreate. In this sense, procreation is a supererogatory or discretionary act and not a duty or a moral obligation. When an action is a duty or an obligation, if the action is morally desirable, the failure to act is morally undesirable. For example, if another human being is in danger, and we have the ability to assist that person without undue hardship, we consider it praiseworthy to render assistance to that person. By the same token, we consider it blameworthy to fail to render assistance, under the same circumstances.

We may contrast the symmetry of this situation with the asymmetry which prevails in the ethics of procreation. Although it is generally a positive act to procreate, the failure to procreate is not, in itself, a

---

[24]I recognize that I am not addressing the question of when a fetus becomes entitled to full consideration as a person, and that this is likely to please neither advocates of the right to choose not opponents of abortion. I do not address this question because the time at which a fetus becomes entitled to full consideration as a person is not relevant to the question I am addressing, namely whether it is just to conceive deliberately and carry to term a child condemned to a miserable existence. My own view is that abortion is an appropriate choice when a fetus is conceived with a genetic disease that would make her or his life a misery. But even those who hold that abortion is never justifiable should still agree that we have an obligation to consider the quality of life a child may have before deciding to conceive children.

[25]See my earlier discussion of the "bone marrow baby" in this chapter.

negative act. The act of procreation has consequences for the being who results from that act, as well as for others who may also be affected. If we choose not to procreate, the consequences of our inaction can fall only on those who already exist or on others who will exist as the result of the actions of others. As Mary Warren has argued, purely "potential persons" are not persons and cannot be harmed by the decision of a couple not to have a child.[26] Therefore, unless the failure to procreate breaches our obligations to other persons, the voluntary decision not to procreate cannot be intergenerationally unjust.

To say that the failure to procreate is not intergenerationally unjust does not mean, however, that the choice of nonprocreation is entirely without moral significance. Even if we exclude the effects of the decision not to procreate on others, nonprocreation may still be a morally significant choice. There is a general moral duty to do good in life.[27] While this does not mean that we are required to do good whenever we can, nor even to do the maximum amount of good possible, nor to perform specific good actions, it does mean that we are generally accountable for how we lead our lives, and for reciprocating some of the good we receive in our lives. We can do good by contributing to the collective welfare. We can also do good by raising children to be decent human beings. We have the freedom to choose the way we live our lives. But with this freedom comes accountability for what we do with our lives. A person who does neither harm nor good in life may not be an unjust person, but such a person might well be considered to be leading a worthless life.

The argument that procreation may have morally desirable consequences, but nonetheless not be obligatory, is inconsistent with the premises of utilitarianism. Utilitarianism requires persons to take actions which have morally desirable consequences (i.e., which produce the greatest happiness for the greatest number of persons). For a

---

[26]Warren, 27–28.

[27]The most direct derivation of this obligation is from the Biblical commandment to Adam and Eve to be fruitful and multiply. Genesis 1:28.

utilitarian to recognize that an action has morally desirable consequences implies that the action is mandatory.

On the other hand, a utilitarian would accept the decision not to procreate if more good would result from pursuing activities other than child rearing. Indeed, for a utilitarian the choice of career over family might be mandatory if the career were one that would benefit a large number of persons. My position is different. The choice of how one leads one's life is not constrained by calculations of comparative utility, but only by the general duty to do good, and perhaps by specific obligations arising from one's relationships with other persons.

The ethics of procreation contain an asymmetry which makes it different from other kinds of actions. Even though the act of procreation may be morally desirable, the failure to procreate is not necessarily morally undesirable. Under most conditions, and certainly under most contemporary conditions, a person may lead a worthwhile life without having children. That the ethics of procreation should have a unique "geometry" should not be altogether surprising in view of the unique nature of the act of procreation.

The sixth position, then, is that

> There is no specific obligation to procreate, but there is a general duty to do good with one's life. To bring children into the world and to raise them so that they may lead happy and fruitful lives is one way of fulfilling this duty. Whether it is desirable to bring a child into existence in any given situation depends both on the expected quality of life of the child and on the effects the child's existence will have on others.

Testing the asymmetrical view of procreation

We can test the plausibility of this position by reflecting on the situation of an imaginary people whom I call "The Ultimate Yuppies."

> The Ultimate Yuppies are mindful of the need to act justly towards future persons, and subscribe to a "person-regarding" understanding of morality. They recognize that it would be unjust for the present generation to bring a new generation into existence without the resources needed to sustain their civilization. The problem this generation faces is that they have

> recently become aware that their planet is running out of vital nonrenewable resources.
>
> In their political debates, they discuss a number of possible courses of action including promoting an ethic of conservation, and the development of new technologies that would lessen their dependence on nonrenewable resources. The disadvantage of all these potential solutions is that they would require the present generation to accept a lower standard of living in order to develop an economy sustainable by future generations.
>
> The present generation is not pleased about having to sacrifice for future generations. After all, they ask, "What has posterity ever done for us?"[28] At the same time, they recognize that it is unjust to deprive other persons of the means to sustain their existence. The Ultimate Yuppies do not want to be accused of acting unjustly.
>
> One day an economist comes along with what appears to be the perfect solution. He argues that there is an alternative to either sacrificing for future generations or acting unjustly towards them. This alternative is to reduce the birth rate to 1.23 children per couple. If each succeeding generation does this, the population will decrease at the same rate as the Earth's nonrenewable resources (given a constant projected per capita rate of consumption). Future persons will not experience scarcity. Therefore, he reasons, future generations will have no grounds to complain that their ancestors acted unjustly towards them.

The consequence of adopting such a policy would be a decrease in the size of the ultimate yuppie population, leading to the eventual extinction of these people. Provided that future generations share the view that population reduction is preferable to sacrifice for posterity, the extinction of the species in this manner would entail no injustice to any "actual" present or future person. According to the narrow person-regarding morality of these people, their actions involve no intergenerational injustice.

But is this how we would actually judge such people? I am convinced it is not. Our reaction might be to find a cruel irony in the

---

[28]This question was posed by Robert L. Heilbroner in his provocative article "What Has Posterity Ever Done for Me?," *Responsibilities to Future Generations*, ed. Ernest Partridge. (Buffalo, NY: Prometheus Books, 1980) 191–194.

fate of these people. We might well conclude that people who prefer voluntary extinction to making the sacrifices necessary to perpetuate themselves deserve precisely the fate they receive. Indeed, we might conclude that such people "know their own worth"; for they would be unfit to survive.

If we were more charitable, we might pity people so poor of spirit that they would choose extinction over sacrifice for posterity.[29] However, in neither case would we say that the actions of the "Ultimate Yuppies" were intergenerationally unjust. We would not say their actions are intergenerationally unjust because it does not seem appropriate to describe as "unjust" a policy by which people determine their own future and which is carried out voluntarily by all generations. Such a policy is more properly taken to be a true reflection or measure of the character of people than an injustice perpetrated by one generation on its posterity.[30]

Our judgment would be different if later generations of these imaginary people did not share the values of their ancestors. More specifically, if later generations preferred sacrifice to extinction, and wished to reverse the decision of their ancestors, they would be faced with the choice of coping with severe scarcity of resources, as a result of the policies of their ancestors, or acquiescing in their ancestor's decision. No matter which choice they made, they would have grounds for arguing that the policies of their Yuppie ancestors were intergenerationally unjust insofar as those decisions effectively deprived them of the right to determine their own future.[31] However, if we

---

[29]The situation would be very different if we believed that the conditions in which people lived were so hard that they had nothing they could give to posterity and, under these circumstances, chose extinction rather than further suffering.

[30]In the language of cultural relativism, we might say that they have a different understanding of intergenerational justice than we do.

[31]Many policies have the effect of shaping the options of future generations, closing off one set of options and opening up another. What makes the decision of the Ultimate Yuppies different is that it is a conscious decision to choose death over life, to close off options without opening up others. In this sense it is possible to argue that the decision of the Ultimate Yuppies involves a procedural intergenerational injustice. To knowingly lock future generations into a decision

assume that each succeeding generation shares its ancestors' views on sacrifice, no generation would be deprived of choice, and therefore no generation would suffer an injustice.

Even if we do not find the actions of the ultimate Yuppies intergenerationally unjust, but instead see poetic justice in their fate, we should not let this understanding obscure the fact that we would judge them to be a morally perverse people. If this is our judgment, it must be because we consider the perpetuation of the human species to be a moral good. Moreover, if we persist in this judgment even in the face of the arguments such as those of Mary Warren (that "if the human race were suddenly and deliberately to stop reproducing altogether no wrong would have been done to merely potential people...."[32]), it can only be because we reject the narrow person-regarding morality which informs her argument.

THE POPULATION PROBLEM: CONCLUSION

How can the principle set forth in the preceding section guide our judgments with respect to population size? The principle that it is morally desirable but not mandatory to procreate appears to translate into a *prime facie* preference for a larger population over a smaller population. But this preference for a larger population is at most a mild one. And this preference can be overridden if increasing the size of the population would result in an unacceptable decrease in the quality of future persons' lives.

On the other hand we still need to ask what constitutes an unacceptable decrease in the quality of future persons' lives. Is any decrease in the quality of life too much? If so, would this principle not

---

without taking due account of the possibility that they may not share the values, which make that choice acceptable, is procedurally unjust. On the other hand, if the Ultimate Yuppies had good reason to believe that each succeeding generation would share its values, and if this turned out to be the case, then no actual injustice would be perpetrated by their actions.

[32]Warren, 28.

lead us to conclude that the decision of the Ultimate Yuppies is morally correct?

The first step in applying this principle is to recognize the importance of the distinction between the survival of the species (or a people), and increases in population size beyond the minimum needed for survival. The moral preference for procreation is relatively mild as long as the survival of the species is not threatened, and as long as others choose to replenish the human population. The moral preference for procreation becomes stronger if a low fertility rate threatens the survival of the species, because the extinction of the human species also extinguishes the possibility of doing good.[33] If the survival of the human species were really endangered by a declining fertility rate, people might have a moral obligation to procreate even though doing so would involve unwanted sacrifice on their part.[34]

Quite clearly this is not the situation today. If anything, the opposite is true. The planet may be said to be overpopulated insofar as the support of the existing population seems to necessitate destructive agricultural and forestry practices inconsistent with the long-term fertility and preservation of the land (including the cultivation of marginal land, irrigation techniques which increase the salt content of soil and the use of toxic fertilizers and pesticides). Under these conditions, no general obligation to increase the population further can exist.

The moral preference for procreation also does not translate into a preference for an agrarian civilization, capable of supporting a larger population, over a nomadic civilization, which is necessarily less densely

---

[33] I am aware of the argument that the human species is so destructive that life on Earth would be better without human beings. The lesson from this is not that the human species ought to commit collective suicide, but that we ought to change our destructive practices. Just as we ought to reject the view that the Earth was created just for us, so we ought to reject the view that our species is so evil it has no right to exist.

[34] On the other hand, the obligation to have children can exist only as long as people find children bearable, since people would have no obligation to perpetuate their species if they did not find life worth living.

populated. The value we place on procreation has meaning only in the context of a particular civilization and in the context of other human relationships. We do not place a value on human beings as numbers but as bearers of cultural values. Therefore, there can be no transcultural imperative to transform a civilization into an agrarian or an industrial civilization merely to allow it to support a larger population (though a particular civilization may have values that would sustain such an imperative).[35] In this context it is worth noting that John Rawls may be wrong to argue that there is an imperative for one generation to set aside savings in order to improve the standard of living of future generations. A nomadic tribe, for example, is not obligated to adopt a different way of life so that their descendants might enjoy greater "liberty" in an agrarian civilization.[36]

The second question we need to examine is how an asymmetrical view of procreation helps us to resolve the "missing victim" problem. By itself, the fact that we place a positive value on procreation does not move us very far in the direction of explaining why genocide and nuclear war are intergenerationally unjust. At most a moral preference for procreation would allow us to say that genocide and nuclear war are morally undesirable. But this type of judgment is too easily overridden, and, in any event, is far too weak. In order to resolve the "missing victim" problem we must move beyond general considerations of potentiality and explain why it is intergenerationally unjust to prevent the existence of future generations by acts of genocide or by unleashing a nuclear holocaust. The fact that we place a positive value on the existence of posterity is critical to explaining the intensity of our judgments of genocide and nuclear war.

What we have seen to this point suggests that an adequate theory of intergenerational justice must differentiate between actions and policies

---

[35]As Terence Ball points out, there can be no transculturally valid theory of intergenerational justice, either. Terence Ball, *Transforming Political Discourse*, (New York: Basil Blackwell, 1988), 143–160.

[36] See John Rawls, *A Theory of Justice*, (Cambridge, MA: Harvard University Press, 1971), 284–293.

such as genocide and nuclear war which ought to be considered to be intergenerationally unjust and policies such as the birth control practices of the "ultimate yuppies" which, however selfish and perverse, do not descend to the level of an intergenerational injustice. Quite clearly, we cannot differentiate between these policies based on the absence of future generations since the extinction of the species is a characteristic of both nuclear war and the population policies of the "ultimate yuppies."

A critical difference between these two types of policies is that the absence of future generations in the case of both genocide and nuclear war is the direct result of an injustice perpetrated on the *present* generation,[37] while the absence of future generations of "ultimate yuppies" is the result of voluntary policies which are *not* unjust to contemporaries. This suggests that we recognize at least two different senses in which actions may be intergenerationally unjust. The first sense is the common one: actions are intergenerationally unjust to the extent that they cause harm to future persons and to the extent that they fail to meet our obligations to future persons. The second sense in which actions may be intergenerationally unjust is when those actions unjustly prevent the existence of future persons. What remains to be explained is why preventing the existence of future generations can be intergenerationally unjust, and not merely unjust to contemporaries.

The first step in this process is to differentiate carefully between the *intra*generational injustice done to members of the existing generation and the *inter*generational injustice done in preventing the existence of future persons. A policy of genocide or a nuclear war necessarily involves harm and injustice to the present generation. Genocide may be committed in a variety of ways including the wholesale execution of a people, the involuntary sterilization of a people, or a combination of these and other policies. At a minimum genocide deprives persons of

[37]It does not seem unreasonable to hold that the deaths of billions of noncombatants in a war between two nuclear powers is unjust.

liberty by preventing them from exercising their right to procreate.[38] Genocide *always* involves *intra*generational injustice.

But genocide also has the *inter*generational effect of preventing the existence of future generations of a people. This aspect of genocide is not incidental but essential. While it is not wrong, in itself, to prevent conception, it *is* wrong to prevent others from procreating unless there are sufficient reasons to do so.[39] Even though there is no specific obligation to procreate, it is generally morally desirable to do so. Genocide prevents others from taking this morally desirable action.

To prevent a person from taking a morally desirable action is very different from merely refraining from taking a morally desirable action oneself. For example, it is morally desirable to save a stranger who is drowning, and it is morally undesirable to fail to attempt to rescue such a person if can. However, our law does not hold a person criminally culpable for failing to rescue a stranger, even if one could have done so at no risk to oneself. It is quite a different matter for a person to prevent another from attempting to rescue the drowning stranger if the other person is able and willing to doing so. A person who intentionally or knowingly prevents another person from rescuing a drowning stranger would be guilty not merely of a morally undesirable action, but, upon proof in a court of law, of the crime of intentional murder.

For similar reasons, to prevent others from procreating makes one morally responsible for the intergenerational consequences of that act.

---

[38]James Hudson argues that there may also be a right to "blameless procreation" which is violated when persons act in ways that make it morally unjust for others to procreate. Thus Hudson argues that a policy of producing and disposing of hazardous waste in a manner which endangers the lives of future generations may make it morally undesirable for the present generation to procreate. This would deprive the present generation of its right to "blameless procreation." James L. Hudson, "Rights and the Further Future," *Philosophical Studies* 49 January (1986), 99–107.

[39] Although the definition of incest varies from culture to culture, the prohibition on incestuous marriage and procreation is widely accepted. On the other hand, decisions such as that handed down by the Supreme Court of the United States in Buck v. Bell 274 U.S. 200 (1927), which upheld the sterilization of Carrie Buck to prevent her from giving birth to retarded children, are now widely condemned.

Since the intergenerational effect of genocide is to prevent the existence of future generations, those who commit genocide are morally responsible for the nonexistence of future generations. Those who commit genocide ought to be held to the same degree of moral responsibility as if they had literally and unjustly killed those persons who would have existed in the future.[40] In this sense it is correct to speak of those persons who never existed as a result of the Holocaust as "virtual" or "missing" victims.

It is now a simple matter to explain why we react as we do to the nuclear war scenarios presented at the beginning of this chapter. We find the two scenarios which projected the extinction of the species to be indistinguishable because the intergenerational effects of these two wars are indistinguishable. It is morally desirable for there to be a posterity, and it is morally wrong to prevent other persons from procreating. Both the first and the third nuclear war scenarios do just that. Therefore, these two scenarios are equal in their intergenerational injustice. By contrast the *intergenerational* effects of the second scenario (which envisions large numbers of casualties from the war, but the ultimate survival of the species) are less heinous, and we judge that scenario accordingly.

---

[40] The Rabbinical commentaries on the slaying of Abel by Cain (Genesis 4, 8) state that Cain not only killed Abel but also all of Abel's descendants as well. Nachmanides *Ad Loc.*

VI

The Identity Problem

THE PRESENT GENERATION HAS THE CAPACITY to affect not only the size of the future population but also the identity of that population. Just as human beings have bred cows which produce more milk, chickens which lay more eggs and dachshunds with short legs (and, not incidentally, weak backs), so we are developing the capacity to engineer a human population which reflects our own understandings of the good life.

There is probably no power, not even the power to destroy our own species, more frightening than the power to alter the identity of future generations. According to Western religious mythology, "man was made in God's image." That we are the product of a creator has meant that we do not bear the full burden of responsibility for our existence. This belief also implies that human beings have the capacity for goodness, for the goodness of God is the fundamental assumption of all Western religions. On the other hand, if we genetically engineer future generations, those generations may still be "created in God's image," but they will also be "recreated" in our image. We will bear a much greater share of the responsibility for who they will be. Indeed, what future generations become will be the truest measure of our own moral worth, though, of course, we will be saved from ever actually having to face this judgment in person.

While it may not be too late to reject the power to genetic engineer our future identity, it is most unlikely that we will do so. Human beings only rarely turn away from the use of power, and then only when its destructiveness is both uncontrollable and undeniable. Such evidence does not exist with respect to genetic engineering. From the vantage point of the late twentieth century, it is far from clear that genetic engineering does not offer the hope of reducing human suffering by ending genetic and other diseases. This hope may prove illusory. We may discover that the price we pay for genetic engineering technology is too high. It is too soon to know, and, in any event, it seems futile to propose that we turn away from the effort.

What we can predict with great confidence is that genetic engineering technology will prove to be a two-edged sword. If the study of human history teaches us anything, it is that power can be used for evil as well as for good. If we are to proceed with the task of remaking ourselves, it is essential that we have adequate moral theories to serve as guideposts.

DEFINING THE IDENTITY PROBLEM

In the context of intergenerational justice, the identity problem has two aspects. The first concerns actions that alter the identity of future generations by preventing the existence of particular categories of persons. The most obvious example of such a policy is genocide. The second aspect concerns actions that alter the identity of future generations by directly affecting the characteristics of those persons who are brought into existence. Examples of the second type of policy include eugenic breeding and genetic engineering.

I divide the identity problem into two aspects because the two ways of altering the identity of future generations raise very different philosophical issues. Attempts to prevent the existence of categories of persons raise the kinds of problems we examined in the previous chapter. Such actions must be examined in terms of whether it is just or unjust to prevent the existence of the relevant category of persons. For example, we want to differentiate between policies which seek to prevent the births of persons with genetically transmitted diseases, such as Tay-Sachs, and genocidal policies aimed at eliminating unpopular groups from the population.

As we saw in the previous chapter, policies which unjustly prevent the existence of future persons typically raise the "missing victim" problem. By contrast, attempts to manipulate the characteristics of those persons who are brought into existence raise very different types of questions. Such actions can raise questions of "wrongful existence" or of "diminished existence." For example, if a eugenicist were to conduct an experiment aimed at breeding more intelligent children and as the result of a miscalculation, children were produced with below normal intelligence, it would be appropriate to ask whether the children who are products of the experiment have been harmed or wronged by the experimenter. The crucial difference between this situation and that of genocide is that if there is a victim of the breeding experiment, the victim is not "missing" but "present." This necessitates a very different type of moral analysis.

One might think there would be no difficulty in establishing that a child born with subnormal intelligence as a result of a negligently run eugenic experiment has been harmed or wronged by the experimenter. But it turns out to be surprisingly difficult to establish this proposition. Despite the fact that the "victim" is present, there are still significant obstacles to pressing the claim that a child (Jane) who is the product of a eugenic experiment that goes wrong is actually a "victim." The most serious obstacle is the fact that if we adhere strictly to person-affecting principles, we have some difficulty explaining in what sense the child (Jane) is "harmed" by the experiment. The reason that we have difficulty explaining how Jane is harmed is that her low intelligence is not the result of something that happened *to* her, but, rather, of her genetic makeup. It is an inseparable part of who she is. If the experiment had been more successful, Jane would not have been more intelligent. Instead, a different (more intelligent) person would have been born. To the extent that Jane could not have benefited from a properly conducted experiment, strict adherence to person-affecting principles makes it impossible for Jane to establish that *she* was harmed by the experiment, unless she finds her life so miserable as to be unbearable. This does not deny that Jane's parents may have a claim against those running the experiment, even if Jane does not. While Jane could not have "benefited" from the experiment had it been conducted properly (because a different person would have existed), Jane's parents could have benefited.

The problem presented by this type of situation is very different from the "missing victim" problem examined in the last chapter. The "missing victim" problem arises when unjust *intra*generational actions prevent the existence of future persons. Even though we may be skeptical of attempts to engage in eugenic breeding, such programs do not necessarily constitute an injustice to contemporaries unless they are carried out coercively. In the case of a "voluntary" eugenic breeding experiment that goes wrong, the strongest claims do not belong to the "purely potential" beings who might have existed had the experiment been conducted differently (or had not been conducted at all); rather, the strongest claims belong to the very real persons of subnormal intelligence who are the "products" of the experiment.[1]

We have very good reason to feel uncomfortable with the notion that the product of a eugenic breeding program is not "harmed" if that program goes wrong. Intuitively, we are inclined to believe that when human beings attempt to breed more intelligent or "better" people, (or otherwise alter the identity of future generations) they are morally accountable for the consequences of their actions, if those actions go wrong due to negligence or recklessness. The problem is to find a coherent explanation for our intuitive judgment.

THE NON-IDENTITY PROBLEM [2]

Among the most systematic attempts to address the problem of identity has been that of Derek Parfit. His efforts have focused on identifying and attempting to resolve what he calls the non-identity problem.[3] The non-identity problem arises from the fact that policies

---

[1]Even where eugenic breeding programs do raise the "missing victim" problem, there may be actual victims as well.

[2]An earlier version of this argument was presented at the 1985 Annual Meeting of the American Political Science Association. Bruce E. Auerbach, "Intergenerational Justice and the Prophetic Tradition," *Annual Meeting of the American Political Science Association*, (New Orleans, LA: 1985).

[3]Gregory Kavka states that the non-identity problem was discovered independently by Derek Parfit, Robert M. Adams, and Thomas Schwartz. I focus on the

which affect the future in ways that alter significantly the conditions of remote generations, also alter the timing of conceptions and therefore the genetic identity of those persons who exist in the future.

We can confirm the existence of the non-identity problem by noting that the genetic makeup of a child born to the same set of parents will be different depending on the month in which that child is conceived.[4] By our choice of social policies we affect the conditions in which people will live. This, in turn, affects the timing of future conceptions. Parfit points out that

> since the choice between ... two policies would affect the timing of later conceptions, some of the people who are later born would owe their existence to our choice of one of the two policies. If we had chosen the other policy, these particular people would never have existed. And the proportion of those later born who owe their existence to our choice would, like the ripples in a pool, steadily grow.[5]

Within three centuries there is little likelihood that anyone alive would have been born had we chosen different public policies.

Because a different set of individuals will exist in the future by virtue of any policies or actions important enough to make life better or worse for future generations, we are unable to make the normally straightforward arguments that a policy, such as energy conservation, is

---

writings of Derek Parfit because his treatment of this question is the most complete. Kavka cites the following articles as the first to discuss the non-identity problem: Robert M. Adams, "Existence, Self-Interest, and the Problem of Evil," *Nous* 13 (1979), 53–65. Thomas Schwartz, "Obligations to Posterity," *Obligations to Future Generations*, ed. R. I. Sikora and Brian Barry. (Philadelphia: Temple University Press, 1978), 3–14. Derek Parfit, "On Doing the Best for Our Children," *Ethics and Population*, ed. Michael D. Bayles. (Cambridge, MA: Schenkman, 1976). However, as Robert Adams points out, Leibniz was also concerned with problem of non-identity. Adams, 53.

Gregory S. Kavka, "The Paradox of Future Individuals," *Philosophy and Public Affairs* 11 Spring (1982), 93.

[4]This understanding of the relationship between genetic makeup and identity assumes that a person would not be who she is if her genetic makeup were different. This does not preclude the possibility that other factors also help determine identity.

[5]Parfit, *Reasons and Persons*, 361.

desirable (or required) because it will "benefit" future persons, or that a policy which lowers the quality of life for future persons is undesirable because it will "harm" future persons. We cannot make these arguments because the future individual making such a claim would not have existed had we not acted as we did.

Parfit contends that it makes no difference whether any individual can claim to have been made worse off by the policy of prior generations.[6] A policy can be wrong even if it will be worse for no one. But Parfit recognizes that some people may not share his intuition, but instead believe that "... what is bad must be bad for someone."[7] In order to meet such objections Parfit suggests that we must abandon "person-affecting principles" in favor of an appeal to more general and impersonal principles of beneficence. We must argue that "it is bad if those who live are worse off than those who might have lived."[8] But as Parfit notes, this is not a familiar moral principle; we still have to explain to those who reject this principle why it should carry any weight.

For those who share Parfit's moral intuition that the non-identity problem makes no moral difference, there is a significant gap between the intuition that it is (*prima facie*) wrong to take actions that will result in future people living in worse conditions than others might have enjoyed, and our moral theories which treat as morally relevant only those actions which affect persons. In order to resolve this dilemma, Parfit suggests that we need to find an accepted moral principle which would allow us to draw the same conclusions as the "person-affecting principle" when the choice is between actions that affect the same individuals differently, and yet would conform to our intuition that it is as wrong to bring about worse conditions for those who will exist as it would be to inflict comparable harm on existing individuals.[9]

---

[6]Ibid., 367.

[7]Parfit cites T. Schwartz, "Obligations to Posterity" in Sikora and Barry, as holding this position. Parfit, *Reasons and Persons*, 363.

[8]Parfit, "The Further Future: The Identity Problem," 175.

[9]Parfit, *Reasons and Persons*, 363–366.

If Parfit's only concern were to find a set of moral principles that supported the moral intuition that it is "bad if those who live are worse off, or have a lower quality of life, than those who would have lived,"[10] he would have to look no further than the utilitarian principle that one should act to produce the greatest amount of happiness for the greatest number of persons. The fact of non-identity does not pose a problem for utilitarianism because utilitarianism is an "aggregate affecting principle" rather than an "individual affecting principle." Utilitarianism is concerned with the total (or average) happiness of a society, not with the happiness of particular individuals. As a result, the fact that the identities of those who make up the two populations may be different is not an issue for utilitarianism.

What complicates Parfit's search is that he is concerned not only with overcoming the non-identity problem, but also with discovering a moral theory that can be applied to actions affecting future generations without leading to other paradoxical, morally repugnant, or otherwise absurd conclusions. Although utilitarianism effectively overcomes the non-identity problem, it does so only at the cost of introducing other paradoxical, absurd, and repugnant conclusions. And while different versions of utilitarianism are able to avoid some of these pitfalls, no single version appears to be able to overcome all of them.[11] In the end Parfit concedes that he is unable to find a principle of beneficence (which he calls "principle X") that can be applied to future generations without succumbing to one of these pitfalls, though he maintains that "if they tried, others could succeed."[12]

---

[10]Ibid., 369.

[11]See Chapter V for a discussion of some of the problems of utilitarianism. For a more systematic discussion of the problems of utilitarianism see Derek Parfit, *Reasons and Persons*, 381–454.

[12]Parfit, *Reasons and Persons*, 443.

THE NON-IDENTITY PROBLEM ANALYZED

On first reading, one might think that Parfit's argument involves some sleight of hand. After all, there is no question that our actions can affect the lives of our descendants. Parfit not only recognizes that our actions affect the lives of future persons, he also recognizes that we are responsible for *how* our actions affect those persons. His point is that we cannot explain *why* we are responsible for the effects of our actions on future persons without appealing to principles other than person-affecting principles. Parfit argues that we do not need to revise our moral intuition that "it is bad if those who live are worse off than those who might have lived."[13] Rather we need to develop different moral principles in order to support those intuitions.

On reflection, then, it might seem that Parfit is right. If we adopt a "depletionist" energy policy which results in a lower standard of living for future generations, we cannot say that future individuals will be made worse off than *they* would have been as a result of our actions. We cannot say this because had we adopted a more forward-looking "conservationist" energy policy, those same individuals would not have existed. If we hold that the only morally relevant aspects of our actions are their effects on persons, the non-identity problem appears to undermine our reason for preferring a conservationist energy policy to a depletionist policy. If no person is *worse off* as a result of our actions, our actions cannot be said to have harmed anyone; and if our actions have not harmed anyone, then, by the standards of person-affecting principles, those actions are not morally wrong.

If the only way out of this paradox were to abandon the assumption that actions are wrong only if they harm individuals, that fact would constitute a powerful reason for seeking other moral principles. But is this conclusion inescapable or even correct? I am convinced that it is not.

---

[13] Parfit, "The Further Future: The Identity Problem," 175.

In its general form, the non-identity problem can be solved without abandoning the person-affecting principles which are the foundation of most of our modern understandings of morality; and if we can resolve the non-identity problem without abandoning person-affecting principles, we ought to do so. To resolve the non-identity problem without abandoning person-affecting principles, we need to be able to demonstrate that we can be responsible for the effects of our actions on future persons, even though altering our public policies would result in the existence of different individuals. In other words, we need to show that we can employ the concepts of harm and benefit, despite the non-identity problem.

Our usual understanding is that in order to be held morally accountable for the effects of our actions, it must have been possible to have taken different actions, with more desirable effects.[14] This understanding of the preconditions for moral accountability can be misleading and even incorrect when applied to intergenerational actions. There are other (more) fundamental interpretations of person-affecting principles which require that we be held morally accountable for the effects of our actions on future persons despite the non-identity problem.

One way we might make this argument is to appeal to ethical principles such as the rights of future persons. Such an argument is made by James Woodward who argues that we can understand the wrongful results of a policy by focusing on the difference between the situation of future persons whose rights are violated and an (unattainable) baseline situation in which the same persons exist and these violations of their rights do not occur.[15] Woodward's position makes it possible to argue that a child who is born into conditions of

---

[14]This is true regardless of the perspective from which one judges the effects of a person's actions.

[15]James Woodward, "The Non-Identity Problem," *Ethics* 96 July (1986), 817–818.

abject poverty is harmed by that fact, even though if the child had not been born into those conditions, the child would not have existed at all.[16]

On the other hand, difficulties arise when we try to resolve the non-identity problem by appealing to the concept of individual rights. In his reply to Woodward, Derek Parfit points out that in some situations it is not appropriate to appeal to an abstract and unattainable baseline against which to measure the rights of persons. More specifically, Parfit points to the situation of an imaginary woman, who knows that if she has a child, that child will be handicapped. If the nature of this handicap is not trivial, but also not so severe as to make life not worth living, can we say that this woman violates the rights of her child by conceiving him? In general, Parfit's answer is that the woman's choice does not violate her child's rights, but Parfit points out that our judgment would be very different if the woman could have avoided giving birth to a handicapped child by waiting two months before conceiving, but chose not to do so. The difference between these two situations cannot be explained by measuring the condition of the child against an abstract and unattainable baseline condition to which the child has a right.[17]

An alternate approach is to examine the non-identity problem as an excuse or justification which a generation might offer if it were accused of harming future persons. If the non-identity problem represents a real obstacle to basing a theory of intergenerational justice on person-affecting principles, it should be possible to phrase the non-identity problem in the form of an excuse or justification which is acceptable to future generations, at least in principle. On the other hand, if the non-identity problem cannot be phrased as an acceptable excuse or justification, this would suggest that the non-identity problem does not represent the type of problem which requires us to abandon person-affecting principles.[18]

---

[16]A similar argument is made by Matthew Hanser, "Harming Future People," *Philosophy and Public Affairs* 19(1) Winter (1990): 47–70.

[17]Derek Parfit, "Comments," *Ethics* 96 July (1986), 859.

[18]Two different grounds for rejecting the position that the non-identity problem releases us from any obligation to promote the well-being of future generations

The non-identity problem can easily be phrased in the form of a justification. To see that this is so, let us imagine a hypothetical dialogue among remote generations. If one generation were accused by its descendants of causing them harm by wasting scarce resources, the older generation could respond by asserting that they were "incapable of acting to improve the conditions for those particular individuals, because any policy which would have resulted in improved conditions for distant generations would also have resulted in the existence of a different set of individuals in the future." To the extent that both generations accept that if no actual individual is made worse off by an action, no harm has been done, the non-identity problem should justify[19] the older generation's failure to act to improve conditions for its descendants.

Intuitively, the non-identity problem sounds like an illegitimate justification. The problem is to understand *why* this justification is illegitimate, and to see whether we can find sufficient reasons to reject it without abandoning person-affecting principles. If there are, then we do not need to look beyond person-affecting principles to support the moral

---

have been proposed by Gregory S. Kavka, "The Paradox of Future Individuals." The first is that it is intrinsically undesirable to bring about conditions that involve persons living restricted lives. (Kavka, 105.) The second is a modified version of the second form of Kant's categorical imperative that "... would forbid treating rational beings *or their creation* (that is, their being brought into existence) as a means only, rather than as ends in themselves." (Kavka, 110.) Both positions have been critiqued in Parfit's "Future Generations: Further Problems," *Philosophy and Public Affairs* 11 Spring (1982), 113–172.

19 Although the terms justification and excuse are often used interchangeably, the argument that we are incapable of benefiting particular future individuals because actions which would improve conditions for future generations would also result in the existence of a different set of individuals is more properly classified as a justification than an excuse. This argument is a justification rather than an excuse because it denies that the failure to improve conditions for future persons is wrong (although, I argue, it does not do so successfully). To argue that an action is permissible because the action in question is not wrong, is to provide a justification for the action rather than an excuse. By contrast, to admit that the action is bad, but to deny that the actor is fully (or even partially) responsible for the action is to provide an excuse. See John L. Austin, "A Plea for Excuses," *Philosophical Papers*, ed. John L. Austin, (London: Oxford University Press, 1961), 123–125.

intuition that it is "bad if those who live are worse off, or have a lower quality of life, than those who would have lived."[20]

The non-identity problem is an illegitimate justification because it seems to imply something that is not true. What the non-identity problem seems to imply is that we are unable to affect the conditions in which future persons will live. But it is quite clear that we *are* capable of affecting the conditions in which future persons will live. What we are not capable of doing is simultaneously to bring into existence a particular set of future individuals *and* to improve the conditions in which those particular individual will live. This is the essence of the non-identity problem.

The non-identity problem would justify a policy such as energy depletion *only* if we had sufficient reason for wanting to being into existence the *precise set of persons* who would exist if we depleted our energy resources. More specifically, the non-identity problem could justify this policy if our reasons for wanting to bring into existence the *precise set of persons* were sufficient to outweigh our obligation to conserve resources for future generations. The non-identity problem might mitigate our responsibility for depleting the Earth's energy resources if an intense desire to bring into existence a specific population led us to pursue an unjust depletionist energy policy. The fact that we cannot simultaneously bring into existence a desired population and improve the conditions in which that population will live, forces us to choose between fulfilling two different obligations or between fulfilling an obligation and a desire. If we make an ethically unjustifiable choice, the existence of extenuating or mitigating circumstances may diminish our responsibility for that choice.[21]

For example, recall the situation of the woman, who knows that if she has a child, the child will be handicapped. This woman is forced to choose between having a handicapped child and not having a biological

---

[20]Parfit, *Reasons and Persons*, 369.

[21]As John Austin points out, in specific situations of diminished responsibility there may be genuine uncertainty or ambiguity whether an action is partially justified or partially excused. John L. Austin, "A Plea for Excuses," 125.

child. This woman's child cannot claim that *he* might have been born free of handicap, nor that *any* child in his position might have been born free of handicap. In this sense, we can say that the woman does not harm her child by bringing him into existence with a handicap, as long as the child finds his life worth living, despite his handicap. On the other hand, the woman can be faulted for wanting a child so much that she does not care for "the child for his own sake," but rather cares about having a child for the sake of the pleasure the child would give *her*. In this sense, her decision violates the modified categorical imperative that Gregory Kavka advances as a theory of intergenerational morality, namely that we are forbidden from "treating rational beings *or their creation* (that is, their being brought into existence) as a means only, rather than as ends in themselves."[22] Even if we conclude that the woman's decision to bear a child is not justified, we are likely to accept that her desire for a child of her own is sufficiently understandable to mitigate her responsibility for her child's suffering.

Despite superficial similarities, the situation we face in choosing an energy policy is very different from that faced by the carrier of a genetic disease. Unlike the woman who wishes to have a child of her own, even at the cost of passing on a genetic defect, we have no *independent* reason to prefer the population which would result from pursuing a "depletionist" energy policy to the population which would result from pursuing a conservationist policy. Indeed, the only basis we can have for distinguishing between the population which would benefit from our conservation of resources and the population which would suffer from our depletion of the Earth's energy resources is that the latter will exist if we pursue second policy while the former will exist if we pursue the first policy.

While it is true that our choice of a depletionist energy policy will not make any specific (distant future) individual *worse off* than she or he would have been had we chosen a conservationist energy policy, this fact cannot be used as a justification because it carries no moral weight.

[22]Kavka, "The Paradox of Future Individuals," 110.

Except for its relationship to our energy policy, we have no basis for distinguishing between the two possible populations.[23] If we can only choose between energy policies and not between populations (because there is no moral basis for preferring one population to the other), we cannot claim that our inability to benefit the population we bring into existence when we deplete energy resources constitutes an excuse or justification for not conserving energy.

In fact, it is disingenuous for the older generation to seek to justify or excuse their actions on the grounds that they could not have improved the conditions *for these particular descendants* by conserving energy resources. Such a justification could be acceptable only if the effects were unintentional. In other words, to make this excuse, the older generation must be prepared to assert that they *would have pursued* a different policy if it had been feasible to do so. But the older generation cannot make this argument because they had the option of pursuing a different policy and chose not to take it.

What complicates the hypothetical dialog among the generations is the fact that even though the older generation has no reason to prefer one future population to the other, those individuals who actually will exist in the future might not be quite so indifferent. Future persons might well be so grateful to be alive that they would be willing to forgive their ancestors' selfishness as the price of their existence. Parfit appears to hold that the fact that many future persons would waive rights to conditions that could have been enjoyed only by different people constitutes an argument against the view that we violate the rights of future persons by causing them to exist with rights that cannot be fulfilled.[24]

---

[23]As Trudy Govier points out, consideration of specific remote future persons is logically out of order because we cannot sensibly consider specific future persons, and because if we decide to conserve, there is "no need to consider specific prospective people identified as 'those who would exist if we deplete but would not exist if we conserve.'" Trudy Govier, "What Should We Do About Future People?," *American Philosophical Quarterly* 16 April (1979), 111.

[24]Parfit, *Reasons and Persons*, 364–365.

There are at least three substantial reasons for rejecting this understanding. The first is that a hypothetical, after-the-fact waiver of rights counts no more than a hypothetical contract. Neither is binding. Second, a waiver of rights in these particular circumstances is not morally relevant because it is based on the same confused understanding of the obligations to future generations as the non-identity problem. To say that someone would agree or does agree to an unjust exchange is not an argument for the fairness of the exchange. Finally, to the extent that certain rights are inalienable, those rights cannot be waived even by the holders of those rights.

Even if Parfit were correct in suggesting that many future individuals might choose to show their gratitude for being alive by "voluntarily" waiving their right to conditions they personally could not have enjoyed in any case, we would have no right to place any moral weight on that hypothetical waiver of rights. On the contrary, for us to do so would be to take advantage of our power to determine the identity of future persons in order to extract unwarranted concessions for our own benefit. It is an affront to human dignity, and arguably a violation of the human rights of future persons, for us to "leverage" our power to shape the identity of future persons into a "justification" for hoarding energy resources.[25] To offer as a justification or excuse to future generations the fact that future persons would not have benefited from our conservation (because if we had conserved energy they would not have existed) is to exploit future individual's natural preference for their own existence. Such an argument not only does not mitigate our responsibility for an unjust energy policy, it might well tend to aggravate that responsibility by demonstrating a high degree of moral callousness. A generation who depletes the energy resources and then claims the non-identity problem as a "moral" justification or excuse, only adds the insult of *chutzpah* to injury it causes to future generations.

---

[25]See Kavka, "The Paradox of Future Individuals," 106–112. Kavka compares this quite correctly to turning life into a commodity.

NON-IDENTITY AND THE PROBLEM OF MEASURING HARMS AND BENEFITS TO FUTURE GENERATIONS

In its general form, the non-identity problem does not pose an insurmountable obstacle to basing a theory of intergenerational justice on person-affecting principles. The fact that different public policies will result in the existence of different individuals means that no specific future person is made better or worse off by our actions. But this fact does not prevent us from recognizing that our actions affect future persons, and that we are responsible for how future persons are affected by our actions.

The most important consequence of our inability to say that our actions will make distant future individuals better or worse off than they otherwise would have been, is that it becomes impossible to measure the effects of our actions either by comparing the condition of particular individuals before and after our actions, or by comparing the actual effects of our actions on future persons with an estimate of how different actions would have affected *those same persons.* The first standard is obviously inappropriate for intergenerational action, since actions that affect future generations necessarily take place prior to the existence of those who will be affected by those actions. But this same standard is also inappropriate for many types of actions that affect contemporaries. For example, if I save a man's life by pulling him back from the edge of a precipice I make him no better off than he was before he wandered to the edge of that precipice. Nevertheless, by my action, I have made him vastly better off *than he would have been*, had I not acted. In this case, the significance of my action is properly judged not by the *actual* change in the man's condition, but by comparing his condition after my action with the best estimate of what his condition would have been had I not acted.

This standard has some relevance for measuring the effects of our actions on proximate future generations, but not on remote generations. When actions and policies affect proximate generations, actions may make some *particular future persons* better or worse off than *they* otherwise would have been. However, as Parfit points out, the non-identity problem prevents us from making this type of statement about actions that affect remote future persons because any policy that has a significant effect on the conditions of future generations will also result in the existence of a different set of future individuals. Nonetheless, our inability to say that any particular individual will be better or worse off than she or he would have been, is not generally morally relevant with respect to social policies that affect remote generations. It is not morally relevant because we may be responsible for the effects of our intergenerational actions, even though it may be impossible for us to affect specific future individuals differently.

What remains to be explained is how we can measure the extent of our moral responsibility for actions that affect distant future persons. It is here that Parfit's search for a "principle X" becomes important. It may be possible to estimate the extent of the harm or benefit resulting from policies that affect future generations by comparing the conditions in which future persons will actually live with conditions in which other future persons might have lived. While it is not a general principle of intergenerational justice that it is "bad if those who live are worse off, or have a lower quality of life, than those who would have lived,"[26] it may well be appropriate to estimate the effects of those actions *for which we are responsible* by this standard. However, it is important to recognize that the issues of measurement and responsibility are distinct. Before we may assess the extent of our responsibility by estimating the effects of our actions, we must first validate the claim that moral responsibility exists, in principle.

The reason that we cannot apply the principle that it is "bad if those who live are worse off, or have a lower quality of life, than those who would have lived,"[27] to all actions that affect future generations is that there are some situations in which this principle is not valid. The history of the United States furnishes an excellent example of such a situation.

---

[26]Parfit, *Reasons and Persons*, 369.
[27]Ibid., 369.

The United States developed as it did, in part because many Native American Indians were killed and the survivors relegated to reservations. One important cause of the near extermination[28] of the American Indians was the fact that they occupied land which persons of European descent wanted for settlement and cultivation.[29] The Indians stood in the way of the economic exploitation of this continent. Let us imagine a white settler who was concerned with the welfare of future (White) Americans and who believed that the land occupied by Indians was less productive than the land occupied by white settlers. Such a settler might have foreseen that if the Indians were pushed off their land, the United States would develop into a great and prosperous nation in which (his) posterity would enjoy great economic prosperity. Such a settler might have argued that "because it is bad if those who will live are worse off, or have a lower quality of life, than those who might live, we have an obligation to future generations to force the Indians off their land."

It is quite clear that a concern with the welfare of white Americans or even of all Americans cannot justify the extermination of the Indians. But I believe we need to go further and argue that the principle that "it is bad if those who live are worse off, or have a lower quality of life, than those who would have lived,"[30] itself is not a valid, universal principle of justice. That, as a consequence of the near extermination of the Indians, we have a higher standard of living than others might have enjoyed, does not count in favor of our ancestor's policy of killing Native American Indians in order to take their land. The reason our higher standard of living does not count in favor of our ancestors' actions is that the composition of the present population differs *in ways that are morally*

---

[28]Russell Thornton estimates that the population of Native American Indians in the United States declined from over five million in 1500 to two hundred fifty thousand in 1900, primarily due to the combined effects of disease, war, and the destruction of the indigenous ways of life. Russell Thornton, *American Indian Holocaust and Survival*, (Norman: University of Oklahoma Press, 1987), 90, 133.

[29]Among the other factors which contributed to the near extermination of the Native American Indians included the fact that many White Americans viewed the Native American Indians as subhuman.

[30]Parfit, *Reasons and Persons*, 369.

relevant from the population which would have existed had our ancestors not adopted a genocidal policy. If the settlers had not nearly exterminated the Indians, the present population of the United States would have included many more Native Americans and presumably fewer persons of European origin. Because the benefits of the present higher standard of living go to a population which is not morally equivalent to the population which would have existed had our ancestors acted justly, the higher standard of living we enjoy cannot serve as a moral justification for the actions of our ancestors.

In order to be able to measure the effects of our actions on future generations by comparing the conditions of future persons with the conditions in which other persons might have lived, future persons must be able to claim that they are *entitled* to the conditions which others might have enjoyed. Such a claim can arise from at least two arguments. The first is when the failure to provide certain conditions violates the fundamental human rights of future persons. For example, intuitively, we want to be able to argue that it is wrong to overpopulate the world because overpopulation harms those who live in that condition. The non-identity problem presents an apparent obstacle to such an argument because a completely different set of persons will exist in the distant future if we practice birth control. However, if we accept that there is a fundamental human right to certain minimal living conditions, then it is possible to argue that we violate the rights of future persons if we permit the world to become so overpopulated that those minimal living conditions cannot be maintained.[31] The argument that there is a fundamental right to live in a world which is not overpopulated would provide a theoretical justification for comparing the actual conditions which prevail in an overpopulated world with our best estimate of what the conditions would be, if the world were not overpopulated.

---

[31]This argument is made by James Woodward in "The Non-Identity Problem," *Ethics* 96 July (1986), 804–831. For a critique, see Derek Parfit, "Comments," *Ethics* 96 July (1986), 854–862.

The claim that future individuals are entitled to the conditions which others might have enjoyed also can be based on the obligation of an earlier generation to provide for the welfare of its descendants. Such an obligation might arise from principles of beneficence.[32] The non-identity problem does not present an obstacle to such a claim as long as the present generation has no independent reason to prefer one possible future population to another. In general, future generations will have a claim to those conditions which others might have enjoyed when our actions affect future persons as *occupiers of a position* rather than as *bearers of identifiable characteristics*.

For example, despite the Clean Air Act, the United States continues to permit industry to emit large quantities of oxides of sulfur and nitrogen into the atmosphere. The resulting acid rain is killing the forests and lakes of the Eastern United States and Canada. These dead lakes and forests will be part of our legacy to posterity. An implication of the non-identity problem is that an indirect effect of the policy of allowing the pollution of the atmosphere is that a different set of persons will exist in the future than would exist if we reduced these emissions. However, the fact that a different set of persons would exist if we reduced emissions will not prevent future generations from claiming that our failure to reduce emissions has caused them harm. Because the present generation has no independent reason to prefer one possible future population to another, the "polluted" future population will have a claim to those conditions which the "unpolluted" future population would have enjoyed. Consequently, we can "measure" or estimate the effects of our actions on the "polluted" population as the difference between the conditions they will actually experience and the conditions the "unpolluted" population would have experienced.

However, there are some circumstances which preclude our measuring the effects of actions in this manner. When the identity of the population and the "conditions" which result from our actions are

---

[32]Derek Parfit argues that an adequate theory of intergenerational justice must include principles of beneficence. Parfit, *Reasons and Persons*, 364–366.

inextricably linked, it may not be legitimate to measure the effects of our actions by comparing how future persons will live with how others might have lived. More specifically, if a generation acts to bring into existence a population with characteristics which it has good reason to prefer, and if acting to improve the conditions of posterity would result in the existence of a different, less desirable population, then those who will exist in the future cannot argue that they were entitled to the conditions that another, less desirable population would have enjoyed.

For example, if a couple wants their own biological child, but knows that such a child will have a genetic defect, the couple must choose between conceiving a child with a genetic defect and not having children who are biologically their own. If the couple chooses to conceive a child, it is not generally open to their child to make the comparative claim that she ought to have been brought into the world with the same genetically healthy constitution another child might have enjoyed. It is not open to the child to make this claim because her identity as the biological daughter of the couple and the condition complained of (the genetic defect) are inseparable.

This is not to say that a child who knowingly is conceived with a genetic defect can never have a claim against her or his parents. In theory, it is possible for a child to advance a claim of "wrongful life" against her parents. But such a claim cannot be based on the general principle that it is "bad if those who live are worse off, or have a lower quality of life, than those who would have lived."[33] Rather the claim must be based on special circumstances which make it appropriate to compare the quality of life of an actual child with the quality of life another child might have enjoyed. One such circumstance would be when the suffering caused by the genetic defect outweighs, or ought to outweigh, the value placed on having one's own biological child. Thus, it is open to the child to claim that she or he was harmed by knowingly having been conceived with a genetic defect, if that defect makes life unbearable. This argument takes the form of a claim that it is a violation

[33]Ibid., 369.

of the child's fundamental rights as a human being knowingly to be brought into an existence of intolerable suffering. Such a claim can only be sustained in the case of severe genetic defects.

The child can also make the claim that she was harmed if there was insufficient reason for the parents to prefer a genetically diseased child who is biologically their own, to adopting a healthy child (or not having children at all). If the child can make a persuasive argument for this position, it becomes appropriate to measure the harm which the parents have inflicted on the child by comparing the actual condition of their child with the condition of another, genetically healthy child.

IDENTITY AND GENETIC MAKEUP

The question of whether it is just knowingly to conceive a child with a genetic defect raises an additional problem which must be addressed. To this point, we have spoken of the genetic makeup of a person as if it were a condition which an individual encounters after birth. But a person's genetic makeup is not something which happens *to* a person after birth. Rather, it is integral to a person's identity. It serves to define *who* a person is. However, genetic makeup and identity are not coextensive. Genetic identity is necessary but not sufficient to define who a person is. It is a necessary aspect of a person's identity insofar as a person would be a different individual if her genetic identity were significantly different.[34] It is not sufficient to define who a person is in that identical twins have the same genetic makeup, but are different persons.

---

[34]The question of what, if *any*, changes could be made in a person's genetic makeup without altering his or her identity is both fascinating and probably unanswerable. It is probable that some genes that control specific physical characteristics (such as eye color) could be altered without altering the "identity" of the person. On the other hand, other genes may have a closer relationship to personality formation. However, we do not need to determine the point at which a person ceased being the same person in order to accept that our genetic makeup serves to define our identity as a person.

Genetic makeup is very different from the environmental conditions one experiences after birth. It is logically possible for a person to have been born into different environmental conditions than she was, and to experience different environmental conditions as she grows up. But it is not possible for a person to be born with an entirely different genetic makeup. If I were born with an entirely different genetic makeup, "I" would be a different person.

The question we must raise is to what extent, and in what sense, it is possible to say that a person is "affected" by her or his genetic makeup. There is no simple answer to this question. On the one hand, one's genetic makeup serves to define the self who experiences the world. In this sense genetic makeup constitutes a precondition for experiencing harms and benefits. On the other hand, genetic makeup is increasingly the object of study and manipulation. To the extent that human beings have developed and will continue to develop the capacity to manipulate genetic identity, it is imperative that we extend our ethical theories to cover these activities.

The alternative to extending our ethical understandings is to hold that human beings can recreate the human and other species without accountability. This would allow human beings to take on the role of God with "ethical impunity." Such an understanding would defy all traditional understandings of morality. For the Greeks, it would have constituted *hubris* for human beings to assume the powers of the gods and, at the same time, to claim inscrutability. Indeed, such a position defies even the common sense understanding of the limits of human wisdom.

Although I believe that the case for extending our ethical theories to cover the creation of human beings is compelling, it is important to recognize that this is indeed an extension of our contemporary morality.[35] How we understand our ability to affect the genetic makeup

[35]See also Gregory S. Kavka, "The Paradox of Future Individuals," 93–112, for another argument for extending our ethical principles to cover the creation of persons.

of a person is a function of what moral postulates we accept. It is logically possible to hold that existence is a precondition for counting as a moral being, and that existence begins only after one's genetic code is set. On the other hand, it is not inconsistent with person-affecting principles to hold that we affect a person *when* we determine her or his genetic identity. This extension of our ethical principles does not deny that what is morally significant is how our actions affect persons. It simply broadens our understanding of what types of actions affect persons.

It is important to recognize that extending our ethical principles to recognize that we affect a person when we determine her genetic identity, has an impact on a variety of contemporary issues, including the debate over abortion. To accept that we affect a person when we manipulate her genetic identity implies a recognition that ethical consideration of another ought to begin at, or even before, conception. This, in turn, might be seen as undergirding an anti-abortion position. However, the impact of this assumption on the debate over abortion is minimal. It is already quite clear that a child, carried to term, can be affected by the actions the mother takes before his or her birth.[36] There is a close relationship between a woman harming her child by drinking alcohol while pregnant and a man or a woman harming his or her child by taking chromosome damaging drugs before conceiving a child. In both cases a child will born with diminished capacities as a result of actions which took place prior to her or his birth.[37]

---

[36]E. Joshua Rosenkranz points out, there is a growing body of case law which permits a child to recover damages for prenatal injuries. Specifically, Rosenkranz cites the Restatement (Second) of Torts § 869 (1982) as stating that "'There now appears to be no American jurisdiction still standing that refuses to recognize the liability to the child for prenatal harm if the child is subsequently born alive.'" E. Joshua Rosenkranz, "Custom Kids and the Moral Duty to Genetically Engineer Our Children," *High Technology Law Journal* 2(1) (1987), 15, note 75.

[37]There are also important differences between these actions, which have to do with knowledge and intent. Thus, a woman who takes chromosome damaging "recreational" drugs while young is likely to be unconcerned about the effects those drugs may have on a child who may or may not be conceived in the future. We might characterize such a person's actions as reckless, but these actions do not

On the other hand, there are also real problems associated with extending the concept of harm to include all actions that affect a person's genetic identity. If one affects a person by determining her genetic identity, it would seem to follow that one can harm a person by conceiving her with a less than "perfect" genetic makeup. If this is true, are we not obligated to engineer children with the best possible genetic constitutions? Once we admit that we affect a person when we determine her or his genetic identity, can we stop from sliding all the way down this slope to compulsory genetic engineering?

As I argued in Chapter V, we ought to accept that when we bring a person into existence, we affect that person. It follows that if we choose to conceive a person with a genetic defect, we affect that person by that decision. This is not to say that we are never justified in doing so. Some genetic defects are not so debilitating as to make life not worthwhile, in spite of the defect (e.g., myopia, flat-footedness, etc.). While it is unquestionably preferable to conceive children free of genetic defects, only in the case of the most severe defects can we make a persuasive case that couples have a moral obligation to forego having children rather than give birth to a child with genetic defects.

Another question we ought to ask is what type of claims a person with a genetic defect might have against her or his parents. Our concern ought to be with claims that are theoretically justified rather than practically enforceable. If we know the types of claims a child might have against her or his parents, we will be in a better position to understand the nature of our obligations with respect to our descendants' genetic constitution.

The claims a child born with a genetic defect might have against her parents (or her mother's physician) depend not only on the severity of

---

rise to the level of knowing or intentional harm, especially since the young woman can prevent the harm to another by not becoming pregnant in the future. By contrast, a woman who knows she is pregnant, yet who persists in drinking (knowing that alcohol is harmful to a fetus), has committed a harm knowingly and not recklessly. However, it is possible to restore the parallel between these two situations by stipulating that the woman taking the chromosome damaging drugs does so fully intending to become pregnant at a later date.

the problem, but also on the nature of the existing genetic technology. If society has developed the capacity to detect and cure specific genetic defects in a fetus, a child born with a preventable defect may well have the claim that she or he was harmed by being born with a defect.[38] Here, the claim of the child is that she had the right to an existence free of a specific genetic defect. Although we might argue that a "different child" would have existed had the child been born with "corrected" genes, this argument does not necessarily defeat the child's claim. The decision whether to correct a genetic defect in a fetus necessarily is made without reference to the actual identity of the child. In this sense, the child occupies a "position" and, therefore, has the claim to benefits which would have accrued to the occupant of that position.

E. Joshua Rosenkranz formulates a different argument for the duty to cure genetic defects. Rosenkranz bases the duty to cure genetic defects on the duty of parents to rescue their children from harm.[39] Because this duty is based on the special relationship between a patient and her or his child, this duty is linked to the identity of the child as the offspring of specific parents. An important consequence of this linkage is the need to establish that a genetic cure does not fundamentally alter the identity of the fetus. If genetic engineering would alter the identity of a fetus, the special (genetically based) relationship of the parents to the child could be destroyed, and with it the duty to rescue the child from the genetic disease.

Rosenkranz argues that minimal changes to the genetic makeup of a fetus do not alter a fetus's identity.[40] But Rosenkranz has great difficulty specifying the point at which identity changes. As he recognizes,

> [w]hat it would take to convert a person into a different person (or what it would take to convert an egg that will become a person into an egg that would become a different person) turns entirely on our subjective valuation of the differing characteristics. ... [T]hat valuation might vary from one society to another. Moreover, valuation of characteristics could

---

[38]For such an argument see Rosenkranz, 1–53.

[39]Ibid.

[40]Ibid., 28.

easily differ among individuals in a given society and will undoubtedly change over a given period of time."[41]

If a society lacks the technology to cure a certain type of genetic disease, but has the capacity to detect that disease in a fetus, the claim of the child is necessarily very different. Here the choice may be between having a child with a defect and aborting the fetus. If a couple decides to have the child, the child is affected by that decision to the extent that the child must live with the genetic disease. If the child has a claim against the parents, it cannot be based on a comparison of her actual life with the life of another child free of the disease. Rather it must be based on a comparison of the actual life of the child, on the one hand, and nonexistence, on the other. If the life of the child is likely to be so miserable that she could reasonably claim that she would have been better off never having been born, then it can be argued that the parents act wrongly by giving birth to the child. On the other hand, if, on balance, the life of the child is likely to be worth living despite the handicap, then the decision to carry a fetus to term is morally sound.

The decision whether to carry to term a fetus with a genetic defect may also be based on factors other than the likely quality of life of the child. A couple may consider how having a genetically diseased child will affect them and their other children. They may also consider the lost opportunities which would result from having such a child. For example, the time and expense of raising a genetically diseased child may preclude their having additional, healthier children. On the other hand, while it may be legitimate to weigh such factors when considering whether to carry a fetus to term, it does not follow that these other factors *must* outweigh the value the couple places on preserving the life of the fetus. Because the question of whether it is morally preferable to carry to term a genetically diseased child depends on many different value judgments, there is often no single morally correct answer to this question in any given situation. Rather, it is a matter for individual moral choice.

---

[41]Ibid., 42.

It is important to note that the question of whether it is morally desirable to carry a genetically defective child to term is very different from the question of whether it is desirable to conceive a genetically defective child intentionally. A couple ought to prefer not to conceive a genetically defective child. On the other hand, if a couple can only conceive a child who has a genetic defect, (or if a couple can only conceive a male or female child who has a genetic disease), then whether or not it is ethical for the couple to conceive a child depends on the nature and extent of the genetic disease. The situation of a couple who can avoid conceiving a genetically damaged child by waiting a few months before conceiving is very different from that of a couple who can only conceive children who have a genetic disease. If a couple can only conceive a child with a genetic disease, then the child of that couple does not belong to a class which includes both genetically healthy and genetically diseased children, but instead belongs to a group which includes only children with the genetic disease.[42]

A problem which underlies this and any other discussion of the application of genetic engineering to human beings is how we define what constitutes a genetic defect. Not every trait people consider to be undesirable is properly considered a defect. In parts of Asia, for example, female children are held to be undesirable; but having two 'X' chromosomes cannot be defined legitimately as a genetic defect, since, at a minimum, the existence of females is necessary for the survival of the species, and what is necessary for the survival of the species cannot be a genetic defect.

More generally, there is a tendency to equate genetic health with conformity to the social standards of the day, and to equate genetic defects with nonconformity to those standards (much as the Soviet Union confined dissidents to mental institutions because they were unable to "adjust" to the Communist system[43]). Yet, at the same time

---

[42]See Derek Parfit, "Comments," 854–862, for a discussion of this problem.

[43]Theresa C. Smith and Thomas A. Oleszczuk, *No Asylum: State Psychiatric Repression in the U.S.S.R.*, (New York: St. Martin's Press, Forthcoming).

we have no other standards but our own. At a minimum we must be aware of this danger and to take care not be overly inclusive in what we classify as a genetic defect.

The final question we need to address is the "Brave New World" problem, namely whether, in a society with advanced genetic engineering technology, it would be intergenerationally just to refuse to have genetically engineered children, if doing so would result in children who are less intelligent and more prone to disease than children who are genetically engineered. What follows from my position is that if genetic engineering comes to be an accepted, reliable practice, it might properly be considered to be a harm (and, therefore, a moral wrong) to a child to be conceived without the "benefits" of genetic engineering.[44]

This conclusion no doubt will strike many readers as odd and disturbing. Anyone who grew up reading Aldous Huxley's *Brave New World* almost instinctively recoils from the view that genetic engineering might become morally obligatory. On the other hand, the fact that this conclusion strikes the reader as disturbing may be an indication that it is unfamiliar rather than wrong. As genetic engineering becomes more common and more available and more effective as a cure for genetic diseases, the acceptance of the practice is likely to increase. While the prospect of popular acceptance of genetic engineering provides no guarantee of its morality, it may be a reason to question whether a blanket rejection of genetic engineering is not premature. On the other hand, the prospect of "genetically designed human beings" remains sufficiently remote as to be an unrealistic concern at this time.

---

[44]My conclusion that we may some day have a duty to genetically engineer our children is considerably broader than Rosenkranz's more limited endorsement of an obligation to engage in "genetic rescue" by curing specific genetic defects. Nonetheless, I certainly would agree that there is no present (or foreseeable) duty to produce genetically designed children. See Rosenkranz, 51–53.

VII

Obligations to Past Generations

When contemporary thinkers discuss the question of intergenerational justice, they are concerned almost exclusively with obligations to future generations. Except for a handful of thinkers who have debated the question of harms to past generations, it is unusual for a contemporary thinker even to raise the issue of obligations to past generations.[1] As we saw in Chapter II, this has not always been the case. Because the classical thinkers understood intergenerational justice to consist of acting justly in an intergenerational community, they were concerned with obligations to past generations as well as with the welfare of posterity.

One possible explanation for the decline in interest in obligations to past generations is that the problems that we face in the late Twentieth Century are very different than those our ancestors faced. Hans Jonas, for one, has argued that the problem of obligations to future generations is not only more pressing than it used to be, but is actually unprecedented in human history.[2] Perhaps we could explain our lack of

---

[1]The participants in the debate over harms to past generations include Joel Feinberg, "The Rights of Animals and Unborn Generations," *Responsibilities to Future Generations*, ed. Ernest Partridge. (Buffalo, NY: Prometheus Press, 1980), 139–150; "Harm and Self-Interest," *Law, Morality and Society: Essays in Honour of H. L. A. Hart*, ed. M. S. Hacker and J. Raz. (Oxford: Clarendon Press, 1977), 284–308; and *Harm to Others, The Moral Limits of the Criminal Law*, Vol. 1, (New York: Oxford University Press, 1984); Barbara Baum Levenbook, "Harming Someone after His Death," *Ethics* 94 (1984), 407–419; and "Harming the Dead, Once Again," *Ethics* 96 October (1985), 162–164; Don Marquis, "Harming the Dead," *Ethics* 96 October (1985), 159–161; Ernest Partridge, "Posthumous Interest and Posthumous Respect," *Ethics* 91 (1981), 243–264; George Pitcher, "The Misfortunes of the Dead," *American Philosophical Quarterly* 21 (1984), 183–188; John O'Neill, "Future Generations: Present Harms," *Philosophy* 68(263) January (1993), 35–51.

[2]Hans Jonas, "Technology and Responsibility: The Ethics of an Endangered Future," *Responsibilities to Future Generations*, ed. Ernest Partridge, (Buffalo, NY: Prometheus Books, 1980), 23–36.

interest in obligations to past generations in terms of a preoccupation with the question of our obligations to posterity.

There is little doubt that we are confronted by different problems from those our ancestors confronted in Biblical times or in the early nineteenth century. But I am not persuaded that these differences explain our lack of interest in obligations to past generations. Our ancestors may not have had the capacity to exterminate the human species in a single day, but they too faced questions of survival, if not of the species, then at least of their tribe or people. Moreover, while interest in obligations to future generations has increased in recent years, it hardly rises to the level of a "preoccupation."

A better explanation for our lack of concern with obligations to past generations is that it is the result of changes in both our moral theories and our understanding of the nature of death. Two widely shared beliefs are particularly important. The first is that morality is concerned with how our actions affect persons. The second is that the actions of the living cannot affect the dead. These two beliefs combine to diminish the salience of obligations to past generations.

In Chapter II we examined the transformation of our concept of intergenerational justice from a concern with justice in an intergenerational community, comprised of past, present, and future persons, to a concern with meeting our obligations to future persons. We saw that a critical element in this transformation was the emergence of person-affecting principles as a cornerstone of our contemporary moral understandings. To the extent that we adhere to person-affecting principles, we hold that actions are morally significant only if they affect actual present or future persons.

The second element in our belief pattern which helps account for our diminished interest in obligations to past generations is the way we have come to understand death. In contrast to the religious understanding of life as a stage in one's passage to an afterlife, the secular understanding of death is that it is the end of existence. A person who is dead has no awareness, and no sensation. The dead do not think. They do not feel. Most importantly, the dead can no longer be affected by the actions of the living.

Because the living cannot affect the dead, it cannot matter *to the dead* whether we keep those promises or not. It follows that the living can have no obligations to the dead based on consequentialist ethical principles. It is true that other (deontological) ethical principles may require the living to keep their contracts with and promises to the dead, but to the extent that our moral theories are based on consequentialist rather than deontological principles, we are unlikely to place great emphasis on obligations to past generations.

It is important to recognize that the secular belief that the dead cannot be affected by the actions of the living is inherently unprovable. To state the obvious, no one is in a position to know that the dead do not feel or are not affected by the actions of the living. The fact that we cannot be certain that our actions do not affect the dead, does not mean that it is wrong to equate death with nonexistence. But it does mean that this is not an empirical proposition which can be tested and proved or disproved, but an article of (secular) faith around which we construct our world view.

We cannot prove that death marks the end of all awareness because we cannot prove that the physical body is necessary for awareness. Many people believe human beings have a soul which survives the death of the body and that this soul is capable of awareness and of experiencing pain and pleasure. While it is not unreasonable to accept the secular view that death marks the end of awareness and sensation, it is also possible to assume precisely the opposite, that the death is not the end of awareness and sensation, and that the actions of the living do affect the dead.

People have not always accepted the secular view that the actions of the living cannot affect the dead. An essential element of the Confucian religion was the belief that the dead could be affected by the actions of the living. It is in this context that the practice of ancestor worship arose and makes sense to its adherents. If the living have the capacity to benefit their ancestors by worshipping them, then it is coherent to hold that each succeeding generation has an obligation to worship its ancestors, and in turn can expect to be worshipped by its descendants.

The belief that the dead can be affected by the actions of the living is not confined to traditional Eastern religions. Many contemporary Christians hold that the human soul survives a person's physical death and that it is possible to intercede with God on behalf of the dead through prayer. While prayer for the dead may not be required, as a matter of justice, a belief in the efficacy of prayers for the dead is an important article of faith and an important part of the mourning process for many people.

Some philosophers have noted that we sometimes speak about the dead as if they can be affected by the actions of the living. Joan Callahan for example writes that "we experience compassion for the dead in the wake of some event, and sometimes we experience what certainly seems to be genuine moral outrage at, for example, the breaking of a promise made to a person before her death."[3] While it is possible that these "recalcitrant intuitions" are merely sentiments which are to be accounted for psychologically,[4] it is also possible that some of the confusion which surrounds the philosophical debate over harming the dead is the result of genuine uncertainty about the nature of death and about whether our actions do affect the dead.

Even though we live in a secular age, religion remains an important part of many people's lives. While most people accept the premises of our secular philosophy in their daily lives, they have not abandoned the religious perspective, altogether. In those areas where secular philosophy speaks unclearly, or where its answers are less than satisfactory, religion remains an important voice. It is at least possible that some of the confusion surrounding the nature of our obligations to past generations is the result not of our failure to apply philosophical principles correctly, but of our inability to decide whether to apply secular philosophical principles or religious beliefs.

---

[3]Joan C. Callahan, 347.

[4]Ibid., 347.

These possibilities do not obviate the need for a secular theory of obligations to past generations. On the contrary, they underscore the need for such a theory. We need a theory of obligations to past generations because we continue to adhere to institutions and practices which seem to imply that we do have obligations to the dead. For example, we have laws which govern the disposition of a person's property after her death. An essential purpose of these laws is to ensure the right of a person to determine how her property will be disposed of, after her death, within the limits of the law. While the executor of a will may exercise some discretion in interpreting a will, she or he generally is bound by custom and by law to abide by the wishes of the deceased.

Another practice which seems to imply the existence of obligations to the dead is the expectation that places of burial will be treated with respect. We need to find some theoretical basis for this practice, if for no other reason than to determine the proper limits of our obligations. For example, Native American Indians have long disputed the right of museums to keep, as part of their holdings, the remains of Native Americans unearthed from their burial sites. The return of those remains has been demanded by American Indians on religious and human rights grounds, "including the right of the dead to remain buried,"[5] but opposed by many anthropologists and archaeologists, on the grounds that "important scientific, medical and demographic research will suffer if major universities and museums return their collections for re-interment."[6]

The disagreement between archeologists and American Indians illustrates not only the potential for conflict among different cultures, but also the potential conflict between our obligations to past generations and the interests of present and future generations. At the

[5]Felicity Barringer, "Major Accord Likely on Indian Remains," *New York Times* August 20, 1989: A 22.

[6]Jane Gross, "Stanford Agrees to Return Ancient Bones to Indians," *New York Times* June 24, 1989: A 1, 6. See also Malcolm W. Browne, "As Deadlines Near, Scientists Seek Data from Indian Bones," *New York Times* September 25, 1989: C 1, 9.

same time, this conflict also illustrates the uncertainty we feel about the concept of obligations to past generations. Even though the Smithsonian and many other institutions have come to the conclusion that the skeletal remains of American Indians ought to be returned to their tribes for reburial, [7] there is no consensus among contemporary thinkers concerning what, if any, obligations we have towards the dead. While some thinkers see the question of obligations to past generations as an essential component of intergenerational justice,[8] others see the very notion of obligations to the dead as without substantive foundation, a manifestation of a superstitious past which ought to be discarded.[9] For still others, the question of obligations to past generations is all too easily ignored.

HARMS TO THE DEAD

The question of whether we can harm the dead undoubtedly will strike many readers as odd. After all, death is generally understood as the cessation of existence, the end of all awareness and sensation. If the dead cannot be affected by the actions of the living, how can it be possible to harm (or benefit) the dead?

Joel Feinberg's response is to point out that sensation and awareness are not necessarily involved when we speak of harming the interests of the living or the dead. It is possible to harm or thwart a living person's interests without that individual being aware of this fact and without causing him frustration. Similarly, it is possible for a person to fulfill his interests without experiencing satisfaction. For these reasons, Feinberg argues that

> harm to an interest is better defined in terms of the objective blocking of goals and thwarting of desires than in subjective terms; and the

[7]Irvin Molotsky, "Smithsonian to Give up Indian Remains," *New York Times* September 13, 1989: A 14

[8]For example, *Harm to Others, The Moral Limits of the Criminal Law*, Vol. 1, (New York: Oxford University Press, 1984).

[9]For example, see Joan C. Callahan, "On Harming the Dead," *Ethics* 97 January (1987), 347.

> enhancement or advancing of an interest is likewise best defined in terms of the objective fulfillment of well-considered wants rather than in terms of subjective states of pleasure.[10]

Because "interests are 'stakes' that are derived from and linked to wants," death can be "a thwarting of the interests of the person who dies, and must be the total defeat of most of his self-regarding interests, even though, as a dead man, he can feel no pain."[11]

According to Feinberg, a person's interests can be harmed not only by his death, but also by events which occur after his death. While some interests die with a person, other self-regarding interests can be fulfilled or thwarted after the death of the person whose wants they were. Feinberg has in mind such wants as the desire to be the object of affection or esteem of others, and particularly the desire to maintain a good reputation. Fulfillment and thwarting of such interests "may still be possible, even when it is too late for satisfaction or disappointment."[12]

One obstacle to accepting the concept of posthumous harm is the problem of how persons can be harmed by that which they are inherently incapable of knowing. If the dead cannot be aware of events as they occur, can they have any stake one way or another in such events? For Feinberg, such objections rest on false premises. The interests of the living can be violated without their ever being aware of that fact.

> If someone spreads a libelous description of me among a group whose good opinion I covet and cherish, altogether without my knowledge, I have been injured in virtue of the harm done my interest in a good reputation, even though I *never* learn what has happened. That is because I have an interest, so I believe, in having a good reputation *as such*, in addition to my interest in avoiding hurt feelings, embarrassment, and economic injury. And *that* interest can be seriously harmed without my ever learning of it.[13]

---

[10]Joel Feinberg, *Harms to Others*, 85.
[11]Ibid., 84–85.
[12]Ibid., 86.
[13]Ibid., 87.

If knowledge is not a necessary condition for harm to one's interests before one's death, why should it become necessary after one's death? If after my death "an enemy cleverly forges documents to 'prove' very convincingly that I was a philanderer, an adulterer, and a plagiarist, and communicates this 'information' to the general public that includes my widow, children, and former colleagues and friends ..., [c]an there be any doubt that I have been harmed by such libels?"[14] Even though it is impossible for the victim of such libels to experience embarrassment or distress, Feinberg argues that libels can harm the dead by thwarting goals in which they had placed great stake.[15]

Perhaps the most convincing argument which Feinberg makes for the possibility of harming the dead is based on three hypothetical cases. Feinberg finds these arguments so compelling that he suggests "the case for posthumous harm can rest with them."[16] They are paraphrased below:

> *Case A* involves a woman who devotes thirty years of her life to the furtherance of certain ideals and ambitions in the form of one vast undertaking. One month before she dies, her project collapses and she is personally disgraced. However, she never learns the truth because her friends conceal or misrepresent the facts to save her from disappointment. She dies contented.
>
> *Case B* is the same as Case A, except that the project in which the woman had so great an interest flourishes until her death. One month later her project begins to flounder, collapsing utterly within a year of her death, and in the process, discrediting her life's work.
>
> *Case C* supposes the same facts as Case B except that the cause of the collapse of the project is a group of malevolent conspirators who, from motives of vengeance, malice and envy, spread damaging lies about her project and otherwise betray her trust in order to bring about the ruin of her interests.[17]

---

[14]Ibid.
[15]Ibid.
[16]Ibid., 88.
[17]Ibid.

Feinberg argues that the woman in Case A suffers a grievous harm to her interests, even though she never learns of the fate of her project. Feinberg argues that those same interests are harmed in Case B, and to the same extent. In this case, the woman does not learn of the news because she is dead, and (so far as we know) "dead people hear no news at all."[18]

Because some people are skeptical that there can be a harm to a person who no longer exists, Feinberg seeks to reinforce this argument by the additional facts presented in Case C. Feinberg points out that in this example

> the woman is not *merely* harmed (if she is harmed at all); rather she is exploited, betrayed, and wronged. When a promise is broken, someone is wronged, and who if not the promisee? When a confidence is revealed, someone is betrayed, and who, if not the person whose confidence it was? When a reputation is falsely blackened, someone is defamed, and who, if not the person lied about? If there is no "problem of the subject" when we speak of wronging the dead, why should there be when we speak of harming them, especially when the harm is an essential ingredient of the wrong?[19]

Ernest Partridge has criticized this line of argument in an article entitled "Posthumous Interests and Posthumous Respect."[20] Partridge focuses on Feinberg's argument that there is no distinction between damaging a living person's interest in a good reputation (by spreading a libelous description without his knowledge in a remote part of the country), and damaging the reputation of a dead person (by spreading a libelous description of him after his death). If a person can have an interest in things which do not affect him directly, his interests can be damaged even when he is unaware of the damage to those interests. If

---

[18]Ibid., 89.

[19]Ibid.

[20]Partridge focused his critique on earlier articles written by Feinberg ("The Rights of Animals and Unborn Generations" and "Harm and Self Interest") in which Feinberg makes substantially the same arguments. Ernest Partridge, "Posthumous Interests and Posthumous Respect," 243–264.

this is the case, it would seem to follow that a person's interests can be damaged even after he is dead.

Partridge is not willing to concede that the interests of a person can survive his death. But Partridge is also not able to insert a "logical wedge" between harms to a person's reputation that have no effect on him while he is alive, and harms to a person's reputation that have no effect on him because he is dead.[21] Therefore, he is forced to choose between accepting that it is possible to harm the dead and concluding that damage to a person's reputation, which has no effect on that individual, does not harm her or him. Partridge suggests that "the case against harming the dead is so strong that the preferable, yet difficult course is to deny that 'the unaffected living' can be harmed, all the while strenuously affirming that the 'unaffecting libels.' etc., are morally wrong on other grounds ...."[22]

Partridge maintains there are good reasons for preserving institutions such as wills quite apart from any alleged "interests" of or "harms" to the deceased. If we do not enforce the wills of persons who have died, those who are alive now will have no reason to believe that their wills will be enforced. This will result in the decay of the practice of making bequests, including bequests such as Alfred Nobel's Prize, which are to the benefit of future generations. Partridge concludes, therefore, that it is wrong to break promises to the dead because doing so undermines social institutions that are highly useful to the living.[23]

Feinberg characterizes Partridge's position as denying "not only that the dead can be harmed but also that they can be wronged, betrayed, or treated unfairly, on the grounds that they do not exist, and nonexistent beings are beyond all wronging."[24] While this is not the only possible interpretation of Partridge's argument, it does seem to be persuasive. At times, Partridge seems to come close to accepting that the

[21]Ibid., 251.

[22]Ibid., 252.

[23]Ibid., 259–261.

[24]Feinberg, *Harms to Others*, 94.

dead can be wronged even though they cannot be harmed. For example, Partridge asks "... if one can 'wrong' the dead and if such 'wrongs' are not 'harms to' or 'invaded interests of' the dead, what are they?"[25] But Partridge never speaks of "wrongs" to the dead without placing that word inside quotation marks. In the final analysis, Partridge holds that it is wrong to break promises to the dead, *because* the failure to keep promises to the dead would cause the erosion of institutions and practices which are of benefit to the living, and will be of benefit to future generations.[26] Partridge's argument is a rule utilitarian defense of the practice of keeping promises to the dead.

Feinberg's critique of Partridge's rule utilitarian approach is telling and worth quoting at length. Feinberg argues that while rule utilitarian arguments

> give the truth about our duties towards the dead, and nothing but the truth, but they do not give the whole truth. The very rules that impose duties on us as promisors, speakers, insurers, and testimonial instruction receivers confer, by the same token, *rights* on the living persons who are the corresponding promisees, parties talked about, insurance buyers, and testimonial instruction givers. These are the rights that can be violated after the right-holder's death by the wrongful behavior of those who violate their own duties. ... Its violation creates a quite distinct and powerful grievance in the right-holder (or his spokesman) which cannot wholly be derived from the more diffuse grievance the rest of us may have that "our practice" has been weakened or threatened. ... It is absurd to think that once a promisee has died, the status of a broken promise made to him while he was alive suddenly ceases to be that of a serious injustice to a victim, and becomes instead a mere diffuse public harm.[27]

I believe Feinberg is correct in holding that we can commit *wrongs* against the dead by breaking promises to them, by defaming their character (more precisely, the character they had when they were alive), or by betraying the trust they placed in us when they were alive. But, it

---

[25]Partridge, "Posthumous Interests and Posthumous Respect," 255.
[26]Ibid., 259–261.
[27]Feinberg, *Harms to Others*, 94–95.

does not follow from this that it is possible to *harm* the dead by breaking our promises to them, by defaming them, or by betraying the trust they placed in us when they were alive. With respect to the possibility of harming the dead, it is Partridge, and not Feinberg, who is correct.

There are important differences between *wronging* a person and *harming* a person. The best indication of this is that it is possible to harm a person without wronging her, and, conversely, to wrong a person without harming her.[28] A person can be harmed by her own actions, as when a person drinks to excess; but we do not generally speak of a person wronging herself. A person can also be harmed by the justifiable actions of another, as when the efforts of a person to defend herself from an attacker result in an injury to the attacker. The injured attacker has suffered a harm, but has not been wronged by the person who defended herself.

It is also possible for a person to wrong another without harming that individual. We can easily verify that this is the case by considering the following scenario:

> It is a time of war and one member of a French army unit is an agent of the enemy. This soldier, Jean, betrays his unit by revealing their location to the enemy. The enemy plans an ambush, but their plans are thwarted and all the enemy soldiers are captured. No French soldier suffers any injury (and some even receive medals of valor for capturing so many enemy soldiers).

It is quite clear that Jean has wronged his fellow French soldiers by betraying their location. If caught, Jean undoubtedly would be tried for treason. Nonetheless, Jean has not harmed those persons whom he has betrayed. No French soldier is any worse off for Jean's actions; some may think themselves better off for having received a medal.

That it is possible to wrong a living person without causing her harm, suggests that it also may be possible to wrong the dead, even though we hold that it is impossible to harm the dead, or their interests.

---

[28]See Feinberg, *Harms to Others*, 31–64, for a general discussion of harms and wrongs to others.

Indeed, this turns out to be the case. We can speak coherently of wronging the dead, even though we recognize that the dead are beyond harm, and even though we recognize that they are no longer capable of having interests (and, therefore, are incapable of having interests which can be harmed).[29] We wrong the dead when we break the promises made to them when they were alive. We also wrong the dead when we betray the trust they placed in us when we were alive. There is nothing particularly mysterious about this. Even though we can no longer harm a person or her "interests" after she has died, we can still be bound by the promises we made to a person when she was alive. This is especially true when we promise to do something after a person's death (or in the event of her death). Traditionally, promises made to a dying person, to perform specific actions after her death were endowed with a special status and name. People were expected to go to great lengths to fulfill such "sacred promises."

We can speak coherently about wronging the dead, but not about harming the dead, because the concepts of a "wrong" and a "harm" have their foundation in different moral theories. The concept of a "wrong" is generally rooted in deontological principles, while the concept of "a harm" is associated with consequentialist principles. In order to harm a person, there must be a person to harm. Because death removes the object of harm, it also removes the possibility of harm.

On the other hand, whether an action is a "wrong" does not depend *directly* on the consequences of the action. It is wrong to spread defamatory lies about a living person because such lies may cause harm to another human being. But it is also wrong to spread defamatory lies about a living person because it is wrong to defame and it is wrong to tell lies. Our judgment that these actions are wrong does not depend directly on the consequences of the lies. We should be prepared to hold that it is wrong to tell lies about a person even without knowing what the actual consequences of those lies are. For similar reasons actions such as breaking a promise or betraying a trust can be a wrong, even when there

---

[29]As Partridge argues in "Posthumous Interests and Posthumous Respect," 246.

is no longer a person who can be harmed by those actions. It is true that in order for there to be a promise or a trust, there must *have been* a person to whom the promise was given, or who placed a trust. But the persistence of the promise or the "trust" is not necessarily tied to the continued existence of that individual.[30]

This is not to say that the consequences of an action are irrelevant for judging its morality. Even though we hold that it is wrong to tell a lie, we accept that a lie may be excused or even justified in order to bring about a desirable end. For example, the friends of the woman in Case A may be justified in concealing the fate of her project in order to save her the anguish of seeing her life work in ruins.

It is also true that there are generally good rule utilitarian arguments which buttress the deontological moral judgment that certain types of actions are wrong. But Feinberg is surely correct in saying that there is a great deal of difference between arguing that the betrayal of a trust wrongs someone, and arguing that it is wrong to betray a trust because it undermines the institutions and practice of placing trust.[31] In the first case, the action is wrong, in itself. In the second case the action is wrong in virtue of the harm done by the publicity which may or may not ensue from the action. How we judge a betrayal of trust should not depend on the extent of the publicity surrounding the betrayal.[32] Rather, our judgment ought to depend on the justification or lack of justification for the action in question.

Another way of arriving at the same conclusion is to argue that it violates the rights of the dead to tell lies about them, or to betray their trust. The problem with a rights based approach is that we generally do not accept that the dead continue to be the bearers of rights. On the other hand, it is possible to argue that the rights of an individual can extend beyond his or her death. In this sense we do not ascribe rights to

---

[30]As we will see in the next section, not all promises survive the death of the person to whom the promise was made. But some promises can and do survive the death of the promisee.

[31]Feinberg, *Harms to Others*, 95.

[32]Ibid.

dead persons, but rather recognize that we may violate the rights of living persons after their death. The distinction may be fine, but it is important. The dead do not have rights insofar as we have no general obligation to consider their claims or rights when planning an action. However, when we are bound by contracts, promises or general ethical principles to do something after a person's death, we may well be obligated to consider the claims of those who formerly lived before acting.

One example of a right which extends beyond the moment of a person's death is the right to have her body disposed of according to her wishes. Like many other rights, this right is circumscribed by law and custom. The law will not permit the executor of the will to honor a request to leave a corpse unburied. Similarly, a request for disposal of one's body in conflict with religious law may not be honored, in practice. However, within the limits set by law and custom, Western culture permits a person to specify the manner of disposition of her body, whether this involves organ donation, cremation, or burial.

The right of an individual to determine the disposition of her body sets important limits on what types of laws are considered just. For example, there is a pressing need for people to donate organs for transplantation. Even though many states provide the opportunity for people to indicate their willingness to donate organs for transplantation by signing donor cards, there are not enough organs to meet the need. One way to increase the rate of donation would be to pass implied consent laws under which permission to "harvest" organs for transplantation is assumed unless a person indicates otherwise. Some states have done precisely this. Most actual laws are careful to preserve the right of the individual to "opt out."

But let us go a step further and assume that even these laws prove to be too burdensome, and in order to meet the growing demand for organs, a state passes an "irrevocable consent" law under which organs may be harvested from a person after her death regardless of her expressed wishes or the wished of her family. Such a law would be unlikely to pass because it would run counter to the wishes and religious traditions of the majority of people in this country. But if such a law were passed, would it be just? It is my sense that given current understandings of privacy and the rights of the individual, such a law would be unjust. In part, it would be unjust because it would do violence to the sentiments of relatives of the person who died. But the law also would be unjust to the dying individual. Our culture recognizes the right of an individual to determine the disposition of her body after her death (within the limits set by reasonable laws). To the extent that this right is accepted by our culture, a law which permits the harvesting of body parts against the wishes of the individual would be unjust *to the deceased*.

Two points should be noted. The first is that given the assumptions of Western secular society, the claim of an individual to determine the disposition her body after her death cannot rest on any harm which might come to the individual from others failing to follow her wishes: for Western secular culture assumes that no additional harm can come to a person after her death. In this sense the claim of a Western secularist must necessarily be different from those of American Indians who believe that the dead cannot rest in peace while their bones lie in museum collections. Rather, the claim of Western secularists must rest on the right of the living individual to determine the disposition of her body after her death.

The second point which should be noted is that the right to determine the disposition of one's body after death is not in any sense a universal right. Not only is this right subject to health and other legal restrictions, it is also a right firmly rooted in local custom. Unlike the rights to a minimum level of food, clothing, shelter, medical care and education, and unlike the right to be free from torture, the claim that one has a right to determine the disposition of one's body after one's death is not easily universalizable. One can advance quite respectable arguments that it is wrong for *any* political system to deprive persons under its jurisdiction of minimal levels of food and shelter or to torture its citizens. But one would be hard pressed to create a persuasive argument that it is always unjust for a state to permit the harvesting of organs from those who have died or that it is always unjust to specify a single mode of burial for all members of a society.

What makes the right to determine the disposition of one's body different from the rights to food, clothing, and shelter is that food, clothing, and shelter are not only desirable in and of themselves, they are also instrumentally necessary for human growth and survival. Persons who are deprived of food, clothing, medicine, and shelter, or who are tortured, not only suffer direct harm, they may also lose the opportunity to pursue other desirable things. By contrast, the right to determine the disposition of one's body may be desired for its own sake, but, at least by the assumptions of Western secular culture, is not instrumentally useful.[33] This is not to say that the right to determine the disposition of one's body after death is unimportant, nor that it would be acceptable, in the United States, to deprive persons of this right. It is simply to argue that the right to dispose of one's body after one's death is neither a "universal" nor a "fundamental" human right.

PROMISES AND CONTRACTS AMONG GENERATIONS

If my analysis is correct, we can have obligations to past generations based on deontological but not consequentialist principles. Even though we cannot harm past generations, it is possible to have obligations to those who have died on the basis of promises or contracts. Thus, if I promise a friend to look after her children in the event of her death, my promise is not rendered moot by the death of my friend. Quite the contrary, the death of my friend is a necessary triggering condition for my having the obligation to take care of her children.

It is true, of course, that my actions have direct consequences for my friend's children and not for my late friend.[34] In this sense, it can be

---

[33]Here, again, we may note the contrast between Western secular culture and such cultures as that of Ancient Egypt which believed that the manner of one's burial had actual effects on the deceased.

[34]This assumes, of course, that we accept the validity of the proposition that the actions of the living do not affect the dead.

argued that I have an obligation to my friend's children (to take care of them) and not to my late friend. But this is an incomplete understanding my obligation. If I had not promised my friend (when she was alive) that I would take care of her children after her death, I would have no special obligation to care for her children. The source of my obligation to my friend's children is the promise I made to my late friend. It is *because* the obligation created by my promise to my friend survives her death, that I am obligated to take care of her children.

Although promises and contracts can be a source of obligation to past generations, both promises and contracts have characteristics which limit their applicability to relations among *remote* generations. Among the limiting characteristics is the fact that while we may be obligated to keep the promises we have made to persons who have died, we can make no new promises to persons once they are dead. The same limitation applies to contracts: the terms of a contract may require us to perform certain actions after the death of an individual, but it is not possible to enter into a new contract with a person once that person has died. From this it would seem to follow that we can have neither promissory nor contractual obligations to our remote ancestors (those who died more than one hundred years ago), for there never was a time when we were both alive.

The fact that it is impossible to make promises to or contracts with distant past generations does not mean that it is impossible to make promises or contracts which *relate to* distant past generations. We can promise our grandparents to tend our great-grandparents' graves after they have died, and we can even promise our grandparents that we will ask our children and grandchildren to make the same promise in turn. But if we make these promises, the obligation we have to tend the graves of our great-grandparents is an obligation we owe to our grandparents and not to our great-grandparents. In this sense the great-grandparents are the quasi-beneficiaries of the promise we make to our grandparents, although, as we have seen, our secular culture holds that it is not possible to benefit or harm the dead in actuality.

The temporal limitation on obligations based on promises and contracts exists because one cannot make a promise or an actual contract without the participation of the person or persons to whom one is making a promise, or with whom one is making a contract. This is clearest in the case of contracts which require the assent of all parties. But it is also true in the case of promises. A promise is a performative utterance or "speech act."[35] As John Austin points out, "[w]hen I say 'I promise', a new plunge is taken: I have not merely announced my intention, but by using this formula (performing this ritual), I have bound myself to others, and staked my reputation in a new way."[36] We make promises to alter the expectations of those to whom the promise is made. If we were incapable of altering the expectations of others, there would be no reason to make promises. It is because it is impossible to alter the expectations of those who have died that we can make no new promises to persons once they are dead.

However, there is a variant on the promise which can be made to the dead; this is the *vow*. Unlike a promise, a vow is not so much made "to" another person as it is made "in the presence of" another. Moreover, those "others" need not be actual persons, and they need not actually be present. Vows can be made to unseen personae, be they God or one's ancestors. Vows, however, belong to a different moral world than the secular world we have been examining.

Another variant on the promise is the promise made to oneself. What is interesting about the practice of making promises to oneself is that it requires the individual play the role of both self and other in an attempt to reinforce the will of the individual. The fact that a promise made to oneself can have greater force than a simple decision to do something is an indication of the extent to which we internalize social norms, in general, and the norms relating to the keeping of promises, in

[35]See John L. Austin, "Performative Utterances," *Philosophical Papers*, ed. John L. Austin. (London: Oxford University Press, 1961), 220–339; "Other Minds," *Logic and Language*, ed. Anthony Flew. (Oxford: Basil Blackwell, 1959), 123–158; John R. Searle, *Speech Acts*, (Cambridge: Cambridge University Press, 1969).

[36]John L. Austin, "Other Minds," 143–144.

particular. However, a promise to oneself may more properly be classified as a vow than as an actual promise.

THE LIMITS OF PROMISES AND CONTRACTS AMONG REMOTE GENERATIONS

If the impossibility of making promises to or contracts with those who are dead limits our ability to establish new obligations to our *ancestors*, the same objections do not apply to the commitments a generation makes to its *descendants*. In theory, it is possible for a generation to make promises to future generations since the promises of one generation can alter the expectations of its descendants. In practice, however, distant future generations are unlikely to be influenced by the promises of their ancestors, since those future generations will be in a position to judge for themselves whether the actions of their ancestors matched their words.

On the other hand, the ways in which future generations understand their history and their world may be altered by the "promises" of past generations. Thus, we speak of the "promise" of equality contained in the Declaration of Independence and its influence on the oppressed throughout American history. We also judge our history in terms of the success of this nation in realizing the "promise" of liberty and justice for all, contained in our "Pledge of Allegiance." However, when we speak of the "promise of liberty," we are using the word promise not so much in its performative sense, of making a pledge, as in its figurative sense, of providing grounds for expecting something to come to pass. Although figurative promises to future generations constitute an important part of our political landscape, performative promises to remote future generations are not generally an important consideration for theories of intergenerational justice.

A different set of considerations would appear to limit the ability of a generation to make contracts with its descendants. Unlike promises, which require only the passive participation of the person(s) to whom the promise is made, contracts require the active agreement of both (all) parties. Because future generations are inherently incapable of agreeing to the terms of a contract until they actually come into existence, there can be no actual contracts among remote generations. At most, the present generation might argue that future generations would agree to the terms of a contract (if they were able to do so). However, to say that future generations would agree to the terms of a contract, if asked, is very different from saying that future generations actually agree to the terms of a contract. As Ronald Dworkin points out in his critique of John Rawls's *Theory of Justice*, in order for a contract to be binding, all parties to the contract must agree to its terms in advance. "A hypothetical contract is not simply a pale form of an actual contract; it is no contract at all."[37] The force of the contractual argument, thus, is significantly diminished by the fact that future generations are inherently incapable of agreeing to the terms which their ancestors put forth.

However, the barriers to intergenerational contracts are not as absolute as they seem, at first. It is possible for members of the present generation to make contracts with or commitments to each other which future generations will inherit. Among these are commitments to the existing distribution of resources in society and existing political institutions. A generation inherits from its ancestors a world in which many resources are already distributed. Future generations may choose to reject the institutions and practices they have inherited, but there is almost always a cost to doing so. The principal cost is in the disruption of people's lives. In general, people expect the future to be like the present. Even when social change is desirable (and desired by large numbers of persons), social upheaval and radical change almost always cause suffering. Thus, even though most of the people of the former East Germany were glad to see the demise of the Communist regime which ran their nation, and even though the change was accomplished largely nonviolently, the transition from a communist system to a market economy and a western style democratic political system has not been an

---

[37]Ronald Dworkin, *Taking Rights Seriously*, (Cambridge Massachusetts: Harvard University Press, 1977), 151.

unmixed blessing. Large numbers of former East Germans have lost their jobs, and people who were accustomed to the security of guaranteed employment now must face the insecurities of a capitalist economy. While the costs associated with social upheaval do not justify the preservation of unjust institutions and practices, they do serve to create a rebuttable presumption in favor of evolutionary rather than revolutionary change.

It is not only the institutions and practices of past generations that one generation inherits from its ancestors. A generation may also inherit financial obligations and other commitments made in its name. For example, a government may choose to finance a building project through the use of long-term bonds. It may also sign treaties with other nations that create obligations for future generations of its citizens.

The question of whether future generations have an obligation to fulfill the commitments their ancestors made in their name is very different from the question of whether a generation has an obligation to fulfill the promises *it* made to its immediate ancestors. Among the questions we should raise is whether a generation has the authority to make promises and to enter into contracts that will bind the actions of its descendants. We also need to ask the complementary question, whether a generation is obligated to fulfill the promises and contracts previous generations have entered into in their name, and if so under what circumstances.

It is my position that while the present generation has the authority to make promises for future generations, these promises are only conditionally binding on future generations. This represents an intermediate position between the Burkean argument that the commitments of past generations are binding on its descendants and the liberal individualist argument that no generation is bound by commitments to which it has not assented. If successful, this argument should serve as the basis for an approach to intergenerational justice which accepts the reality of conceptual and moral change while at the same time leaving room for intergenerational community and moral commitment.

THE AUTHORITY OF PAST GENERATIONS AND THE OBLIGATIONS OF FUTURE GENERATIONS

A strong case can be made that the present generation has the authority to make "promises" and "contracts" for future generations. This case is based on the fact that the present generation has the obligation to act justly towards future generations. In order to fulfill this obligation, the present generation must be able to take those actions which are necessary and proper to ensure justice for future generations. For example, if intergenerational justice requires the present generation to preserve wilderness areas for future generations, it must follow that the present generation has the authority to take those actions and make those promises which are necessary to set aside wilderness areas for preservation (provided that those actions and promises are not unjust for other reasons). If preserving wilderness represents too great a financial burden to be funded through the normal budgetary process, it may be necessary for the government to finance the acquisition and preservation of wilderness lands through the sale of long-term bonds.

Because long-term bonds represent contractual obligations that future generations will be expected to meet, we need to ask whether it is just for the present generation to incur debts that future generations will inherit. This question has been examined extensively by Nobel Prize-winning economist, James Buchanan.[38] Buchanan argues that the practice of financing the *consumption* of the present generation through large scale borrowing is unjust to future generations. Such deficit financing is unjust because it shifts the costs of the present generation's prosperity onto future generations. However, when the purpose for which debt is incurred is a *long-term benefit*, which the present generation seeks to provide for itself and for future generations, Buchanan argues

[38]See James M. Buchanan, *Public Principles of Public Debt*, (Homewood: Irwin, 1958); "The Ethics of Debt Default," *Deficits*, ed. James M. Buchanan, Charles K. Rowley and Robert D. Tollison. (New York: Basil Blackwell, 1986), 361–373; and James M. Buchanan, and Richard Wagner, *Democracy in Deficit*, (New York: Academic Press, 1977).

that deficit financing not only may be justifiable, it even may be desirable.[39]

One problem with this position is that it seems to open the door to the Cold War argument that it was just to require future generations to bear a significant part of the cost of the arms race because winning the arms race was necessary to ensure that future generations of Americans would enjoy the freedoms their ancestors had enjoyed. The proper reply to this argument is not that it is never just to incur debt which future generations will inherit, but that the specific purposes for which debt was incurred may not be the unadulterated benefit its advocates held it to be. A strong case can be made that the deficit spending associated with the arms race not only will make future generations financially poorer, but that it also has increased the risk and destructiveness of war for ourselves *and* for future generations.

If we accept that one generation has the authority to enter into long-term contracts when there is reason to believe that doing so will benefit future generations, it would seem to follow that future generations have the obligation to fulfill the terms of that contract. Our understanding of the nature of contracts and of the relationship between authority and obligations is such that, if A has the authority to enter into a contract for B, then B is obligated to fulfill the terms of that contract.

However, the question of whether a generation is obligated to fulfill the commitments of its ancestors is one on which thinkers may disagree. The most traditional response calls for preserving the symmetry between authority and obligations. This is the response of classical conservatism. It holds that if a generation has the authority to act in the name of posterity, then future generations have a corresponding obligation to fulfill the commitments of their ancestors. This is very much the view of Edmund Burke, who argues that society is an intergenerational partnership among the living, the dead, and those who are to be born.[40]

---

[39]James Buchanan, "The Ethics of Debt Default," 363.
[40]Edmund Burke, *Reflections on the Revolution in France*, 110.

One consequence of Burke's position is that it tends to amplify the "natural imbalance" which exists between a generation and its descendants. The source this "natural imbalance" is the fact that the actions of the present generation can affect its descendants but not vice versa. Because this is the case, to hold that the present generation is obligated to honor the commitments of its ancestors may lead to a restriction of the sovereignty of later generations over their own affairs as compared to that of their ancestors.

This danger may be seen clearly in the deficit crisis brought about by the policies of the Reagan and Bush administrations. An immediate consequence of the debt crisis has been a cutback in spending on social welfare programs. This consequence is consistent with the inentions of the Reagan administration when they proposed cutting taxes in the early 1980s. Even as late as 1990, former Nixon and Reagan advisor, Patrick Buchanan, argued in favor of additional tax cuts as a way of ensuring further curtailment of social welfare spending.[41] A long-term consequence of the debt crisis may well be a permanent reduction in the ability of the American people to spend for the welfare of society. By 1990, the cost of financing the national debt had risen to approximately fifteen percent of the total federal budget.[42] To the extent that interest payments on the national debt diminish the capacity of future generations to spend for their social welfare, the Reagan administration may have succeeded in making permanent the so-called "Reagan revolution." The price of this victory, however, is a loss of future generations' sovereignty over their own affairs.

While the danger of the loss of sovereignty is real, this danger can also be exaggerated. It is possible for future generations to renounce the commitments of their ancestors. Future generations may default on the debts they inherited from their ancestors, much as some Third World

---

[41] Patrick Buchanan, "Moynihan's Tax Cut: A No-Lose Proposition for Bush & Co.," *Times Leader, Wilkes-Barre, PA,* January 29, 1990, 8A.

[42] Based on data from the U.S. Office of Management of Budget, *Budget in Brief* (Washington, D.C.: U.S. Government, 1990).

nations have done on their debts to Western banks.[43] Even Edmund Burke does not argue that a generation must always adhere to the commitments prior generations had made in their name. If earlier generations acted without regard for what is just to posterity, Burke would allow future generations to correct the "mistakes" of their ancestors. This may necessitate renouncing some of the commitments of past generations. Burke would seem to consider this to be acceptable only if it is directed at restoring a tradition which had been allowed to erode by prior generations or if it is aimed at adapting a society's traditions to changed conditions.[44]

Although the classical conservative understanding of the social contract is less rigid than might be supposed, it remains at odds with the liberal understanding that no person can make promises or enter into contracts for another without that person's consent. The liberal model permits a competent individual to authorize another to enter into a contract for her by granting the power of attorney. However, unless an individual *explicitly* authorizes another to act on her behalf, there is a strong presumption that no one has the authority to act for another. Since it is impossible for distant future generations to give their (prior) consent to the actions of their ancestors, it would seem to follow that no generation can ever claim the authority to enter into contracts or to make promises for its descendants.

This understanding of intergenerational obligations has disturbing implications for the stability of intergenerational relations. It would mean that even though a generation has the moral obligation to attempt to act justly towards its descendants, that generation's descendants would be under no obligation to honor the commitments their ancestors made in their name. What makes this position unstable is that if future

---

43 For an argument defending the right of future generations to modify inherited contracts and property distributions see David Braybrooke, "The Social Contract and Property Rights across the Generations," *Justice between Age Groups and Generations*, ed. Peter Laslett and James S. Fishkin. (New Haven: Yale University Press, 1992) 107–126.

44 Burke, 290–291.

generations refuse to honor the commitments made by prior generations (in an attempt to act justly towards posterity), it would not be long before the practice of making commitments for future generations, itself, became discredited. This, in turn, would diminish the capacity of all generations to act justly towards their descendants by restricting their capacity to undertake projects which are intergenerational in nature.[45]

However, just as the conservative understanding of intergenerational obligations is not as rigid as it appeared to be, the liberal understanding is more flexible than it at first appears. The source of this flexibility is the rebuttability of the presumption that only the individual may act in her own behalf. This presumption can be overridden in special circumstances, such as when an individual is not competent to act in her own behalf. The classical examples of conditions associated with noncompetence are youth and mental deficiency (whether due to retardation or mental illness).[46] Moreover, when an individual is not competent to act on her own behalf, that individual is also unlikely to be competent to authorize another to act on her behalf. Thus, a child is presumed to be incapable of determining not only what is in her best interests, but also which individuals are best able to preserve her interests.[47] The same is true for individuals judged mentally incompetent. In such circumstances, the State may appoint a guardian to act on her behalf and in her interests. In the case of a minor, this responsibility is generally placed where it had been placed traditionally, in the hands of the child's parents.[48]

---

[45]If we accept Burke's argument that society itself is an intergenerational endeavor, then a good case can be made that the acceptance of a radically liberal understanding of intergenerational obligations threatens to undermine the possibility of society itself.

[46]Other classes of persons who, historically, have been considered incompetent include women and blacks.

[47]In the case of a custody battle, a child's wishes may be solicited and considered. However, the authority to award custody of a child belongs to the Court and not to the child, herself.

[48]Parental authority is now understood to be more limited than it was in previous centuries. The State restricts parental authority in several important respects.

The situation of remote future generations is analogous in some respects to that of a child who is incompetent to act on her own behalf. Some of the special circumstances which permit or require a parent (or guardian) to act for a minor also exist in the case of remote future generations. For example, future generations have (or will have) interests which can be affected by the actions others may take at present. At the same time, remote future generations are incapable, at present, of acting on their own behalf or otherwise defending their own interests. The present generation may be in a position to foresee how its actions are likely to affect its descendants and to act to defend their interests. Given the undeniable noncompetence of future generations to act on their own behalf (due to their nonexistence), the present generation must assume the responsibility for protecting the interests of future generations. To the extent that the present generation has this responsibility, it would seem to follow that it must also have the authority to make those promises and contracts in the name of future generations which are reasonably necessary to protect the interests of their descendants.

Even though the argument that a generation has the authority to make decisions and commitments for posterity is based on a well-established exemption to the liberal principles of autonomy and consent, there remains a fundamental tension between the authority of one generation to act on behalf of its descendants and the belief that only the consent of those future generations can legitimize promises and contracts made in its name. One way we might attempt to resolve this tension is by separating the question of the *authority* of the present generation to make commitments for posterity from the question of the *obligation* of future generations to fulfill the commitments made by its ancestors. We might accept that the inability of future generations to act on their own behalf gives the present generations the authority to act on behalf of its descendants, without conceding that future generations

---

The State requires the parents to provide a child with a particular kind of education. It also prohibits certain forms of discipline.

are obligated to fulfill all the commitments their ancestors made in their name. Once a generation becomes competent to act on its own behalf, the question of its consent becomes paramount. A generation may consent to the commitments its ancestors had made, but it may also renounce those commitments.

The right to renounce the commitments which others have made in one's name (but without one's own consent) can be understood to be an inalienable (liberal) right. From this characterization as an inalienable right, it follows that no one ought to be surprised if future generations renounce the commitments their ancestors made in their name. On the other hand, we have seen that the acceptance of this model may seriously undermine the ability of a generation to make commitments for its descendants, and consequently, restrict its ability to act justly towards posterity.

OBLIGATIONS TO PAST GENERATIONS AND THE SOCIAL CONTRACT

Neither the conservative nor the liberal understanding of obligations to past generations is entirely satisfactory. The conservative argument, which stresses the authority of past generations and the corresponding duties of future generations, may result in an exploitation of the natural imbalance among generations. The fact that the present generation can affect the future, but not the other way around, leaves future generations vulnerable to the unjust and self-serving actions of their ancestors. One example of this problem is that the United States is spending far more money than it receives in taxes. The result of this imbalance is that future generations will be saddled with a sizeable debt, which will inevitably reduce their ability to pursue public policies of their own choosing. While it is possible to argue that this debt is the future generation's "fair share" of the benefits they will receive from us, the better view is that future generations are not the principal beneficiaries of our expenditures, and in any event have no say in how these resources are being spent.

These arguments do not deny that the present generation has the authority to incur debt in the name of future generations. But they do suggest that future generations may be deprived of sovereignty over their own affairs if we maintain that they have a duty to fulfill all the promises and contracts their ancestors had the authority to make.

The liberal individualist understanding that future generations are not bound by the commitments of their ancestors avoids this difficulty, but only at the cost of eroding of the bonds which make justice among generations possible. To the extent that each generation is free to renounce the obligations incurred by their ancestors, and to the extent that they actually do so, long-term planning becomes practically impossible—to the detriment of future generations.

The answer to this dilemma, if any answer exists, lies in finding a middle ground between the conservative emphasis on authority and the liberal emphasis on consent. Such an understanding of the relations among generations would avoid exacerbating the natural imbalance among generations, while at the same time laying the groundwork for a more expansive understanding of the obligations among generations.

In this regard, two questions need to be addressed by any theory of obligations to past generations. The first is "What duties does the present generation owe to its ancestors?" The second is "What is the relationship between the obligations the present generation has to its descendants and the duties which future generations will have to their ancestors (including the present generation)?"

One way of answering the first question is to begin with the liberal argument that the commitments of a generation are ultimately based on the consent of that generation. This would mean that the commitments and promises of prior generations are binding on a generation only if it assents to those commitments and promises.

The liberal emphasis on consent can be balanced by the recognition that assent to the commitments of past generations is not to be given or withheld arbitrarily, but is itself subject to moral constraints. More specifically, the present generation has an obligation to assent to the arrangements undertaken by past generations (in the belief that those arrangements were intergenerationally just), provided that those arrangements are not unjust by their standards.

This understanding leaves important areas of discretion for future generations. Future generations are not obligated to fulfill commitments that were unjust by the standards of their ancestors. Thus, future generations of Americans may not be obligated to pay the interest on the debt they inherited, if they can establish that it was intergenerationally unjust, by our standards, to incur this debt. Future generations also would not be obligated to fulfill commitments that were just by our standards, but unjust by their standards. Of the two exemptions, the second is the more important since it is their own standards which will be most relevant and most apparent to future generations.

The right of each generation to judge for itself what actions are just and unjust is a corollary of the principle that all generations are morally equal. There is a natural imbalance in the powers of the generations which makes it possible for earlier generations to affect their descendants but not vice versa. However this imbalance in power does not imply the *moral* superiority of earlier generations to later generations. The moral equality among the generations is reflected in the right of each generation to judge the actions of its ancestors. Just as past generations had the authority (and indeed the obligation) to act towards future generations in ways that were just by *their* (past generations') standards, so future generations will have the right to judge the actions of their ancestors by their own standards.

But the right of the each generation to judge the actions of its ancestors does not give the present generation the license to do as it pleases. If past generations have acted in ways they had reason to believe were just to future generations, then their descendants are bound to honor the promises and contracts of their ancestors unless there is good reason to abrogate those promises and contracts. There is always a *presumption* that the good-faith commitments of past generations are binding on posterity. While this presumption can be overridden, it can be overridden only by a reasoned argument based on principles of justice.

An important question is what evidence and arguments are sufficient to justify abrogating promises or contracts made by previous generations. Must future generations be able to argue that the commitments of their ancestors were unjust before the presumption that they are bound by the promises of past generations may be overridden? Or is a lesser standard acceptable? May they argue, for example, that even though the intentions of their ancestors were just (by both their own and their ancestors' standards), the actual effects of the policies are unjust and, therefore, not morally binding?

It makes a great deal of difference which standard we adopt. No generation can foresee all possible effects of its actions. This suggests that it is inappropriate to judge the actions of previous generations based solely on the actual effects of those actions. On the other hand, it is difficult to give up the advantages of hindsight when judging the actions of previous generations. It is always open to future generations to argue that their ancestors *should have* anticipated the possibility that their actions would have unjust consequences. It is not always possible to determine when such an argument is appropriate and when it is inappropriate. But we do need to recognize that overriding the promises of past generations always has a cost, and that such an action ought not to be undertaken lightly. Moreover, the cost may well be greatest in those cases in which the cause is most marginal.

Among the costs of overriding the promises of past generations is the cost to those who have relied on those promises. If future generations default on bonds issued to finance the consumption of their ancestors, those who hold the bonds at the time of default will be hurt by that decision. Even if the deficits of past generations were intergenerationally unjust, those who invested in government bonds are not necessarily implicated in this injustice. Those who hold government securities at the time of the default may well be innocent victims. However, as James Buchanan has argued, the holders of risky investments are generally compensated for those risks by the higher interest rates that market forces assign to bonds which are perceived to be at risk of default. To the extent that the market has already "compensated" those who buy risky bonds through higher interest rates, the debtor's "sense of moral obligation towards holders of debt claims is attenuated," perhaps to the point that a partial default may be morally justifiable.[49]

The cost of overriding the promises of past generations may also fall on the descendants of those generations who break the promises of their ancestors. As Ernest Partridge has argued, when we break promises and contracts we undermine the institution of promises and contracts.[50] There are good rule utilitarian reasons for not overturning the just contract and promises of past generations. But the reasons for assenting to the just promises and contracts of our ancestors go beyond rule utilitarian considerations. There are important deontological principles which require us to honor the commitments of past generations, especially when those commitments are made for the benefit of posterity.

The most obvious grounds for holding that we are obligated to honor the contracts and fulfill the promises past generations made for our benefit is that to do otherwise violates our deepest sense of justice. To the extent that we have an obligation to act justly towards future generations, it may be necessary to make long-term commitments which will bind future generations. If we hold that a generation has the obligation to promote the welfare of its descendants, we cannot complain that it is wrong, *in principle*, for one generation to make commitments and contracts that bind its posterity. Moreover, to the extent that past generations were substantially correct in their view that the benefits to future generations of a specific long-term commitment would exceed the cost to future generations of that commitment, we cannot say that these commitments were wrong, *in fact*. The only ground we could have for refusing to acknowledge the validity of such

[49]James Buchanan, "The Ethics of Debt Default," 371.

[50]Ernest Partridge, "Posthumous Interests and Posthumous Respect," 259–261.

commitments is that honoring those commitments is inconvenient. Indeed, to the extent that a generation may already have received the benefits of the commitments which past generations made, paying for those benefits may well seem inconvenient! But there can be no principled ground for refusing to acknowledge the validity of commitments and contracts past generations made in our name and from which we have benefited. This does not mean that there may not be practical reasons for abrogating these commitments. A generation may lack the means to fulfill the obligations its ancestors made in its name. Nonetheless, to the extent that we have no principled ground for refusing to acknowledge the validity of the commitments past generations made for our benefit, we must recognize that it is unjust to do so. At a minimum, our obligations to past generations include keeping those promises and contracts which are intergenerationally just, and from which we have benefited.

VIII

Reconceptualizing Intergenerational Justice

"That which has saved us,
we cannot defame it,
by doing less than that which is our all."

Cecil Taylor, jazz artist,
speaking of Duke Ellington and other jazz greats

AN ADEQUATE THEORY of intergenerational justice must address four issues. The first is the nature and extent of our obligations to future persons. Are our obligations limited to not causing harm to future persons, or do we have a broader obligation to promote the welfare of our descendants? The second issue is the nature and extent of our responsibility for the existence of future persons. Do we have an affirmative duty to perpetuate the human species, or merely the "negative" duty to avoid taking actions which would cause the extinction of the species? The third issue is the nature and extent of our responsibility for the identity of future generations. To what extent are we responsible for the effects of our actions on the identity of future generations; and under what circumstances, if any, can we be said to benefit or harm future persons by adopting policies which "alter" their identity? The fourth and final issue is the nature and extent of our obligations to past generations. Does our inability to affect persons after their death absolve us of all obligations to the dead, or do some obligations persist across generations?

Judged by the standard of whether it addresses adequately these four fundamental issues, the dominant contemporary understanding, that intergenerational justice consists of not causing harm to future persons, falls short in several important respects. First, it represents too narrow a view of our obligations to future persons. To limit our obligations to not causing harm to future persons, as most contemporary approaches do, treats future persons as strangers to whom we have only minimal responsibilities. It is more appropriate to recognize distant future persons as members of our extended community, for whose welfare we have affirmative responsibilities.

Many contemporary understandings of intergenerational justice also fail to address adequately the issue of the perpetuation of the human species. To the extent that we define intergenerational justice as not causing harm to future persons, we fail to address such fundamental questions as whether we have an affirmative duty to perpetuate the human species or even whether it is *intergenerationally* unjust to prevent the existence of future generations. Despite the fact that questions such as nuclear war and genocide have been explored extensively in both the popular and academic literature, the narrow person-regarding ethics, which serves as the foundation for most academic theories of intergenerational justice, does not lend itself to defining nuclear war and genocide as *intergenerational* injustices.

We have also seen that a narrow understanding of person-affecting principles makes it difficult to address adequately the ethical significance of our power to affect the identity of future generations. The actions of the present generation can have a dramatic effect on the genetic makeup of our descendants. We know that some of the chemicals we use in our homes and places of work can cause genetic mutation. We can also affect the genetic makeup of future generations by encouraging certain groups within the population to procreate or by discouraging others from doing the same. In addition, we have begun to develop the technologies which will make it possible to manipulate the genetic identity of future persons. Because many of the actions that affect the genetic identity of future persons take place before those persons exist, it is difficult—or, as Parfit argues,[1] perhaps even impossible to—define the effects of our actions on the genetic identity of future generations in

---

[1]Parfit, *Reasons and Persons*, 351-379.

strictly person-affecting terms. Nonetheless, our power to affect the identity of future generations raises important ethical issues, at least some of which are properly understood to be questions of intergenerational justice.

Finally, our contemporary approaches to intergenerational justice encourage us to ignore the issue of obligations to past generations altogether. The understanding that justice is concerned with how our actions *affect* persons leads to a general skepticism towards the claim that we have any obligations to past generations. While a few thinkers do argue that our actions can harm the dead (or the interests of the dead), most contemporary writings on intergenerational justice have focused on questions other than obligations to past generations. Indeed, for many contemporary thinkers, the notion that we have obligations to past generations remains problematic, at best.

The fact that contemporary understandings of intergenerational justice are often too narrow to address a number of important issues has not prevented contemporary thinkers from raising some of these issues in other forms. For example, the ethical issues which arise from our power to determine whether future generations will exist have received considerable attention in the later half of the twentieth century. The danger that the human species may exterminate itself in a nuclear holocaust has forced us to confront the fact that the survival of our species depends on whether we find a way to avoid nuclear war. The absence of a theory of intergenerational justice capable of explaining clearly *why* nuclear war is *intergenerationally* unjust has not prevented most contemporary thinkers from condemning nuclear war as an immoral policy. Contemporary thinkers also have had little difficulty condemning genocide as an intergenerational injustice, even though a narrow person-regarding understanding of intergenerational justice makes it difficult to explain *why* genocide is intergenerationally unjust (and not unjust only to its contemporary victims). In these and other cases, our moral intuitions seem to be ahead of our moral theories.

The fact that we have been able to address a variety of intergenerational issues, despite the failings of our theories of intergenerational justice, does not mean that the weakness of these theories is without consequence. Quite the contrary, the inability to develop a more adequate theory of intergenerational justice may be implicated in the muted response of the world to the Cambodian, Bosnian, Rwandan, and other contemporary genocides; and it contributes to the confusion and uncertainty with which we react to the development of genetic engineering technology. There is a pressing need to develop a more adequate theory of intergenerational justice. Our capacity to shape the future has increased dramatically in this century, and continues to increase at an undiminished pace.[2] With this increased capacity comes a corresponding need to develop a more robust theory of intergenerational justice.

One area where this need is most apparent is in the field of biomedical ethics. We are on the threshold of developing new technologies which will allow us to manipulate the genetic characteristics of future generations. An important factor influencing the development of this technology is the potential for private corporations to profit from developments in this field. There exists the very real danger that unless the development and use of this technology is circumscribed by well-designed laws, the profit motive may overwhelm ethical considerations. The other side of the coin is that the fear of emerging genetic technologies may lead to excessive restrictions on the development of desirable therapeutic techniques. A coherent and persuasive understanding of intergenerational justice could contribute substantially to guiding our judgment and calming our unfounded fears of appropriate genetic engineering practices.

Before we realistically can expect legislators to adopt wise public policies, we need to develop a more adequate understanding of what constitutes the course of wisdom in these matters. An essential step in this process is to extend our contemporary understanding of

---

[2]For an argument that these changes require a transformation of our ethical theories, see Hans Jonas, "Technology and Responsibility: The Ethics of an Endangered Future," *Responsibilities to Future Generations*, ed. Ernest Partridge. (Buffalo, NY: Prometheus Books, 1980), 23–36.

intergenerational justice so that it addresses questions beyond the effects of our actions on the conditions in which future persons will live.[3]

The deficiencies of our contemporary understanding of intergenerational justice do not become visible only in the extreme cases of genocide and nuclear war, or in the "novel cases" of emerging technologies such as genetic engineering. These deficiencies also are apparent in more familiar surroundings such as the ethics of birth control and population planning. As we have seen, the contemporary understanding that intergenerational justice consists of avoiding actions which will harm future persons is open to several interpretations with respect to the question of population size.

The dominant contemporary understanding is that we have no obligation to procreate, but if we do procreate, we have an obligation not to permit the size of the human population to exceed the capacity of future generations to feed, clothe and shelter themselves. According to this understanding, our obligations to posterity are conditional in nature. We have no obligation to bring future generations into existence, but *if* we do procreate, *then* we (may) have obligations to those individuals who will exist and to their descendants. While this understanding is not incoherent, it does not conform to the moral intuition of many persons that the perpetuation of the human species is ethically desirable or even obligatory. The lack of agreement between contemporary ethical theories and widely shared moral intuition represents a significant

[3]There is a growing body of literature on these questions. Of particular interest are studies of bio-medical ethics and the law, including D. Suzuki, and P. Kundtson, *Genetics: The Clash Between the New Genetics and Human Values*, (Cambridge, Mass.: Harvard University Press, 1989); E. Joshua Rosenkranz, "Custom Kids and the Moral Duty to Genetically Engineer Our Children," *High Technology Law Journal* 2(1) (1987), 1–53; Aubrey Milunsky, and George J. Annas, ed., *Genetics and the Law II*, (New York: Plenum Press, 1979); *Genetics and the Law III*, (New York: Plenum Press, 1984); Cynthia J. Dreeman, "Designer Genes: An Ethical Perspective on Genetic Manipulation," *Rutgers Computer & Technology Law Journal* 15(447) (1989); John C. Fletcher, and Dorothy C. Wertz, "Ethics, Law and Medical Genetics: After the Human Genome is Mapped," *Emory Law Journal* 39(747) (1990); and Gerald Coleman, "Note: Genetic Engineering: Should Parents Be Allowed to Design Their Children?," *Howard Law Journal* 34(153) (1991).

weakness in our secular ethical theories. This weakness is accentuated by the existence of competing understandings of our duties with respect to procreation. One such competing understanding is that of the Catholic Church, whose teachings hold that the use "artificial" means of contraception is a sinful interference with the natural reproductive process.

The strengths and weaknesses of the Catholic Church's understanding are the opposite of those of the contemporary secular view. The Catholic Church's position conforms to the common view that procreation is desirable, but departs from the moral intuition of many persons that a concern for the welfare of future generations may require that we limit the size of the human population.[4] It is likely that the appeal of the secular view, that justice to future generations requires that we limit population size, would be greater if the secular understanding also recognized that the existence of future generations is a morally desirable end, in itself, rather than a *morally neutral precondition* for our having obligations to future generations.

In general, we can characterize the deficiencies of contemporary understandings of intergenerational justice as being of one of two types. The first is the failure to recognize the full extent of our responsibility for how we shape the future. The second is the failure to understand how the different aspects of intergenerational justice are interconnected.

Our capacity to shape the future is not limited to affecting the conditions in which future persons will live. Therefore, our

---

[4] A 1994 report on population by the Pontifical Academy of Sciences, a lay panel of the Catholic Church, concluded that "'There is a need to contain births in order to avoid creating the insoluble problems that could arise if we were to renounce our responsibilities to future generations.' Increases in life-span and advances in medical care 'have made it unthinkable to sustain indefinitely a birth rate that notably exceeds the level of two children per couple—in other words the requirement to guarantee the future of humanity.'" Alan Cowell goes on to say that "Pope John Paul II was reportedly infuriated by the report, which emerged just as the Vatican was intensifying its campaign against several proposals to be discussed [at the population conference] in Cairo. Alan Cowell, "Scientists Associated With Vatican Call for Population Curbs," *New York Times* June 16, 1994: A6.

understanding of intergenerational justice ought not to be limited to a concern with how our actions affect the conditions of those who actually will exist in the future. Because our actions determine whether future persons will exist, how many persons there will be, as well as the identity of the future population, our theories of intergenerational justice ought to address our responsibilities for ensuring the continued existence of the human species, for implementing an ethical population policy, as well as for how our actions affect the identity of future generations. While the survival of the human species is unquestionably a precondition for having responsibility to future persons, the survival of the species is also an important ethical issue in its own right. The value we place on the continued existence of humanity is a fundamental ethical choice which serves to define our other ethical values, as well as the "moral worth" of our species.

For similar reasons, we ought to be concerned with how we use our power to alter the identity of future generations. Because our actions can affect the identity of future generations, our understanding of intergenerational justice ought to be broad enough to guide our actions in this area, as well. The alternative to extending our theories of intergenerational justice is to accept that our power to reengineer the human species is unconstrained by moral principles. In light of the unacceptability of this alternative, the case for extending our contemporary understanding of intergenerational justice becomes compelling.

Contemporary understandings of intergenerational justice also suffer from the failure to recognize how the different aspects of intergenerational justice are interconnected. Examples of the interconnection of the components of intergenerational justice abound. For example, it is possible to act to improve the welfare of future persons by limiting the size of the population, by acting to improve the infrastructure of the planet (so that a larger population can be accommodated) or, at least theoretically, by altering the genetic characteristics of the population to make future persons better suited to life on an overpopulated planet. Any of these "solutions" may increase the happiness of future persons. Which solution (or combination of solutions) is preferable depends not only on the effects of each policy on those who actually will live in the future, but also on other ethical constraints on intergenerational actions, such as we have examined in this book. A sound theory of intergenerational justice ought to be able to provide guidance for policy makers and critics alike. In too many areas of public policy, our contemporary approaches to intergenerational justice fail to provide more than minimal guidance to policy makers and their critics, alike.

THE NEED FOR A MORE COMPLETE THEORY OF INTERGENERATIONAL JUSTICE

At times the approach to intergenerational justice which my analysis suggests seems like a four-headed creature. It includes a concern with the welfare of future persons, with the perpetuation of the human species and of sub-groups within the species, with the ethics of altering the identity of future generations, and with our obligations to past generations. The obvious question is whether it is possible to integrate these four components into a unified theory which includes not only a concern with these four components of intergenerational justice, but also a concern with justice to contemporaries.

The traditional approaches to intergenerational justice were very much of this sort. The Hebraic understanding of intergenerational justice focused on the obligation to act justly in an intergenerational community. Their understanding of justice included not only a love of and respect for the patriarchs of the past, but also a concern with how the actions of each generation affected the welfare of future members of the community.

A return to the theories of the ancient Hebrews or the ancient Greeks is not possible, and we would not consider it desirable, even if it were possible. A return is not possible because the traditional understandings of intergenerational justice grew out of a world and a world view we no longer share. An essential part of the ancient understanding of intergenerational justice was the belief that human beings occupied a special place in a divinely created cosmos and the belief that God punishes (or the gods punish) those who transgress those limits. Few contemporary thinkers understand the world in these terms.

The fact that we no longer accept the world view of our ancestors does not mean we are incapable of reconciling and integrating a concern for justice to contemporaries with a concern for justice to past and future generations. However, while it is possible for us to develop a unified understanding of justice, there are significant obstacles to doing so. One way we might seek to develop a unified theory would be to view human relationships as existing in a matrix that extends in time and space and even species.[5] According to this understanding, justice consists of meeting our obligations to other beings in the matrix. Our greatest obligations are to those closest to us in the matrix. Specifically, our greatest obligations are owed to contemporaries who are members of our immediate community, with whom we share mutual dependencies and common understandings. As we move away from our immediate community in time, space or species, our obligations diminish. Thus, we have fewer obligations to those who live on other continents than to our fellow Americans;[6] we have fewer obligations to our distant descendants than to our immediate descendants; and we have fewer obligations to other species than to our fellow human beings.[7]

---

[5]I am indebted to Professor Edwin Fogelman for the suggestion that we may understand both justice to distant persons and justice to future generations in terms of the problem of justice on a time–space matrix.

[6] In a world made smaller by air travel, distance has a different meaning than it once did. Traditionally, persons who were remote in distance were also likely to be person of different lineage and different cultures. While there remains some relationship between physical distance and culture, this relationship is more attenuated than it once was. Thus, my brother may live half a world away from me, but my bonds to him may be stronger than my bonds to the person who lives next door.

[7]To say that we have fewer obligations to other species than to our fellow human beings *does not* imply that it is just for us to hunt other species to the point of extinction.

Although a unified theory of justice would certainly incorporate many of the elements of this approach, the understanding that our obligations vary with our proximity to others in a time/space/species matrix is not a substitute for a unified theory of justice. One deficiency of the matrix approach is that the relationship among generations remote in time is not identical to, and cannot be reduced to, that of peoples remote in distance. As I argued in Chapter III, future generations stand in a different relationship to us than do persons distant in space. Even though both may seem like strangers to us, the fact that the cultures of future generations will develop out of contemporary cultures means that future generations may stand in a more intimate relationship to us than do contemporaries distant to us in space. Even more important is the fact that our actions shape the future in ways that have no *intra*generational parallel. For example, our actions determine the size and identity of future generations, but not those of the present generation. Consequently, a theory of intergenerational justice must address questions different from those we ordinarily address in theories of (intragenerational) justice.

The most significant of the obstacles to developing a unified theory of justice, however, is our commitment to ethical theories based on person-affecting principles. As I have argued throughout this book, many important questions of intergenerational justice cannot be addressed easily, if at all, in the language of person-affecting principles. For example, we cannot explain why nuclear war and genocide are *intergenerationally* unjust, nor can we resolve many of the difficult questions raised by genetic engineering without moving beyond person-affecting principles.

Unfortunately, person-affecting principles remain the foundation of most contemporary approaches to justice and intergenerational justice. Most contemporary thinkers approach intergenerational justice as a special case of justice to contemporaries, seeking to extend understandings rooted in person-affecting principles in an effort to address the special circumstances which exist when our actions involve remote generations. Because person-regarding ethics are now well established in Western thought, it is "natural" for us to approach intergenerational justice in this manner. However, even though such an approach may be "natural," it is not adequate. This approach inevitably yields too narrow an understanding of intergenerational justice.

None of this makes it impossible for us to develop a unified theory of justice. However, to the extent that most contemporary approaches to justice are wedded to person-affecting principles, these conclusions do suggest that such a unified theory is most unlikely to take the form of an extension of contemporary approaches of justice. If anything, the opposite is more likely to be true: we would likely be more successful if we approached justice to contemporaries as a special case of intergenerational justice rather than the other way around.

What makes this alternate approach attractive is the fact that our actions affect future generations in more and different ways than they affect proximate generations. Another way of saying this is that *inter*generational actions have greater "degrees of freedom" than *intra*generational actions. It would seem to follow that if we can develop an adequate theory of intergenerational justice, it might be a relatively simple matter to apply that theory to the more circumscribed moral universe of contemporaneous action.

This suggests that the task of developing a unified theory of justice may require a radical rethinking of our ethical theories, such as occurred in the field of physics in the early twentieth century when Einstein's theory of relativity replaced the Newtonian understanding of time and space.[8] To say the very least, the task of reconstructing our theories of justice in intergenerational terms is a major undertaking with no

[8]For a discussion of the dimensions of such a restructuring of our ethical theories, see Derek Parfit, "Energy Policy and the Further Future: The Identity Problem," *Energy and the Future*, ed. Douglas MacLean and Peter G. Brown. (Totowa, NJ: Rowman and Littlefield, 1983), 178–179. See also Hans Jonas, "Technology and Responsibility: The Ethics of an Endangered Future," *Responsibilities to Future Generations*, ed. Ernest Partridge. (Buffalo, NY: Prometheus Books, 1980), 23–36.

guarantee of success. Nonetheless, it is appropriate to begin this journey with a few small steps in what I believe is the right direction.

TOWARDS A RECONSTRUCTED UNDERSTANDING OF INTERGENERATIONAL JUSTICE

A good place to begin the task of reconstructing a theory of intergenerational justice is by recognizing that there is a close relationship between how we act towards future generations and whether future generations will have obligations to us. If the present generation acts justly and to the benefit of our descendants, our descendants are likely to value the traditions they have inherited from us and to recognize an obligation to fulfill the intergenerational commitments we have made in their name. By contrast, if we act selfishly and without consideration for how our actions will affect our distant descendants, those who inherit the planet from us are unlikely to recognize a moral obligation to preserve the institutions and practices they have inherited, or to honor our commitments.

Although engendering in our descendants a sense of obligation to their ancestors is not an end in itself, acting in a manner that future generations will have something to be grateful for is! Our goal should not be to constrain the choices of future generations; nor should we seek to "coerce" future generations into preserving the institutions and practices they will inherit. On the contrary, we ought to condemn as intergenerationally unjust policies such as the deficit spending of the Reagan and Bush years, which was undertaken with the knowledge that increasing the national debt would serve to make it all but impossible for future generations to restore social welfare by depriving those generations of the discretionary resources needed to do so. Instead, our goal should be to pass on to future generations traditions, institutions, and practices that *they* are likely to find worthy of preservation.

It is true, of course, that it can make no difference *to us* whether distant future generations recognize an obligation to preserve our institutions and honor our commitments. But this does not mean it will make no difference *to future generations and their descendants* whether they find the institutions and commitments they will inherit worthy of preservation. By attempting to act justly towards future generations, and by occasionally succeeding in doing so, we do more than provide material benefits to future generations; we also establish the institutional and cultural foundations for a just intergenerational community. This should be our most important legacy to posterity.

An essential feature of a just intergenerational community is that remote generations recognize obligations to one another. This is most obvious in the relationship between a generation and its descendants. All but a very few contemporary thinkers recognize that we have some responsibility for how our actions will affect distant future generations and some obligation to act in their interests. What is much less widely accepted is that the present generation also has obligations to its ancestors. If past generations have sacrificed for our benefit—and if we have actually benefited from their actions—the most fundamental principles of comity require that we be grateful for those benefits. Even as committed an individualist as Thomas Hobbes recognized that gratitude for benefits received is an important human obligation. Indeed, Hobbes described gratitude as the fourth law of nature, placing it immediately after justice:

> As justice dependeth on antecedent covenant; so does GRATITUDE depend on antecedent grace; that is to say, antecedent free gift; and is the fourth law of nature; which may be conceived in this form, *that a man which receiveth benefit from another of mere grace, endeavour that he which giveth it, have no reasonable cause to repent him of his good will.*[9]

The ingratitude of distant descendants cannot, of course, cause past generations to repent their good will towards them; but this fact does not absolve later generations of the obligation to be grateful for the benefits they have received from their ancestors.

---

[9]Thomas Hobbes, *Leviathan*, ed. Michael Oakeshott (New York: Collier Books, 1962), 118.

The other side of the obligation to be grateful for the benefits we have received is that we should be prepared to criticize the failures of our ancestors or even to condemn their injustices. If the actions of our ancestors have proved to be harmful to us, or if past generations have acted without regard to their obligations to posterity, criticism or even condemnation is appropriate. Here, too, it cannot make any actual difference to past generations whether we condemn their actions as unjust. But the possibility that future generations *might* condemn the actions of their ancestors can have a beneficial effect on a people concerned with the "judgment of history."[10] Moreover, a willingness to criticize the failures of past generations is an essential part of living in an intergenerational community. Not only does such criticism serve as a cathartic, it also reminds us that our descendants will be affected by our actions, just as we have been affected by the actions of past generations.

While the questions of gratitude to and criticism of past generations present few conceptual problems, the question of repaying the debts we owe to our ancestors presents more difficulties. Because our actions cannot affect the dead, it is impossible for us to reciprocate directly either the benefits or harms we have received from past generations. On the other hand, *successive reciprocity* can exist among remote generations.[11] This is to say, the debts we owe our ancestors can be paid to our descendants, who in turn can repay to their descendants the debt they owe us.[12] In this manner, a truly intergenerational community can develop in which the just actions of past generations bind future

---

[10]It is notable, however, that an almost obsessive concern with how history would view him did not prevent the late President Richard Nixon from obstructing justice or from committing what amount to war crimes in Southeast Asia.

[11]For a discussion of the applicability of successive reciprocity to questions of intergenerational justice, see John Rawls, *A Theory of Justice*, (Cambridge, MA: Harvard University Press, 1971), 284–293.

[12]It is noteworthy that only the benefits we have received from past generations may be repaid justly to future generations. For it would be most unjust of us to harm future generations as "repayment" for the harm past generations might have caused us.

generations not to the status quo, but to a tradition of intergenerationally just action.

The notion that the existence of an intergenerational community is closely linked to intergenerational justice is not new. A concern with acting justly in an intergenerational community informed the writings of both Plato and the ancient Hebrews. Edmund Burke, too, saw an intergenerational contract or partnership "between those who are living, those who are dead, and those who are to be born"[13] as the cornerstone of just intergenerational community. Although we may disagree with the way Burke formulated his intergenerational contract, we should recognize that Burke was correct to emphasize the intergenerational nature of civilization.

However, we must go beyond merely recognizing the links between the existence of an intergenerational community and intergenerational justice. We must also recognize that the existence of an intergenerational community is essential to achieving intergenerational justice. Consequently, we should acknowledge an affirmative obligation to establish an intergenerational community where one does not already exist, and to preserving and strengthening that community where it already exists.

The recognition that we have an obligation to establish or sustain an intergenerational community does not, by itself, determine the extent of our obligations to future generations, nor does it provide us with much information about the nature of this intergenerational community. How we should define our intergenerational community is properly the subject of public debate, in the same way that how we define the "social contract" among contemporaries is an essential part of the political debate in every nation that aspires to popular sovereignty. The importance of recognizing an obligation to establish or sustain an intergenerational community is not that it provides us with a detailed blue print for achieving intergenerational justice, but that it provides us

[13]Edmund Burke, *Reflections on the Revolution in France*, (New York: Bobbs-Merrill, 1955), 110.

with a framework by which we can understand, evaluate, and develop just intergenerational policies.

Our power to shape the future is too great to permit us to shirk or minimize our responsibility for how our actions shape the future by treating future generations as strangers to whom we have only the minimal obligation not to cause harm. If we are to act morally in the intergenerational sphere, we must accept that future generations are members of our moral community, and we of theirs. If we suspect that future generations are unlikely to recognize us as members of their moral community, we should treat this as a condemnation of our actions and not as granting us license to ignore their needs and interests. The truest test of the morality of our intergenerational actions is future generations' recognition of those actions as just, and their recognition of us as their moral ancestors.

Future generations are unlikely to recognize many of our actions as just if we continue along our present course. Quite clearly, part of the problem is that we are not acting justly even by our own minimal standards. We know full well that the burdens of the pollution of our environment, the rapid consumption of nonrenewable resources, and overpopulation will fall (unjustly) on future generations. But even if we address these issues, our actions would fall short of intergenerational justice in several important respects. We must still address such essential questions as the ethics of genetic engineering and the shape and direction of our industrial civilization. At a minimum, for example, our consumption of the Earth's nonrenewable resources obligates us to seek to develop alternative, renewable energy resources to replace the nonrenewable resources we have depleted.

The task of addressing these and other fundamental questions of intergenerational justice will not be easy. As I have argued throughout this work, the individualistic understanding which lies at the base of our moral theories prevents us from addressing adequately many important questions of intergenerational justice. Only by shifting to a more relational understanding of intergenerational justice can we begin to make significant progress in overcoming these deficiencies. But shifting to a relational understanding at best only points the way. The most serious underlying problem is that we do not now have an intergenerational community, at least we do not have one in the United States. We do not see ourselves in our own future.

One reason we do not now have an intergenerational generational community is that we do not have a true community among contemporaries in the United States. Although it is only one manifestation of our lack of community, perhaps the worst legacy of the Reagan-Bush era in American politics was the abandonment of the concept of the common good in favor of a view of politics which stresses the individual good of those who are capable of winning the economic competition. This glorification of individual economic achievement aggravated the racial and ethnic tensions within our multi-ethnic and multi-cultural society. To the extent that many people do not identify the future majority population of this country as their posterity (especially because it may not look like them), it becomes difficult to establish a sense of common welfare, without which no community, let alone an intergenerational community, can exist. The passage of Proposition 187 in California (in 1994), which prohibits the state from providing education or health care benefits to children of illegal immigrants, represents another manifestation of this process, as indeed does the so-called "Contract with America," which would further dismantle the social contract established by the New Deal.

Any civilization which has an impact on its environment more enduring than its own life span must be concerned with the effects of its actions on future generations. Unless the present generation takes into consideration and gives due weight to the interests of future generations when framing its public policies, its actions will not be just to its descendants. While the obligations of future generations to their ancestors are more subtle, they are hardly less important. Unless future generations acknowledge, respect, and build upon the just intergenerational commitments of their ancestors, their actions may undermine their own ability to act justly towards their descendants.

Little stock will be placed in the commitments of a generation which abrogates unjustly the commitments of their ancestors.

As we saw in Chapter II, a just intergenerational community cannot be founded on a true contract among generations, because future generations cannot give their consent to the terms of a contract until they come into existence. A better model by which to understand intergenerational relations is that of a covenant, in which commitments made by one generation are agreed to and assumed voluntarily (or rejected) by its descendants. The present generation can do no more than offer a covenant to future generations in belief that its terms are just and beneficial to posterity, and in the hope that this covenant will be acceptable to future generations. Future generations, for their part, may either renew the covenant their ancestors made, modify it, or reject it entirely in favor of charting their own path. If they renew the covenant, their choice is voluntary, insofar they had the option of rejecting it. However, there is no contradiction in recognizing that the decisions of future generations are constrained by moral obligations and characterizing those decisions as voluntary, at least to the extent that those decisions are determined by the moral principles of future generations themselves and not by necessity.

Of course, it is not always possible for one generation to adopt policies which leave future generations constrained only by moral obligations. Renunciation of the commitments and institutional arrangements inherited from prior generations always comes at a cost, and some policies are reversible only at high cost to future generations. Inherent in any intergenerational policy is the risk that future generations will not share the judgments of their ancestors. When the present generation chooses to pursue a path from which it is difficult, costly, or perhaps even impossible to turn back, it has a special obligation to consider the interests of future generations. Under such circumstances, the present generation is making a choice not only for itself, but also for its distant descendants who, almost by definition, will live in a world very different from that of their ancestors. It adds nothing to the morality of such decisions to speak of an intergenerational "contract" between the present generation and its descendants.

For those who are uncomfortable with the concept of a covenant, an alternative approach is to understand our intergenerational obligations in Kantian terms. More specifically, we can define our intergenerational obligations in terms of the following categorical imperative: *We ought to act towards future generations in such a way that future generations are most likely to choose voluntarily to honor the commitments and build upon the moral traditions of their ancestors.*[14] If our actions towards future generations are just, if we give due consideration to their interests and act towards them as towards members of our own community, future generations are likely (though not certain) to feel gratitude for our actions and an obligation to preserve the institutions and traditions which have served them well. On the other hand, if we ignore the interests of future generations and instead treat them as strangers to whom we owe little or nothing, future generations are likely to give us our due by reviling us and abandoning our institutions as unworthy of preservation.

If a community is a set of persons bound together by common understandings and mutual obligations, intergenerational justice requires that we seek to establish and preserve a truly intergenerational community. We do this by taking into consideration the interests of future generations when framing public policies, just as we take into consideration, or should take into consideration, the interests of contemporary members of our own community when framing present policies. While there is no guarantee that future generations will in fact see us as members of *their* intergenerational community, it is far more likely that they will do so if we treat them as members of *our* community to whom we have obligations and for whose welfare we bear some

---

[14]For a general discussion of the concept of a categorical imperative, see Immanuel Kant's "Introduction to the Metaphysic of Morals and Preface to the Metaphysic Elements of Ethics," *Kant's Critique of Practical Reason*. trans. Thomas Kingsmill Abbott. 6th ed, (London: Longmans, Green and Co., 1923), 265–322.

responsibility, than if we treat them as strangers for whom we have no obligations but the obligation not to plan.[15]

Indeed, for us to treat future generations as strangers for whom we bear no moral responsibility and to whom we have no obligations can be seen as the paragon of intergenerational injustice. For this view of posterity misrepresents our actual relationship to future generations and our responsibility for how our actions will affect the future. Future generations are neither our subordinates whom we are justified in treating as means to our own ends, nor strangers towards whom our only responsibility is not to cause harm. Rather, they are members of our extended community who will feel the effects of our actions. This does not mean that there is always an affirmative obligation to seek to improve the conditions in which future persons will live.[16] It is intergenerationally just to tread lightly on the Earth, limiting the effects of our actions to our remote generations as much as possible, and leaving the Earth in the essentially same condition we found it.[17] Societies we call "primitive" have done so for tens of thousands of years.

On the other hand, the time is long past when we have treaded lightly on the Earth. The effects of many of our actions will be felt by persons living centuries from now. Under these circumstances there is no moral alternative to taking the interests of future persons into account when framing our public policies. Indeed, so profound are the effects of some of our actions (such as the decision to produce energy by nuclear fission) that they are almost certain to outlast our own community and be felt by generations who, in fact, *will be* strangers to us. To the extent that some present policies can be so characterized, we must conclude that these policies are intergenerational unjust.

The question of population size also fits quite comfortably into the understanding that we have an obligation to act to create an

---

[15]See Golding, "Obligations to Future Generations," 69–70.

[16]John Rawls, *A Theory of Justice*, 284-293.

[17]In this sense John Rawls's argument that there is an obligation to save for future generations so that they may enjoy greater liberty than we, is not a valid principle of intergenerational justice. John Rawls, *A Theory of Justice*, 284–293.

intergenerational community. For it is quite clear that the size of the community can affect the quality of life in the community. Consequently, our efforts to create a just intergenerational community must incorporate our understanding of what constitutes a desirable population policy.

What is striking about the question of population size is that there is no single answer to what size population is most desirable. It is coherent to say that, other things being equal, a larger population is preferable to a smaller one. It is even coherent to hold that some sacrifice in material well-being is desirable (though presumably not mandatory) in order to accommodate a larger population. On the other hand, it is also quite clear that a preference for a larger population can be taken to extremes. If population size is not limited, it can exceed the carrying capacity of the land, leading to disease and mass starvation. Thus, it is consistent to hold that while it is morally desirable to procreate, in many circumstances it is preferable to limit population size in order to raise the standard of living of a nation. This, too, can be taken to extremes, as I attempted to demonstrate with the story of the "Ultimate Yuppies."

Between the extremes of unlimited population growth and the solipsism of the Ultimate Yuppies lie a large number of approaches each of which can be defended as desirable. What constitutes the optimal solution is an open question on which people may disagree. Indeed, the attempt to answer this question is a part of the process of defining who we are as a people. As we gain some control over the reproductive process, as individuals and as a society, the determination of the "optimal" population size is increasingly a part of the process of self-definition for an intergenerational community.

The question of identity raises some of the most difficult and dangerous questions of intergenerational justice. The greatest outrages of the twentieth century have occurred in the name of determining the identity of future generations of a community. Yet, from the fact that a power can be abused, it does not follow that a power can never be used ethically. Genetic engineering technology, for example, may allow us to eliminate inherited diseases and improve the lives of our descendants. A strong case can be made that such changes in the "identity" of the future population would be ethically desirable.

On the other hand, genetic engineering raises many different ethical questions. As in the case of population size, there is no single correct answer to what constitutes a genetic defect which ought to be "engineered" out of the population. The danger of imposing the perverse and narrow understanding of one generation on its descendants is undoubtedly greater in the case of identity than in the case of population size, since changes in genetic identity are harder to reverse and are often more focused than changes in population size.

It is not clear that the categorical imperative I have suggested would be sufficient to guide actions in this difficult area. The underlying assumption of this imperative is that future generations are most likely to honor commitments and build upon moral traditions which have been of genuine benefit to them. In the cases of such genetic diseases as hemophilia and Tay-Sachs, we can feel relatively confident that future generations would find their elimination through gene therapy or other techniques, a genuine benefit. On the other hand, it would not be unjust or unreasonable for a people to reject the use of genetic engineering altogether, as ethically too dangerous for humans to engage in wisely. Certainly, it is not foreordained that a people could not rise to the challenge of using the power of genetic technology wisely and for the benefit of its descendants. However, it is also plausible to argue that our species lacks the self control to make wise and safe use of the powers that genetic engineering is unleashing, just as our species seems to lack the self control to make wise use of the power of nuclear energy. On the whole I find the arguments of the skeptics more persuasive, though I am convinced that, at least in principle, genetic engineering can be undertaken ethically.

One issue which is not addressed as fully as one might wish by the Kantian approach I have outlined is the possibility that a people will act in the name of "ethnic purity" to prevent disfavored groups within the population from procreating. It is possible, for example, that the Serbian descendants of the perpetrators of genocide in Bosnia will "honor the commitments and build upon the traditions of their ancestors." If this turns out to be the case, it would not make the actions of the Bosnian Serbs any less immoral. If the actions future generations honor are unjust and the traditions upon which they build are immoral, the willingness of future generations to honor those actions and build upon those traditions justifies neither the actions of the ancestors nor the those of their descendants.

The categorical imperative I have proposed must be qualified by the recognition that it is subject to two interpretations, one salutary, the other perverse. Kant notes a similar dualism in his work, "Perpetual Peace." There, Kant contrasts two forms of perpetual peace, the first represented by the graveyard, is achieved by force and war, the second, the peace of a world federation of free states, guarantees the rights of nations, thereby making war unnecessary.[18] The immorality of the first form of perpetual peace, and the moral desirability of the second was clear for Kant. "...[F]rom the throne of its moral legislative power, reason absolutely condemns war as a means of determining the right and makes seeking the state of peace a matter of unmitigated duty."[19] Let us hope, at least, that we will have no difficulty differentiating between the two interpretations of the intergenerational imperative when the choice between them is presented in stark form, as it often is.

While a theory of intergenerational justice based on a Kantian categorical imperative falls short of the goal of a truly unified theory of justice, it does lend itself more than most other approaches to addressing coherently the four central issues essential to an adequate theory of intergenerational justice. This approach directly links and gives recognition to the obligations of one generation to its descendants and the obligations of those descendants to their ancestors. It also makes clear, as do few other approaches to intergenerational justice, that our

---

[18]Immanuel Kant, "To Perpetual Peace: A Philosophical Sketch," *Perpetual Peace and Other Essays*, tr. Ted Humphrey. (Indianapolis: Hackett Publishing Co., 1983), 107–143.

[19]Ibid., 116.

responsibility is not limited to a concern with the effects of our actions on future persons who stand as strangers to us, but envisions a broader responsibility for how our actions shape the future of our human community—including such questions as the existence, size, and identity of the future population.

IX

CONCLUSION

ALTHOUGH THIS BOOK HAS FOCUSED on the conceptual difficulties surrounding intergenerational justice, it seems appropriate to conclude by looking more broadly at the prospects of achieving something approximating intergenerational justice. For in the end, it is not enough to understand how we ought to act, we must actually act that way!

Conceptual clarity is undoubtedly an important first step towards achieving this goal. Without a coherent and adequate understanding of intergenerational justice, we are almost certain to misapprehend the nature of the challenges we face and ignore fundamental problems. We need to understand our relationship to other generations in a way which makes clear the important questions of intergenerational justice and which makes it natural to address these questions in the course of debate over public policy.

A critical element in any adequate understanding of intergenerational justice is the recognition that human existence is inherently intergenerational. Our civilization is built on the achievements and the failures of past generations, and our actions, in turn, affect the lives of our descendants. Unless we understand ourselves to be a part of an intergenerational community which extends from past to future, we are unlikely to devote sufficient attention or resources to policies which shape that community and its future.

However, it is not sufficient to develop a better understanding or theory of intergenerational justice. In any modern political system in which public opinion plays an important role, popular acceptance of that understanding is also essential. Unless people come to understand the importance of intergenerational justice, not merely intellectually, but viscerally, the prospects of implementing intergenerationally just public policies are poor, at best.[1]

In this area we seem to have far to go. Our society remains committed to a philosophical individualism which makes it difficult to demand collective sacrifice for the sake of our children, let alone for the sake of remote future generations. Indeed, political careers have been built on opposition to all manner of tax increases, while other careers have been cut short by support for even modest tax increases designed to reduce the debt future generations will inherit. It is difficult to imagine a more self-absorbed time in our history or a period more destructive of the rights of future generations than the 1980s in the United States.

While I am not generally optimistic that the type of conceptual revolution I have been describing will take place in the near future, there are at least some signs of movement towards a greater concern with intergenerational justice. One such sign is that the generation now coming into adulthood seems to have a more intuitive understanding than their parents of many of the issues critical to intergenerational justice, among these are the need for recycling and other more ecologically sound public policies. The concept of intergenerational justice has also found a place in popular political parlance, in recent years. President Clinton's 1992 inaugural address, for example, gave prominent play to the question of intergenerational justice. Concern for the effects of present policies on future generations has even been voiced in the halls of Congress. Indeed, the concept of intergenerational justice has had an easier time gaining acceptance in popular political discourse than it has at the meetings of learned political science associations.[2]

---

[1] Tyler Cowen, and Derek Parfit are undoubtedly correct in arguing that the extent of our obligations to future generations is a moral question and not a political question which should be decided democratically. Nonetheless, intergenerational justice will only be achieved, if it will be achieved at all, through the political process. Tyler Cowen, and Derek Parfit, "Against the Social Discount Rate," *Justice between Age Groups and Generations*, ed. Peter Laslett and James S. Fishkin. (New Haven: Yale University Press, 1992), 144–161.

[2] There have been very few convention panels on intergenerational justice at either national or regional political science association meetings in the United States.

But intergenerational justice cannot be achieved by speech and good will alone. If we are to implement intergenerationally just public policies, we must also have the capacity to determine the course of wise and just intergenerational action. This requires, among other things, that we be able to predict and control future population growth, that we study the likely effects of different courses of action on posterity, and that we develop a better understanding of the needs of future generations. But there is also a need for more traditional historical knowledge. To create, or more accurately recreate[3] an intergenerational community takes time. An essential feature of an intergenerational community is its institutional memory. The successes and failures of past policies must be remembered and future policies shaped accordingly. One generation can only plant the seeds of a just intergenerational community by acting towards future generations in a manner which makes it more likely that future generations will seek to perpetuate and build upon the traditions they inherit. However, a truly intergenerational community cannot be said to exist until future generations have chosen to preserve and build upon the works of their ancestors. Only future generations can determine whether we will have succeeded in recreating an intergenerational community.

GUIDING ACTIONS WHICH SHAPE THE FUTURE

An essential task for those concerned with intergenerational justice is to move from normative theory to prudential guidance.[4] Prudential guidance requires, among other things, that we enunciate standards by

---

On the other hand, philosophical associations have been well ahead of political scientists in recognizing the importance of intergenerational justice. Most of the journal articles on intergenerational justice have been published in philosophy journals; and philosophical association meetings have had panels on obligations to future generations for several years.

[3]I say recreate because, as I have argued, traditional societies saw themselves as intergenerational communities.

[4]See Neal Riemer, *The Revival of Democratic Theory*, (New York: Appleton-Century-Crofts, 1962), and *The Future of the Democratic Revolution*, (New York: Praeger, 1984), for discussions of prudential guidance.

which to judge policies and actions which honor the past and shape the future.

Although no set of standards is beyond criticism, a reasonable starting point is the conservationist principle that we must pass on to future generations a world no worse than the one we inherited. The conservationist principle conforms well to the contemporary understanding that intergenerational justice consists of avoiding causing harm to future generations. As such, it is capable of attracting broad support within our society. At the same time, conservationism represents a base on which we can build, rather than a limitation on our obligations to future generations.

Conservationism does not require that we preserve all that we have inherited from our ancestors, regardless of its worth. If it did, we would be little more than the servants of our ancestors. Even Edmund Burke did not counsel so slavish an understanding of intergenerational justice. We have the right, and even the obligation, to evaluate the world we have inherited from our ancestors and to modify that world according to *our* best judgment of what is good and what is bad in our inheritance. But if we have this right and this obligation, future generations also have the right to judge us, based on how we have exercised our discretion. If we choose wisely, future generations are likely to view us as ancestors worthy of emulation. On the other hand, if we make unwise or selfish choices, future generations are likely to revile our actions.

The authority to exercise discretion in evaluating our inheritance and in reshaping the world does not imply that we have the right to use up our (and future generations') inheritance, without replenishing it. No generation has such a right. Moreover, because time and nature erode all human artifacts, future generations will inherit a world as good as the one we inherited only if we are productive. Unless we ourselves are prepared to return to a subsistence economy, we must work to maintain and build upon what we have inherited from our ancestors. In fact, we have not been content merely to stand still; we have continued to transform the world through our life activity. In the process, we not only build, we also destroy. When we build cities, we remove land from agricultural use. When we rebuild cities, we tear down old buildings and replace them with new ones.

It can be difficult to judge the value of our contributions to the inheritance of future generations. Because this is the case, it is important to articulate standards by which we may measure the quality of the world we inherited and that of the world we will pass on to future generations. Not everything we inherit is desirable, and not every change we make is an improvement.

There is no certain yardstick against which to measure the quality of our contribution to civilization. But at least it is possible to suggest a perspective with which to judge our own actions and those of our ancestors. The changes we make should be judged for how they are likely to affect remote future members of our community; for only by treating future generations as members of our community do we make it possible for future generations actually *to be* members of that community, who will choose to honor our commitments and build on our moral traditions.

It should be acknowledged that the principle that we ought to treat future generations as members of our community provides only a very general standard by which to judge actions that affect future generations. Because different cultures have different traditions and different understandings of the good, they are likely to judge the same intergenerational actions differently. But this fact does not render the concept of intergenerational justice incoherent. It merely acknowledges that all standards of justice—intragenerational as well as intergenerational—arise within cultural communities. It is within those communities that the essential details of a theory of intergenerational justice must be articulated; and it is within these communities that it becomes meaningful to ask whether our actions make it more or less likely that future generations will choose to honor commitments and to build upon moral traditions.

THE PROBLEM OF NON-RENEWABLE ENERGY RESOURCES

Although this book has focused on the conceptual problems associated with the concept of intergenerational justice, and with how these problems might be resolved, it seems appropriate to conclude by addressing at least one of practical problems of intergenerational justice we now face. Specifically, it is worth examining how the approach to intergenerational justice I have suggested might inform our thinking on the problem of non-renewable energy resources.

Some of the most difficult moral dilemmas and some of the greatest opportunities for just intergenerational action arise from the use of scarce and non-renewable resources. The use of non-renewable energy resources poses a classical dilemma of intergenerational distributive justice: how to allocate finite resources among an indefinite number of future persons. Many of the thinkers who have examined the problem of intergenerationally just energy use have argued that a just energy policy requires that we seek to ensure that future generations will have energy opportunities at least equal to those of the present generation.[5] This would require the present generation to do one or more of the following: (1) explore for previously undiscovered deposits of oil and natural gas (and other non-renewable energy resources), (2) develop the technology needed to extract resources that we are unable to extract at present, (3) improve the efficiency of our use of energy, (4) develop new sources of renewable and non-renewable energy.

Any of these four policies would be more just than our present policy of consuming the non-renewable resources of the planet with little regard for the interests of future generations. However, I would argue that only a policy of developing renewable energy resources is

---

[5]See for example, Brian Barry, "Intergenerational Justice in Energy Policy," *Energy and the Future*, ed. Douglas MacLean and Peter G. Brown. (Totowa, NJ: Rowman and Littlefield, 1983), 23, and Talbot Page, "Intergenerational Justice as Opportunity," *Energy and the Future*, ed. Douglas MacLean and Peter G. Brown. (Totowa, NJ: Rowman and Littlefield, 1983), 56.

truly intergenerationally just. To see why this is the case, we need to examine, at least briefly, the problem of the intergenerationally just use of energy resources.

At present, the energy policy of the United States is characterized by its reliance on non-renewable energy resources such as petroleum, natural gas, coal and non-breeder reactor nuclear fission. Renewable resources, such as active solar, wind, and geothermal energy represent a small fraction of the total energy generation capacity of this nation.

There are two grounds for arguing that our consumption of *non-renewable* energy resources is unjust to future generations. The first is that our consumption of non-renewable resources may have adverse consequences for future generations if it leaves them without the resources necessary to sustain a modern civilization. Because our urban civilization is built around the availability of abundant energy resources, there will be a significant decline in living standards as those resources becomes more scarce and more expensive. One needs only a little imagination to understand the suffering which might result from running low on energy resources. As we run low on energy, the cost of transportation, food, and shelter will rise dramatically, leaving only the wealthy able to afford to travel or to maintain current living standards. It will be increasingly difficult for the poor to afford to heat their homes in northern climates. Many families will find it necessary to share living quarters in order to afford utility bills. With increasing disparities in wealth will come an increased risk of civil disorder.

The second reason for arguing that our consumption of energy resources is unjust to future generations is deontological. If we start with the moral postulate that the resources of the planet belong in common to all generations,[6] it follows that one intergenerationally just

6 This moral postulate is clearly rooted in a rights-based theory which has its origin in the writings of John Locke. While rights-based approaches have their critics, they also have their defenders. For a defense of rights-based approaches to intergenerational justice see, for example, Ernest Partridge, "On the Rights of Future Generations," *Upstream/Downstream: Issues in Environmental Ethics*, ed. Donald Scherer. (Philadelphia: Temple University Press, 1990), 40–66. For a fuller discussion of the application of Lockean principles to the question of the

energy policy would be to share the available energy resources equally with all future generations. However, we cannot determine what each generation's share of the planet's resources is, because we cannot know how many generations there will be. Nor is this the most serious problem. If we assume that humanity will survive for many generations, rationing the non-renewable resources of this planet among a large number of generations would so diminish the value of each generation's share of those resources as to render those resources nearly worthless.

If we accept these calculations, it is possible to make the contrarian argument that we do not harm future generations in any significant way when we consume the non-renewable resources of this planet. If each generation's share of those resources is so small that it cannot be exploited effectively by any one generation, the "value" of the Earth's non-renewable resources to each generation is its value in the natural state. While, in principle, a generation which consumes non-renewable resources is obligated to compensate future generations for the lost value of those resources, in practice the natural resources of this planet are almost free for the taking, because the value of each generation's share of the non-renewable resources is minimal.

This, of course, is the logic of all exploiters throughout human history. What is wrong with this argument is that there is no reason to determine the value of the Earth's non-renewable energy resources based on their value to an undeveloped society rather than their value to a developed society. On the contrary, there is every reason to hold that the value of non-renewable resources ought to be appraised based on the use to which they are actually put by the society which consumes those resources.

To place a higher and more honest value on non-renewable energy resources does not, by itself, move us any closer to solving the basic dilemma posed by non-renewable energy resources, namely, that we can

---

intergenerationally just use of non-renewable resources see Clark Wolf, "Contemporary Property Rights, Lockean Provisos, and the Interests of Future Generations," *Ethics* (Forthcoming).

either render those resources virtually worthless by taking no more than "our fair share," or we can consume non-renewable resources in sufficient quantity to produce great benefits in the short term, while depriving future generations of the opportunities those resources represent. These, and other arguments, have led some people to conclude that industrial civilization itself is unjust.[7] Quite clearly, this is a minority opinion; but it is easy to understand the logical appeal of this argument. If civilization is nothing more than a temporary phenomenon, doomed to fail catastrophically (like Charlie's operation in *Flowers for Algernon*[8]), then it is not unreasonable to conclude that we would have been better off never having gone down this road at all.

But is it the case that civilization is doomed to fail catastrophically? Is it doomed to run out of energy resources? While we can never guarantee against the catastrophic failure of civilization, the risk that such a failure will result from the scarcity of energy resources can be minimized if we convert our civilization from dependence on non-renewable energy resources to dependence on renewable energy resources. Such a policy would go a long way towards placing civilization on a more solid foundation, at least with respect to the availability of the energy resources essential to its survival.

Not only is a policy of developing renewable energy resources desirable for its consequences, it is ethically mandatory for other reasons as well. From the belief in the moral equality of all persons of all generations, it is possible to conclude that the non-renewable resources of this planet belong in common to all generations. Because these resources are non-renewable, any generation which consumes those resources incurs a debt to future generations. This debt can be diminished by developing technology which permits the remaining non-renewable resources to be exploited more efficiently or by developing new sources of non-renewable energy. But the debt to future generations can never be repaid merely by expanding the (non-

---

[7]See for example, Daniel Quinn, *Ishmael*, (New York: Bantam Books, 1992).

[8]Daniel Keyes, *Flowers for Algernon*, (New York: Bantam Books, 1970).

renewable) resource opportunities for the next generation.[9] Inevitably, some future generation will find itself holding the bag, as it were, unable to make the technological improvements needed to leave as much and as good for the next generation. It is possible to repay our debt to posterity only by expanding the resource opportunities of all future generations. It is likely that this can be accomplished only by beginning immediately to convert from dependence on non-renewable energy resources to dependence on renewable energy resources.

The existence of relatively abundant and inexpensive non-renewable energy resources represents a window of opportunity for civilization. Sophisticated renewable energy technologies could not have been developed prior to the technological revolution which took place and is continuing to take place in the late twentieth century. It is entirely possible that the development of such technology will become impossible, once again, if we wait until non-renewable energy resources are nearly depleted before undertaking the development of alternate energy technologies. Only by using the opportunity which relatively abundant and inexpensive non-renewable energy resources provides, to place civilization on a stable foundation based on renewable energy technology, can future generations be compensated for the non-renewable energy resources we have consumed. If we pursue such a policy, we would be acting towards future generations in a manner which makes it more likely that they will choose to honor our commitments and build on our moral traditions. Intergenerational justice requires nothing less.

---

[9]Brian Barry argues that our obligation to future generations can be met if each generation leaves as much and as good energy resources for future generations. Barry holds that this condition can be met by a generation devoting resources to any of several projects, including energy exploration, increasing the efficiency with which energy is used, or improving the technology by which energy resources are produced, Brian Barry, "Intergenerational Justice in Energy Policy," *Energy and the Future*, ed. Douglas MacLean and Peter G. Brown. (Totowa, NJ: Rowman and Littlefield, 1983), 15–30.

BIBLIOGRAPHY

Adams, Robert M. "Existence, Self-Interest, and the Problem of Evil." *Nous* 13 (1979): 53–65.

Ahrens, John. *Preparing For the Future: An Essay on the Rights of Future Generations*. Bowling Green: Bowling Green Social Philosophical Center, 1983.

Anglin, William. "In Defense of the Potentiality Principle." *Obligations to Future Generations*. Eds. R. I. Sikora and Brian Barry. Philadelphia: Temple University Press, 1978. 31–37.

__________. "The Repugnant Conclusion." *The Canadian Journal of Philosophy* 7 (1977): 745–754.

Asahi, Joji I. "Intergenerational Justice and Economic Growth." Ph.D. Thesis. University of Kansas, 1981.

Auerbach, Bruce E. "Intergenerational Justice and the Prophetic Tradition." *Annual Meeting of the American Political Science Association*. New Orleans, LA, 1985.

__________. "Standing for Future Generations." *Pennsylvania Political Science Association Annual Meeting* . Harrisburg, PA, 1992.

Austin, John L. "Other Minds." *Logic and Language*. Ed. Anthony Flew. Oxford: Basil Blackwell, 1959. 123–158.

__________. "Performative Utterances." *Philosophical Papers*. Ed. John L. Austin. London: Oxford University Press, 1961. 220–339.

__________. "A Plea for Excuses." *Philosophical Papers*. Ed. John L. Austin. London: Oxford University Press, 1961. 123–152.

Baier, Annette. "The Rights of Past and Future Persons." *Responsibilities to Future Generations*. Ed. Ernest Partridge. Buffalo, NY: Prometheus Books, 1980. 171–183.

Ball, Terence. "The Incoherence of Intergenerational Justice." *Inquiry* 28 (1985): 321–337.

__________. *Transforming Political Discourse*. New York: Basil Blackwell, 1988.

Bandman, Bertram. "Do Future Generations Have the Right to Breathe Clean Air?" *Political Theory* 10, 1 (1982): 95–102.

Barry, Brian. "Circumstances of Justice and Future Generations." *Obligations to Future Generations*. Eds. R. I. Sikora and Brian Barry. Philadelphia: Temple University Press, 1978. 204–248.

__________. "Intergenerational Justice in Energy Policy." *Energy and the Future*. Eds. Douglas MacLean and Peter G. Brown. Totowa, NJ: Rowman and Littlefield, 1983. 15–30.

__________. "Justice Between Generations." *Law, Morality and Society*. Eds. P. M. S. Hacker and Joseph Raz. Oxford: Clarendon Press, 1977. 268–284.

__________. *The Liberal Theory of Justice*. Oxford: Clarendon Press, 1973.

__________. "Rawls on Average and Total Utility: A Comment." *Philosophical Studies* 31 (1977): 317–325.

Bayles, Michael D. "Famine or Food: Sacrificing for Future or Present Generations." *Responsibilities to Future Generations*. Ed. Ernest Partridge. Buffalo, NY: Prometheus Books, 1980. 239–245.

__________. *Morality and Population Policy*. Alabama: University of Alabama Press, 1980.

Bennett, Jonathan. "On Maximizing Happiness." *Obligations to Future Generations*. Eds. R. I. Sikora and Brian Barry. Philadelphia: Temple University Press, 1978. 61–73.

Bentham, Jeremy. *An Introduction to the Principles of Morals and Legislation*. New York: Methuen, 1982.

Berry, Thomas. "Towards Tomorrow's Mankind: Reflection on the Earth Process and Its Newly Emerging Phase." *Journal of Dharma* 3, January-March (1978): 53–66.

Bickham, Stephen. "Future Generations and Contemporary Ethical Theory." *The Journal of Value Inquiry* 15 (1981): 169–177.

Braaten, Carl E. "Caring for the Future: Where Ethics and Ecology Meet." *Zygon* 9, December (1974): 311–322.

Braybrooke, David. "The Social Contract and Property Rights across the Generations." *Justice between Age Groups and Generations*. Eds. Peter Laslett and James S. Fishkin. New Haven: Yale University Press, 1992. 107–126.

Buber, Martin. *I and Thou*. Trans. Walter Kaufmann. New York: Charles Scribner's Sons, 1970.

Buchanan, James M. "The Ethics of Debt Default." *Deficits*. Eds. James M. Buchanan, Charles K. Rowley and Robert D. Tollison. New York: Basil Blackwell, 1986. 361–373.

__________. *Public Principles of Public Debt*. Homewood: Irwin, 1958.

Buchanan, James M., and Richard Wagner. *Democrary in Deficit*. New York: Academic Press, 1977.

Burke, Edmund. *Reflections on the Revolution in France*. New York: Bobbs-Merrill, 1955.

Callahan, Daniel. "What Obligations Do We Have to Future Generations?" *Responsibilities to Future Generations.* Ed. Ernest Partridge. Buffalo, NY: Prometheus Books, 1980. 73–85.

Callahan, Joan C. "On Harming the Dead." *Ethics* 97, January (1987): 341–352.

Cameron, J. R. "Do Future Generations Matter?" *Ethics and the Environmental Responsibility.* Ed. Nigel Dower. Aldershot: Avenbury, 1989. 57–78.

Care, Norman S. *On Sharing Fate.* Philadelphia: Temple University Press, 1987.

Cochran, Thomas B., and David L. Brodde. "Conflicting Views on a Neutrality Criterion for Radiactive Waste Management." *Energy and the Future.* Eds. Douglas MacLean and Peter G. Brown. Totowa, NJ: Rowman and Littlefield, 1983. 110–128.

Cohen, Avner, and Steven Lee, eds. *Nuclear Weapons and the Future of Humanity.* Totowa: Rowman & Allanheld, 1986.

Coleman, Gerald. "Note: Genetic Engineering: Should Parents Be Allowed to Design Their Children?" *Howard Law Journal* 34, 153 (1991).

Condit, Steven Huntley. "Survival or Community: A Critique of Garrett Hardin's 'Lifeboat Ethics' Based upon Paul Tillich's Ontological Theology." Ph.D. Thesis. Rice University, 1983.

Cowen, Tyler. "Consequentialism Implies a Zero Rate of Intergenerational Discount." *Justice between Age Groups and Generations.* Eds. Peter Laslett and James S. Fishkin. New Haven: Yale University Press, 1992. 162–168.

Cowen, Tyler, and Derek Parfit. "Against the Social Discount Rate." *Justice between Age Groups and Generations*. Eds. Peter Laslett and James S. Fishkin. New Haven: Yale University Press, 1992. 144–161.

Dagger, Richard. "Rights." *Political Innovation and Conceptual Change*. Eds. Terence Ball, James Farr and Russell L. Hanson. Cambridge: Cambridge University Press, 1989. 292–308.

Dasgupta, Partha. "Savings and Fertility: Ethical Issues." *Philosophy and Public Affairs* 23(2), Spring (1994): 99–127.

Dasgupta, Partha, and John Broome. "Discounting the Future." *Philosophy and Public Affairs* 23(2), Spring (1994): 128-156.

Davies, Kim. "The Conception of Possible People." *Cogito* 2, September (1984): 53–60.

Davis, Richard S. "The Morally Relevant Future." *Ecological Consciousness*. Ed. Robert C. Schultz. Washington: Washington University Press of America, 1981. 371–389.

De George, Richard T. "The Environment, Rights, and Future Generations." *Responsibilities to Future Generations*. Ed. Ernest Partridge. Buffalo, NY: Prometheus Books, 1980. 157–165.

De-Shalit, A. "Bargaining with the Not-Yet-Born: Gauthier's Contractarian Theory of Inter-Generational Justice and Its Limitations." *International Journal of Moral and Social Studies* 5(3), Autumn (1990): 221–234.

Delattre, Edwin. "Rights, Responsibilities, and Future Persons." *Ethics* 82, April (1972): 254–258.

Derr, Thomas Sieger. "The Obligation to the Future." *Responsibilities to Future Generations*. Ed. Ernest Partridge. Buffalo, NY: Prometheus Books, 1980. 37–44.

Dipert, Randall R. "Reflections on the Rights of Future Generations." *Rights and Regulation*. Ed. Tibor Machan. Cambridge: Ballinger, 1983. 203–216.

Dooley, Patrick K. "The Ambiguity of Environmental Ethics: Duty or Heroism." *Philosophy Today* 30, Spring (1986): 48–57.

Dreeman, Cynthia J. "Designer Genes: An Ethical Perspective on Genetic Manipulation." *Rutgers Computer & Technology Law Journal* 15, 447 (1989).

Durkheim, Emile. *Suicide: A Study in Sociology*. Trans. George Simpson. New York: Free Press, 1951.

Dworkin, Ronald. *Taking Rights Seriously*. Cambridge Massachusetts: Harvard University Press, 1977.

Dyck, Arthur. "An Analysis of Population Policy Alternatives." *Monist* 60 (1977): 29–46.

Earle, William. "The Future of Civilization?" *Philosophy Forum (Dekalb)* 13, June (1973): 209–231.

Elliot, Robert. "Future Generations, Locke's Proviso and Libertarian Justice." *Journal of Applied Philosophy* 3, October (1986): 217–227.

Epstein, Richard A. "Justice across the Generations." *Justice between Age Groups and Generations*. Eds. Peter Laslett and James S. Fishkin. New Haven: Yale University Press, 1992. 84–106.

Feinberg, Joel. "The Child's Right to an Open Future." *Whose Child*. Ed. William Aiken. Totowa: Littlefield, 1980. 124–153.

__________. "Harm and Self-Interest." *Law, Morality and Society: Essays in Honour of H. L. A. Hart*. Eds. P. M. S. Hacker and J. Raz. Oxford: Clarendon Press, 1977. 284–308.

__________. *Harm to Others.* Vol. 1. New York: Oxford University Press, 1984.

__________. "The Rights of Animals and Unborn Generations." *Responsibilities to Future Generations.* Ed. Ernest Partridge. Buffalo, NY: Prometheus Press, 1980. 139–150.

Fishkin, James S. "The Limits of Intergenerational Justice." *Justice between Age Groups and Generations.* Eds. Peter Laslett and James S. Fishkin. New Haven: Yale University Press, 1992. 62–83.

Fletcher, John C., and Dorothy C. Wertz. "Ethics, Law and Medical Genetics: After the Human Genome is Mapped." *Emory Law Journal* 39, 747 (1990).

Freedman, Benjamin. "On the Rights of the Voiceless." *The Journal of Medicine and Philosophy* 3, September (1978): 196–210.

Fullinwider, Robert K. "Hare on Rawls: A Worry About Possible Persons." *Philosophical Studies* 29, March (1976): 199–205.

Galston, William A. *Justice and the Human Good.* Chicago: University of Chicago Press, 1980.

George, Rolf. "Who Should Bear the Cost of Children?" *Public Affairs Quarterly* 1, January (1987): 1–42.

George, William P. "Regarding Future Neighbours: Thomas Aquinas and Concern for Posterity." *Heythrop Journal* 33(3), July (1992): 283–306.

Glover, Jonathan. "Future People, Disability, and Screening." *Justice between Age Groups and Generations.* Eds. Peter Laslett and James S. Fishkin. New Haven: Yale University Press, 1992. 127–143.

Golding, Martin P. "Ethical Issues in Biological Engineering." *UCLA Law Review* 15, 267 (1968): 443–479.

__________. "Obligations to Future Generations." *Responsibilities to Future Generations.* Ed. Ernest Partridge. Buffalo, NY: Prometheus Books, 1980. 61–72.

__________. "Towards a Theory of Human Rights." *The Monist* 52, 4 (1968): 521–549.

Golding, Martin P., and Naomi Holtzman Golding. "Ethical and Value Issues in Population Limitation and Distribution in the United States." *Vanderbuilt Law Review* 24 (1971): 495–523.

Gotesky, Rubin, and Ervin Laszlo, eds. *Human Dignity: This Century and the Next.* New York: Gordon & Breach, 1970.

Govier, Trudy. "What Should We Do About Future People?" *American Philosophical Quarterly* 16, April (1979): 105–113.

Gower, Barry S. "What Do We Owe to Future Generations?" *The Environment in Question: Ethics and Global Issues.* Ed. David E. Cooper. New York: Routledge, 1992.

Green, Ronald M. "Intergenerational Distributive Justice and Environmental Responsibility." *Responsibilities to Future Generations.* Ed. Ernest Partridge. Buffalo, NY: Prometheus Books, 1980. 91–101.

__________. "Justice and the Claims of Future Generations." *Justice and Health Care.* Ed. Earl E. Shelp. Dordrecht, Holland: D. Reidel, 1981. 193–211.

Grossman, Peter Z., and E.S. Cassedy. "Cost-Benefit Analysis of Nuclear Waste Disposal: Accounting for Safeguards." *Science, Technology, and Human Values* 10, Fall (1985): 47–54.

Gunn, Alastair S. "Engineering Ethics and Hazardous Waste Management: Why Should We Care About Future Generations?" *Research in Philosophy and Technology* 12 (1992): 135–146.

Hanser, Matthew. "Harming Future People." *Philosophy and Public Affairs* 19(1), Winter (1990): 47–70.

Harblin, Thomas Devaney. "Mine or Garden: Values and the Environment—Possible Sources of Change in the Next Hundred Years." *Zygon* 12, June (1977): 134–150.

Hardin, Garett. "Who Cares for Posterity." *Responsibilities to Future Generations*. Ed. Ernest Partridge. Buffalo, NY: Prometheus Books, 1980. 221–234.

Hare, R. M. "Abortion and the Golden Rule." *Philosophy and Public Affairs* 4(3), Spring (1975): 212.

Hartmann, Nicolai. *Ethics*. Vol. Vol. 2. Atlantic Highlands, NJ: Humanities Press, 1932.

__________. "Love of the Remote." *Responsibilities to Future Generations*. Ed. Ernest Partridge. Buffalo, NY: Prometheus Books, 1980. 305–308.

Hartshorne, Charles. "The Ethics of Contributionism." *Responsibilities to Future Generations*. Ed. Ernest Partridge. Buffalo, NY: Prometheus Books, 1980. 103–107.

Hauerwas, Stanley. "The Moral Limits of Population." *Thought* 49, September (1974): 237–249.

Heilbroner, Robert L. "What Has Posterity Ever Done for Me?" *Responsibilities to Future Generations*. Ed. Ernest Partridge. Buffalo, NY: Prometheus Books, 1980. 191–194.

Heyd, David. "Procreation and Value: Can Ethics Deal with Futurity Problems?" *Philosophia (Israel)* 18, July (1988): 151–170.

Hobbes, Thomas. *Leviathan*. Ed. Michael Oakeshott. New York: Collier Books, 1962.

Horowitz, George. *The Spirit of Jewish Law*. New York: Central Book Co., 1973.

Houck, Margaret McKenna. "Derek Parfit and Obligations to Future Generations." Ph.D. Thesis. Georgetown University, 1988.

Hubin, D. Clayton. "Justice and Future Generations." *Philosophy and Public Affairs* 6, Fall (1976): 70–83.

Hudson, James L. "Rights and the Further Future." *Philosophical Studies* 49, January (1986): 99–107.

Hurka, Thomas. "Value and Population Size." *Ethics* 93, April (1983): 496–507.

Jecker, Nancy S. "The Extended Nonidentity Problem." *Auslegung* 14, Summer (1988): 185–196.

__________. "Obligations to Future Generations: A Critical Study of Teleological and Deontological Moral Theories." Ph.D. Thesis. University of Washington, 1986.

Jonas, Hans. "Technology and Responsibility: The Ethics of an Endangered Future." *Responsibilities to Future Generations*. Ed. Ernest Partridge. Buffalo, NY: Prometheus Books, 1980. 23–36.

Jones, Hardy. "Genetic Endowment and Obligations to Future Generations." *Responsibilities to Future Generations*. Ed. Ernest Partridge. Buffalo, NY: Prometheus Books, 1980. 247–259.

Kant, Immanuel. "Critical Examination of Practical Reason." *Kant's Critique of Practical Reason*. Trans. Thomas Kingsmill Abbott. 6th ed. London: Longmans, Green and Co., 1923. 87–262.

__________. *Foundations of the Metaphysics of Morals*. Trans. Lewis White Beck. New York: Bobbs-Merrill, 1959.

__________ . "Introduction to the Metaphysic of Morals and Preface to the Metaphysic Elements of Ethics." *Kant's Critique of Practical Reason*. Trans. Thomas Kingsmill Abbott. 6th ed. London: Longmans, Green and Co., 1923. 265–322.

__________ . "To Perpetual Peace: A Philosophical Sketch." *Perpetual Peace and Other Essays*. Ed. tr. Ted Humphrey. Indianapolis: Hackett Publishing Co., 1983. 107–143.

Katz, Eric. "The Moral Justification for Environmentalism." Ph.D. Thesis. Boston University Graduate School, 1983.

Kavka, Gregory S. "The Futurity Problem." *Responsibilities to Future Generations*. Ed. Ernest Partridge. Buffalo, NY: Prometheus Books, 1980. 109–122.

__________ . "The Paradox of Future Individuals." *Philosophy and Public Affairs* 11, Spring (1982): 93–112.

__________ . "Rawls on Average and Total Utility." *Philosophical Studies* 27 (1975): 237–253.

Keyes, Daniel. *Flowers for Algernon*. New York: Bantam Books, 1970.

Kline, George L. "'Past', 'Present', and 'Future' as Categorical Terms, and the 'Fallacy of the Actual Future.'" *Review of Metaphysics* 40, December (1986): 215–235.

Kneese, Allen V., Shaul Ben-David, and William D. Schulze. "The Ethical Foundations of Benefit-Cost Analysis." *Energy and the Future*. Eds. Douglas MacLean and Peter G. Brown. Totowa, NJ: Rowman and Littlefield, 1983. 59–74.

Landsberg, Helmut. "Energy Use and the Atmosphere." *Energy and the Future*. Eds. Douglas MacLean and Peter G. Brown. Totowa, NJ: Rowman and Littlefield, 1983. 91–109

Lappé, Marc. "Ethical Issues in Manipulating the Human Germ Line." *Journal of Medicine and Philosophy* 16(6), December (1991): 621–639.

Laslett, Peter. "The Conversation Between the Generations." *Philosophy, Politics and Society*. Eds. Peter Laslett and James Fishkin. New Haven: Yale University Press, 1979. 36–56. 5th Series.

_________. "Is There a Generational Contract?" *Justice between Age Groups and Generations*. Eds. Peter Laslett and James S. Fishkin. New Haven: Yale University Press, 1992. 24–47.

Laslett, Peter, and James S. Fishkin. "Introduction: Processional Justice." *Justice between Age Groups and Generations*. Eds. Peter Laslett and James S. Fishkin. New Haven: Yale University Press, 1992. 1–23.

Laslett, Peter, and James S. Fishkin, eds. *Justice between Age Groups and Generations*. New Haven: Yale University Press, 1992. *Philosophy, Politics and Society*. 6th Series.

Laszlo, Ervin. "Goals for Global Society." *Main Currents* 31, May-June (1975): 138–144.

Levenbook, Barbara Baum. "Harming Someone after His Death." *Ethics* 94 (1984): 407–419.

_________. "Harming the Dead, Once Again." *Ethics* 96, October (1985): 162–164.

Lifton, Robert J., and Eric Markusen. *The Genocidal Mentality*. New York: Basic Books, 1990.

Locke, Don. "The Parfit Population Problem." *Philosophy* 62, April (1987): 131–157.

Mackenzie, Michael. "A Note on Motivation and Future Generations." *Environmental Ethics* 7, Spring (1985): 63–70.

Macklin, Ruth. "Can Future Generations Correctly Be Said to Have Rights?" *Responsibilities to Future Generations.* Ed. Ernest Partridge. Buffalo, NY: Prometheus Books, 1980. 151–155.

MacLean, Douglas. "A Moral Requirement for Energy Policies." *Energy and the Future.* Eds. Douglas MacLean and Peter G. Brown. Totowa, NJ: Rowman and Littlefield, 1983. 180–197.

MacLean, Douglas, and Peter G. Brown, eds. *Energy and the Future.* Totowa, NJ: Rowman and Littlefield, 1983.

Marquis, Don. "Harming the Dead." *Ethics* 96, October (1985): 159–161.

Mattlage, Alan. "Response to Jecker's 'The Extended Nonidentity Problem.'" *Auslegung* 14, Summer (1988): 197–200.

Mayo, Bernard. "Traces and Portents." *Philosophical Quarterly* 18, October (1968): 289–298.

McMahan, Jefferson. "Nuclear Deterrence and Future Generations." *Nuclear Weapons and the Future of Humanity.* Ed. Avner Cohen. Totowa: Rowman & Allanheld, 1986. 319–339.

Mill, John Stuart. "On Liberty." *Essential Works of John Stuart Mill.* Ed. Max Lerner. New York: Bantam Books, 1961. 249–360.

Milunsky, Aubrey, and George J. Annas, eds. *Genetics and the Law II.* New York: Plenum Press, 1979.

__________. *Genetics and the Law III.* New York: Plenum Press, 1984.

Mueller, Dennis C. "Intergenerational Justice and the Social Discount Rate." *Theory and Decision* 5 (1974): 263–273.

Muller, Herbert J. "Modern Civilization and Human Survival." *Philosophy Forum (Dekalb)* 12, September (1972): 1–26.

Narveson, Jan. "Future People and Us." *Obligations to Future Generations.* Eds. R. I. Sikora and Brian Barry. Philadelphia: Temple University Press, 1978. 38–60.

__________. *Morality and Utility.* Baltimore: John Hopkins Press, 1967.

__________. "Semantics, Future Generations, and the Abortion Problem: Comments on a Fallacious Case Against the Morality of Abortion." *Social Theory and Practice* 3, Fall (1974): 461–485.

__________. "Utilitarianism and Future Generations." *Mind* 76 (1967): 62–72.

Ng, Yew-Kwang. "What Should We Do About Future Generations? Impossibility of Parfit's Theory X." *Economics and Philosophy* 5(2), October (1989): 235–253.

Nielson, Kai. "The Enforcement of Morality and Future Generations." *Philosophia (Israel)* 3, October (1973): 443–448.

Norton, Bryan G. "Environmental Ethics and the Rights of Future Generations." *Environmental Ethics* 4, Winter (1982): 319–338.

Nozick, Robert. *Philosophical Explanations.* Cambridge, Mass.: Harvard University Press, 1981.

O'Neill, John. "Future Generations: Present Harms." *Philosophy* 68(263), January (1993): 35–51.

Odum, Howard T. "The Ecosystem, Energy, and Human Values." *Zygon* 12, June (1977): 109–133.

Page, Talbot. "Intergenerational Justice as Opportunity." *Energy and the Future*. Eds. Douglas MacLean and Peter G. Brown. Totowa, NJ: Rowman and Littlefield, 1983. 38–58.

Parfit, Derek. "Comments." *Ethics* 96, July (1986): 832–872.

__________. "Energy Policy and the Further Future: The Identity Problem." *Energy and the Future*. Eds. Douglas MacLean and Peter G. Brown. Totowa, NJ: Rowman and Littlefield, 1983. 166–179.

__________. "Energy Policy and the Further Future: The Social Discount Rate." *Energy and the Future*. Eds. Douglas MacLean and Peter G. Brown. Totowa, NJ: Rowman and Littlefield, 1983. 31–37.

__________. "Future Generations: Further Problems." *Philosophy and Public Affairs* 11, Spring (1982): 113–172.

__________. "On Doing the Best for Our Children." *Ethics and Population*. Ed. Michael D. Bayles. Cambridge, MA: Schenkman, 1976.

__________. *Reasons and Persons*. Oxford: Clarendon Press, 1984.

__________. "A Reply to Sterba." *Philosophy and Public Affairs* 16, Spring (1987): 193–194.

Partridge, Ernest. "Environmental Ethics: Obstacles and Opportunities." *Ecological Consciousness*. Ed. Robert C. Schultz. Washington: Washington University Press of America, 1981. 325–349.

__________. "On the Rights of Future Generations." *Upstream/Downstream: Issues in Environmental Ethics*. Ed. Donald Scherer. Philadelphia: Temple University Press, 1990. 40–66.

__________. "Posthumous Interest and Posthumous Respect." *Ethics* 91 (1981): 243–264.

__________. "Rawls and the Duty to Posterity." Ph.D. Thesis. University of Utah, 1976.

__________, ed. *Responsibilities to Future Generations: Environmental Ethics*. Buffalo, NY: Prometheus Books, 1980.

__________. "Why Care About The Future." *Responsibilities to Future Generations*. Ed. Ernest Partridge. Buffalo, NY: Prometheus Books, 1980. 203–220.

Passmore, John. *Man's Responsibility for Nature*. New York: Charles Srcibner's Sons, 1974.

Peterson, E. Wesley F. "Time Preference, the Environment and the Interests of Future Generations." *Journal of Agricultural and Environmental Ethics* 6, 2 (1993): 107–126.

Pitcher, George. "The Misfortunes of the Dead." *American Philosophical Quarterly* 21 (1984): 183–188.

Pitkin, Hanna Fenichel. *Wittgenstein and Justice*. Berkeley: University of California Press, 1972.

Pletcher, Galen K. "The Rights of Future Generations." *Responsibilities to Future Generations*. Ed. Ernest Partridge. Buffalo, NY: Prometheus Books, 1980. 167–170.

Quinn, Daniel. *Ishmael.* New York: Bantam Books, 1992.

Rawls, John. *A Theory of Justice.* Cambridge, Massachusetts: Harvard University Press, 1971.

Regan, Tom, ed. *Earthbound: New Introductory Essays in Environmental Ethics*. New York: Random House, 1984.

Reichenbach, Bruce R. "On Obligations to Future Generations." *Public Affairs Quarterly* 6(2), April (1992): 207–225.

Rescher, Nicholas. *Distributive Justice*. Indianapolis: Bobbs-Merrill, 1966.

Richards, David A. J. "Contractarian Theory, Intergenerational Justice, and Energy Policy." *Energy and the Future*. Ed. Douglas MacLean and Peter G. Brown. Totowa, NJ: Rowman and Littlefield, 1983. 131–150.

Riemer, Neal. *The Future of the Democratic Revolution*. New York: Praeger, 1984.

__________. *The Revival of Democratic Theory*. New York: Appleton-Century-Crofts, 1962.

Riepe, Dale. "The Civilization of the Future: Ideals and Possibility." *Philosophy Forum* 13, June (1973): 179–208.

Rissmiller, Kent James. "Law, Morality and Intergenerational Justice." Ph.D. Thesis. Syracuse University, 1986.

Rolston III, Holmes. "The River of Life: Past, Present, and Future." *Responsibilities to Future Generations*. Ed. Ernest Partridge. Buffalo, NY: Prometheus Books, 1980. 123–132.

Rosenkranz, E. Joshua. "Custom Kids and the Moral Duty to Genetically Engineer Our Children." *High Technology Law Journal* 2, 1 (1987): 1–53.

Routley, Richard, and Val Routley. "Nuclear Energy and Obligations to the Future." *Responsibilities to Future Generations.* Ed. Ernest Partridge. Buffalo, NY: Prometheus Books, 1980. 277–301.

Rubinoff, Lionel. "Obligations to Future Generations." *Ethics and Justification*. Ed. Douglas Odegard. Edmonton: Edmonton Academic, 1988. 147–165.

Sagan, Carl. "Nuclear War and Climatic Catastrophe: Some Policy Implications." *Foreign Affairs* 62, Winter (1983): 257–292.

__________. *Nuclear Winter and Its Implications.* Washington: G.P.O.: 99th Congress, 1986.

Sartorius, Rolf E. "Government Regulation and Intergenerational Justice." *Rights and Regulation.* Ed. Tibor R. Machan. Cambridge: Ballinger, 1983. 177–202.

__________. *Nuclear Fission Power and the Rights of Members of Future Generations.* Unpublished Manuscript.

Schwartz, Thomas. "Obligations to Posterity." *Obligations to Future Generations.* Eds. R. I. Sikora and Brian Barry. Philadelphia: Temple University Press, 1978. 3–13.

Scott, Robert, Jr. "Environmental Ethics and Obligations to Future Generations." *Obligations to Future Generations.* Eds. R. I. Sikora and Brian Barry. Philadelphia: Temple University Press, 1978. 74–90.

Searle, John R. *Speech Acts.* Cambridge: Cambridge University Press, 1969.

Selk, Eugene E. "Toward an Environmental Ethic: Royce's Theory of Community and Obligations to Future Generations." *Transactions of the Charles S. Peirce Society* 13, Fall (1977): 253–276.

Shapiro, Michael H. "The Technology of Perfection: Performance Enhancement and the Control of Attributes." *Southern California Law Review* 65, 11 (1991).

Sher, George. "Ancient Wrongs and Modern Rights." *Justice between Age Groups and Generations.* Eds. Peter Laslett and James S. Fishkin. New Haven: Yale University Press, 1992. 48–61.

Sikora, R. I. "Classical Utilitarianism and Parfit's Repugnant Conclusion: A Reply to McMahon." *Ethics* 92, October (1981): 128–133.

__________. "Is it Wrong to Prevent the Existence of Future Generations?" *Obligations to Future Generations.* Eds. R. I. Sikora and Brian Barry. Philadelphia: Temple University Press, 1978. 112–166.

Sikora, R. I., and Brian Barry, eds. *Obligations to Future Generations.* Philadelphia: Temple University Press, 1978.

Silverman, William A. "Pre-Zygotic Rights." *Bioethics* 2, January (1988): 70–71.

Singer, Peter. "Utilitarianism and Vegetarianism." *Philosophy and Public Affairs* 9 (1979): 325–337.

Smith, Janet Farrell. "Responsibility and Future Generations: A Constructivist Model." *Philosphy of Technology.* Ed. Paul T. Durbin. Norwell: Kluwer, 1989. 169–186.

Smith, Theresa C. and Thomas A. Oleszczuk. *No Asylum: State Psychiatric Repression in the U.S.S.R.* New York: St. Martin's Press, 1995.

Sprigge, Timothy L. S. "Professor Narveson's Utilitarianism." *Inquiry* 11, 3 (1968): 332–346.

Steiner, Hillel. "The Rights of Future Generations." *Energy and the Future.* Eds. Douglas MacLean and Peter G. Brown. Totowa, NJ: Rowman and Littlefield, 1983. 151–165.

Sterba, James P. "Abortion, Distant Peoples and Future Generations." *Journal of Philosophy* (1980): 424–440.

__________. "Explaining Asymmetry: A Problem for Parfit." *Philosophy and Public Affairs* 16, Spring (1987): 188–192.

__________. "The Welfare Rights of Distant Peoples and Future Generations: Moral Side-Constraints on Social Policy." *Social Theory and Practice* 7, Spring (1981): 99–119.

Stinchcombe, Arthur L. "On Softheadedness on the Future." *Ethics* 93, October (1982): 114–128.

Strole, Donald. "Rights, Obligations and Future Generations." *Auslegung* 9, Winter (1982): 283–299.

Sumner, L. W. "Classical Utilitarianism and the Population Optimum." *Obligations to Future Generations.* Eds. R. I. Sikora and Brian Barry. Philadelphia: Temple University Press, 1978. 91–111.

Surber, Jere Paul. "Obligations to Future Generations: Explorations and Problemata." *The Journal of Value Inquiry* 11, Summer (1977): 104–116.

Suzuki, D., and P. Kundtson. *Genetics: The Clash Between the New Genetics and Human Values.* Cambridge, Mass.: Harvard University Press, 1989.

Temkin, Larry S. "Intergenerational Inequality." *Justice between Age Groups and Generations.* Eds. Peter Laslett and James S. Fishkin. New Haven: Yale University Press, 1992. 169–205.

__________. "Intransitivity and the Mere Addition Paradox." *Philosophy and Public Affairs* 16, Spring (1987): 138–187.

Thompson, Thomas H. "Are We Obligated to Future Others?" *Responsibilities to Future Generations.* Ed. Ernest Partridge. Buffalo, NY: Prometheus Books, 1981. 195–202.

Thornton, Russell. *American Indian Holocaust and Survival.* Norman: University of Oklahoma Press, 1987.

Vetter, Hermann. "The Production of Children as a Problem of Utilitarian Ethics." *Inquiry* 12, Winter (1969): 445–447.

__________. "Utilitarianism and New Generations." *Mind* 80, April (1971): 301–302.

Vogely, William A. "Long-Term Supplies of Nonrenewable Fuels." *Energy and the Future*. Eds. Douglas MacLean and Peter G. Brown. Totowa, NJ: Rowman and Littlefield, 1983. 77–90.

Walter, Edward. "Liberalism, Morality, and the Future." *The Philosophical Forum* 15 (1977): 91–110.

Walzer, Michael. *Spheres of Justice*. New York: Basic Books, 1983.

Warren, Mary. "Do Potential People Have Moral Rights?" *Obligations to Future Generations*. Eds. R. I. Sikora and Brian Barry. Philadelphia: Temple University Press, 1978. 14–30.

Wenz, Peter. "Ethics, Energy Policy, and Future Generations." *Environmental Ethics* 5, Fall (1983): 195–209.

Westra, Laura. "Let It Be: Heidegger and Future Generations." *Environmental Ethics* 7, Winter (1985): 341–350.

Williams, Mary B. "Discounting Versus Maximum Sustainable Yield." *Obligations to Future Generations*. Eds. R. I. Sikora and Brian Barry. Philadelphia: Temple University Press, 1978. 169–185.

Wilson, Edward O. "Species Diversity as an Ethical Goal." *Wilderness* 1984: 12–17.

Wolf, Clark. "Contemporary Property Rights, Lockean Provisos, and the Interests of Future Generations." *Ethics* (Forthcoming).

Wolff, Robert Paul. *Understanding Rawls*. Princeton, NJ: Princeton University Press, 1977.

Woodward, James. "The Non-Identity Problem." *Ethics* 96, July (1986): 804–831.

Index

—D—

—E—

—F—